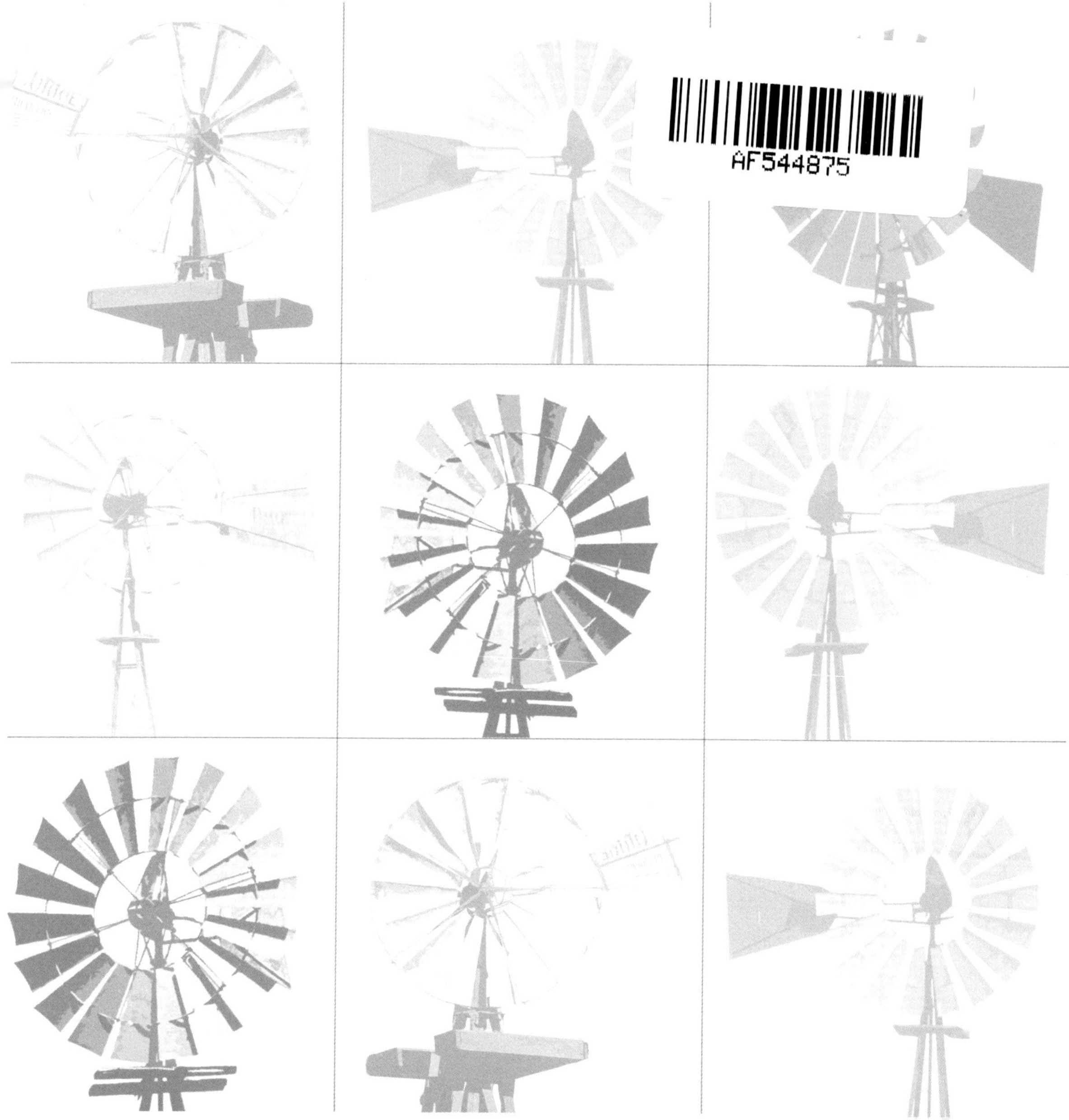

WINDMILLS OF THE WEST

Rural America's Most Important Invention

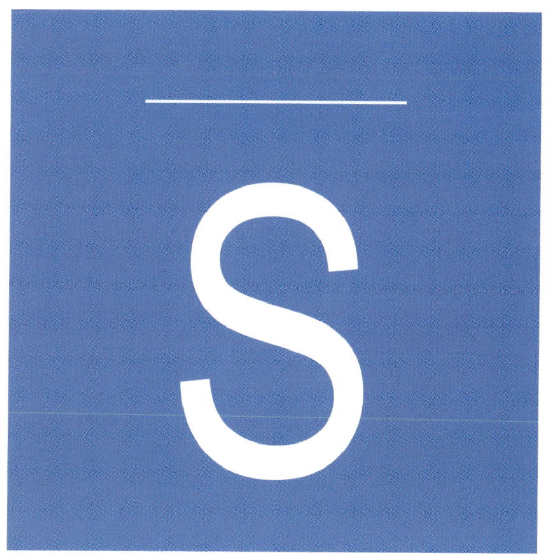

Photography by David R. Stoecklein
Text by Jack Goddard

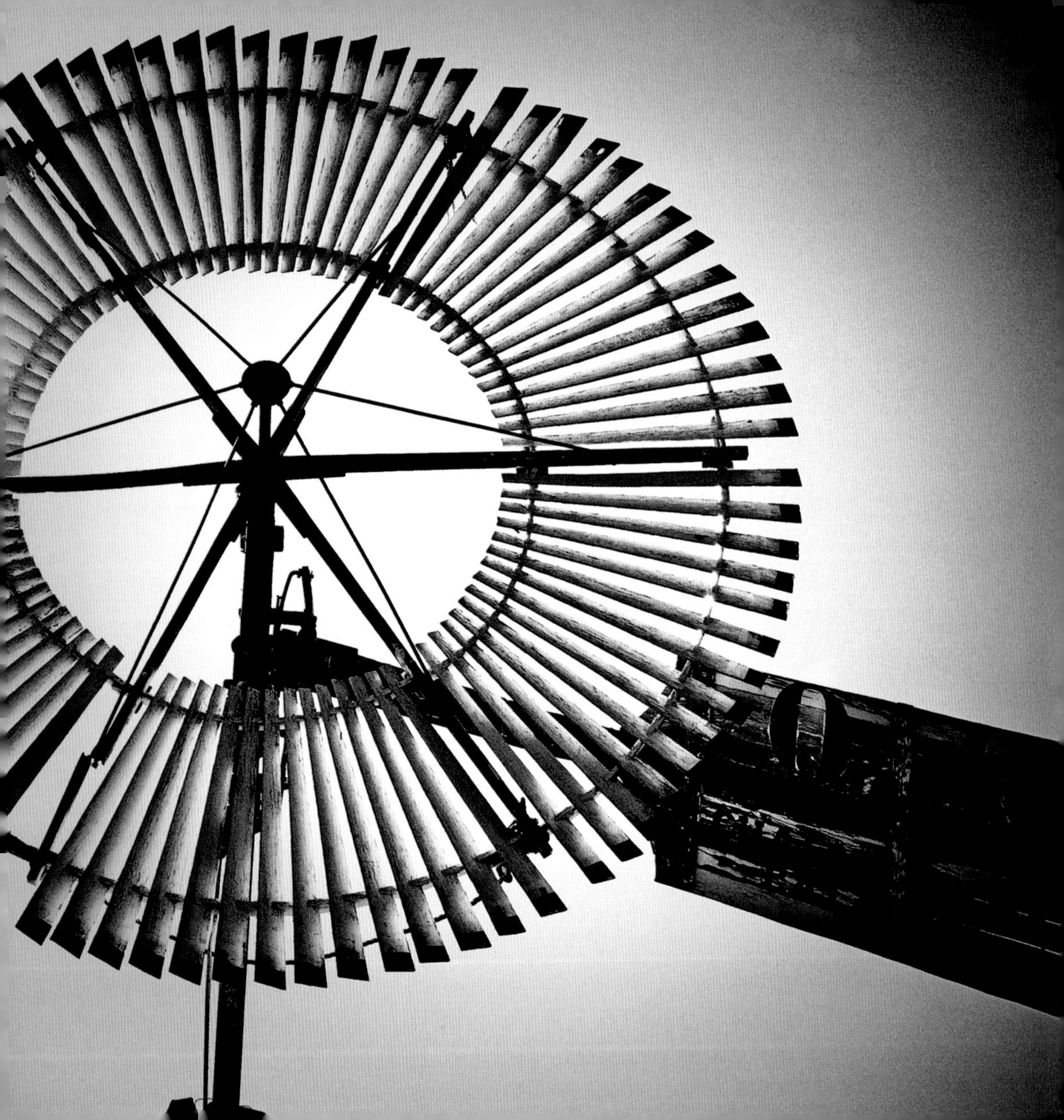

WINDMILLS OF THE WEST

Rural America's Most Important Invention

Photography	David R. Stoecklein
Text	Jack Goddard
Editor	Carrie Lightner
Art Direction & Design	Mark Epstein

Other books by Stoecklein Publishing include *The Cowboy Hat, Fly Fishing in Idaho, The American Quarter Horse, Cattle, The Cowboy Boot, Barns of the American West, Brands of the West, Outhouses, Western Fences, Saddles of the West, California Missions, Dude Ranches of the American West, The Spur, The Western Buckle, Ranch Style, Cowgirls in Heaven, The Performance Horse, Cow Dogs, Lil' Buckaroos, The American Paint Horse, The Idaho Cowboy, Cowboy Gear, Don't Fence Me In, The Texas Cowboys, The Montana Cowboy, The Western Horse, Cowgirls, Spirit of the West,* and *The California Cowboy.*

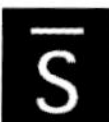

Stoecklein Photography & Publishing
1730 Lear Lane, Unit A
Hailey, Idaho 83333

tel 208.788.4593 fax 208.788.4713 toll-free 800.727.5191

WWW.THESTOECKLEINCOLLECTION.COM

Printed in Korea through Four Colour Printing Group, Louisville, Kentucky

ISBN-10: 1-935269-00-3
ISBN-13: 978-1-935269-00-7
Library of Congress Catalog number 2009902830

Antique Windmill
J.B. Buchanan Windmill Park
Spearman, Texas

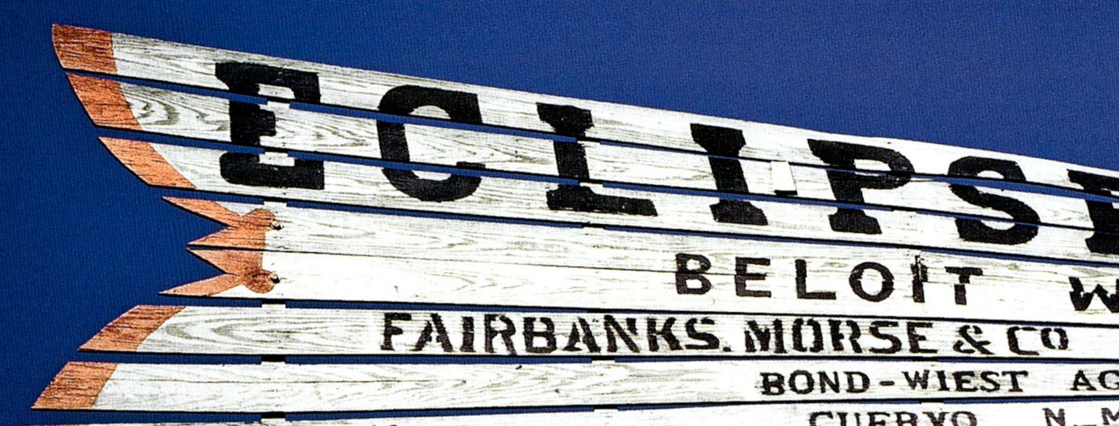

Antique Windmill
J.B. Buchanan Windmill Park
Spearman, Texas

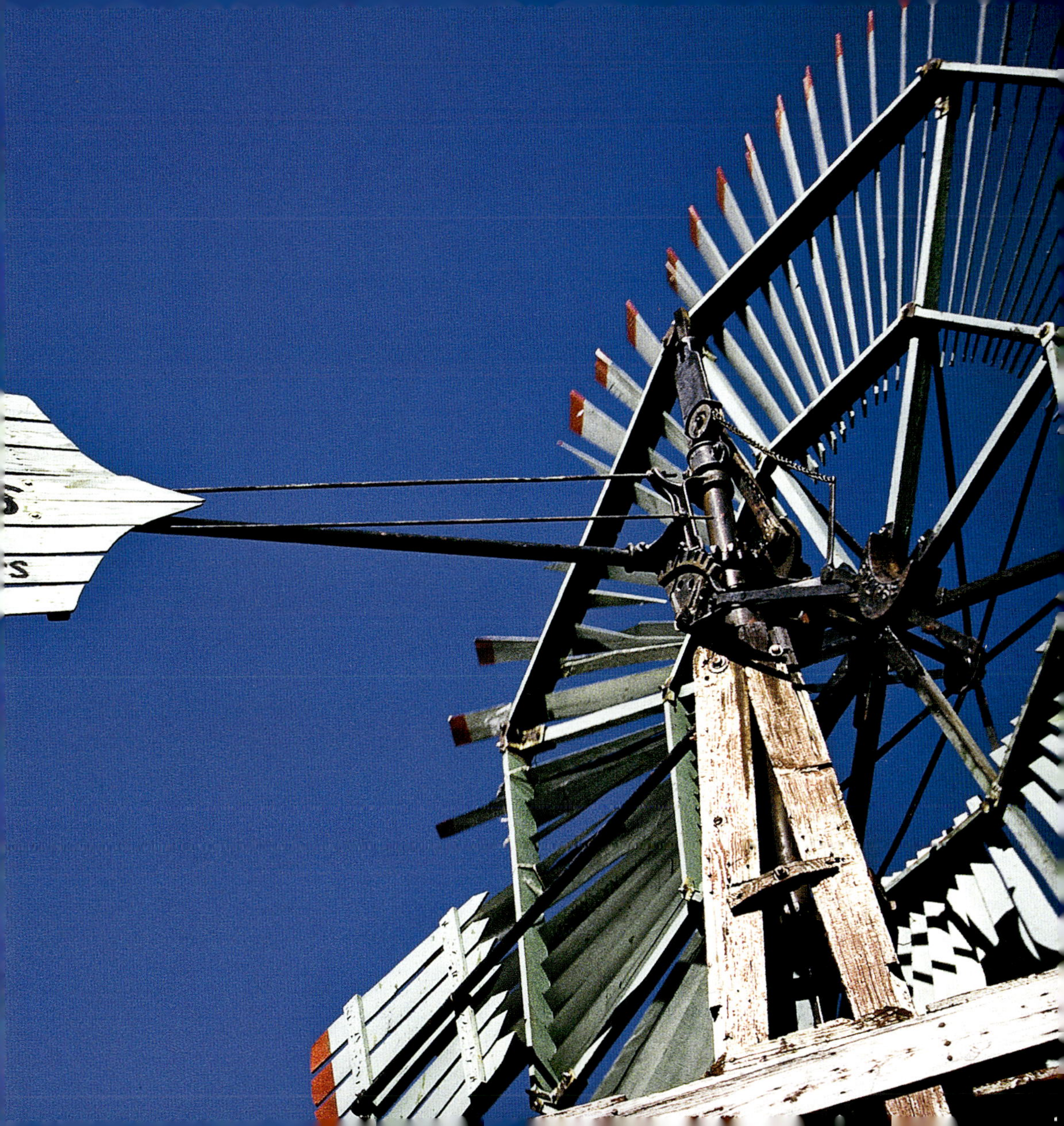

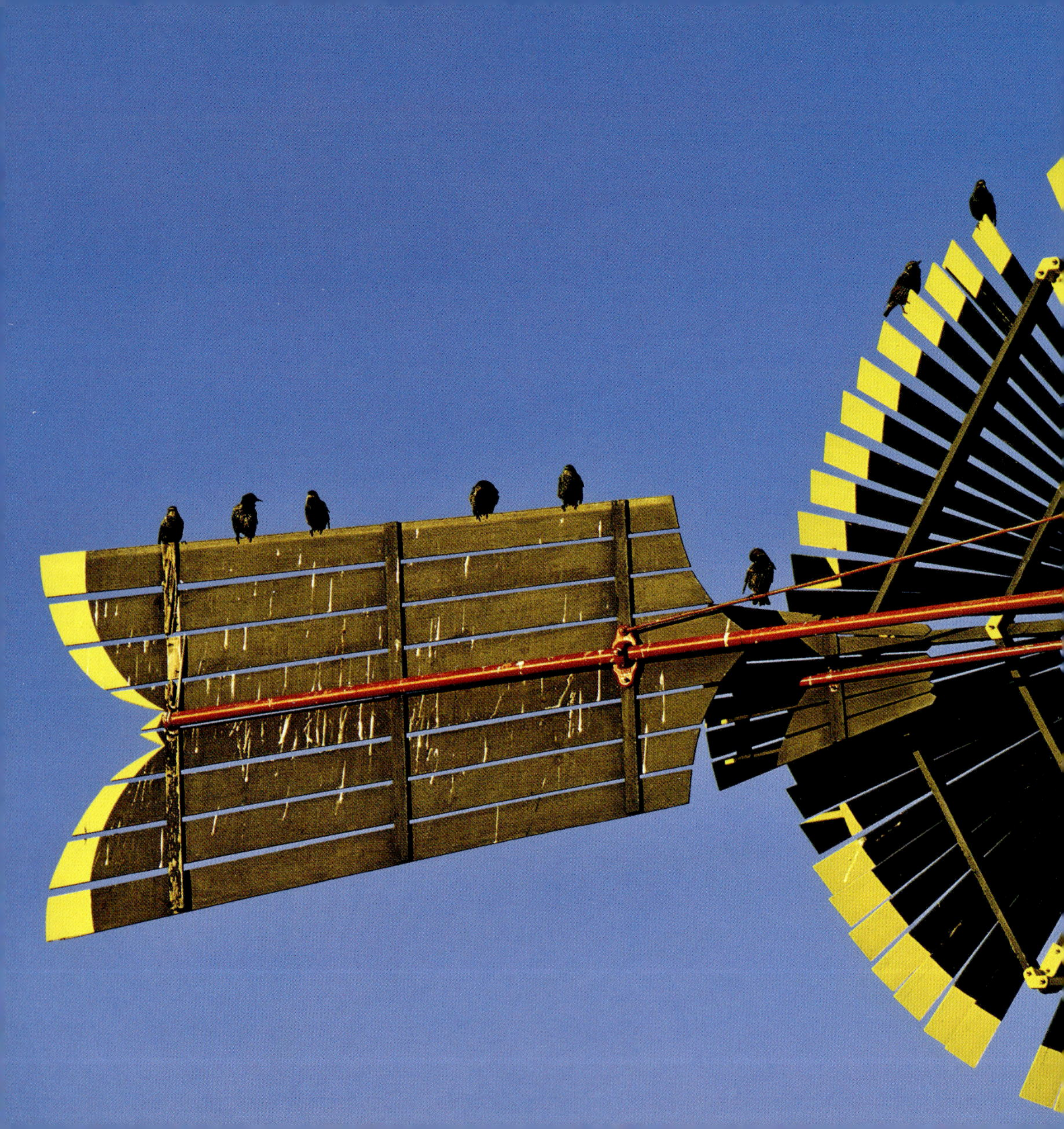

Foreword

The windmill is one of the most important inventions that contributed to the settling of the American West. The windmill delivered water to the thirsty settlers, their livestock, and the parched landscape. I have been photographing windmills for more than thirty years and I have been documenting the West—its people, landscapes, and ranches—for over forty years. Windmills have always stood out in the western landscape and cowboys have always posed in front of them or sat on the tanks to have their pictures taken. They have gathered their horses and cows around the tanks and I have been there to photograph them.

Windmills are an icon of the West as much as anything. But most of all, the structures provided the pioneers of the region with water, the most essential necessity. Please enjoy this small volume as a tribute to the windmill.

Keep the spirit of the West alive,

David R. Stoecklein

Antique Windmill
J.B. Buchanan Windmill Park
Spearman, Texas

Dedication

I believe that this is the first photograph of a windmill that I ever took. I was antelope hunting with my good friends Alex Higgins, Jed Gray, Brian Barsotti, and Andy Slough in Lusk, Wyoming. The year was 1981. We were on our way home to Sun Valley when I saw these cowboys herding their cattle by the windmill. I jumped out of the car and leaped over the fence to take the photo. This book is dedicated to my friendship with Alex, Jed, Brian, and Andy.

Last Light
Lusk, Wyoming

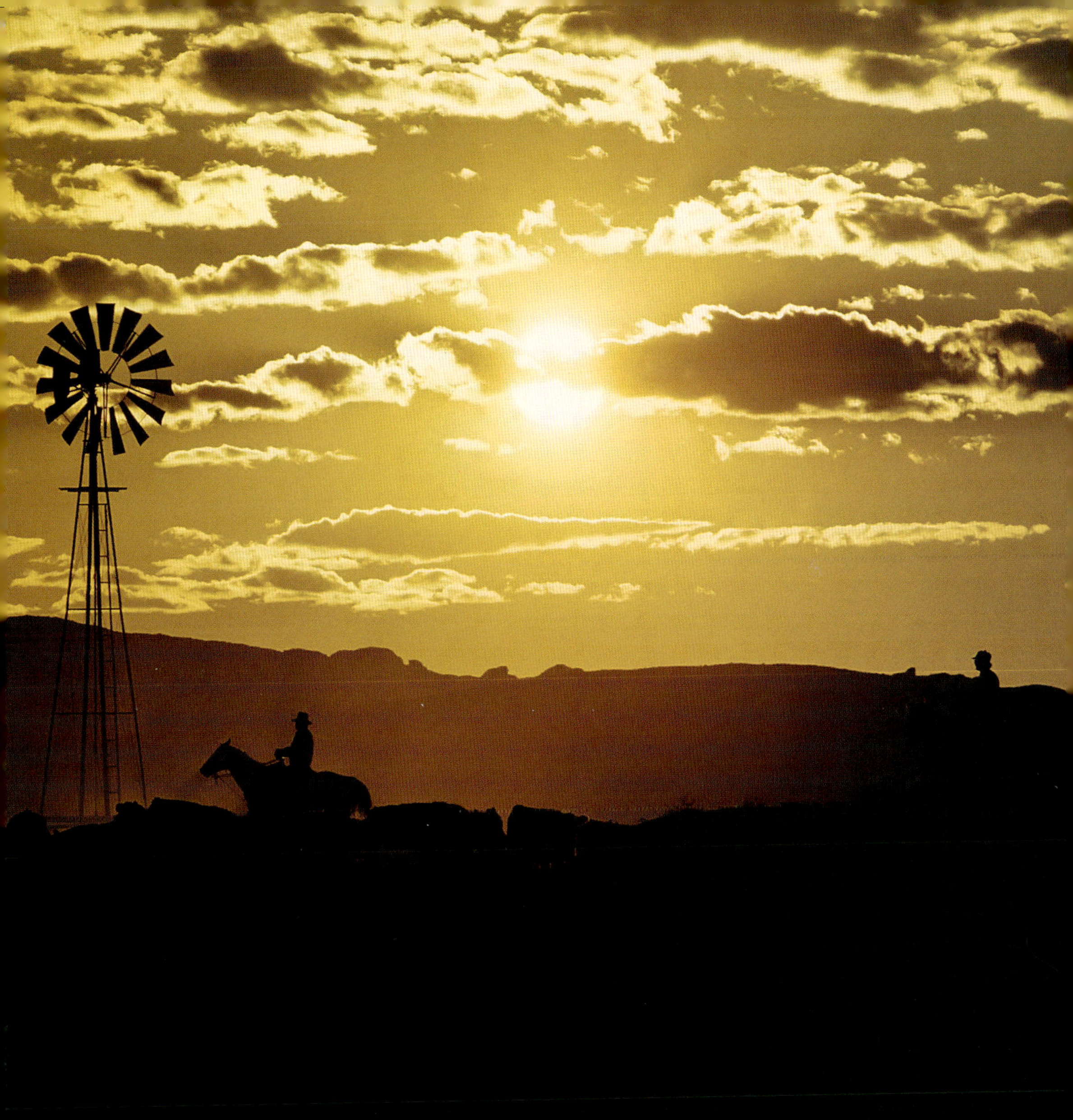

Special Thanks

I would like to give special thanks to my good friend Butch Morgan who introduced me to Patrick Gottsch, Founder and President of RFD-TV, at the 2008 National Finals Rodeo in Las Vegas, Nevada. During our brief conversation, Patrick asked me if I had ever published a book on windmills. I told him that I hadn't but that I sure would love to.

Patrick's love for windmills is the reason this book exists. The windmill is the logo and trademark for RFD-TV. The book was his vision and idea.

Thank you Patrick and Butch.

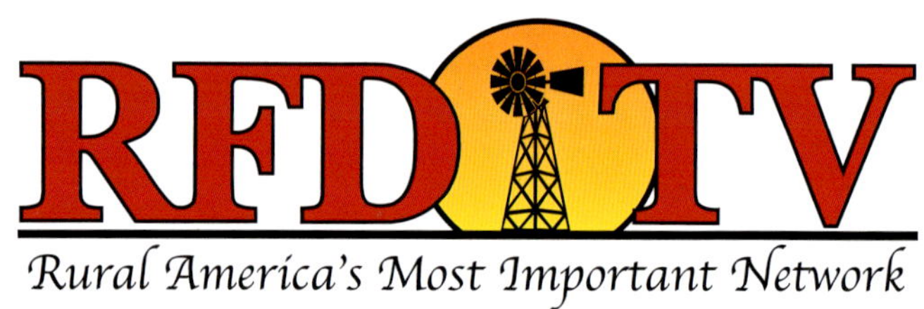

Antique Windmill
J.B. Buchanan Windmill Park
Spearman, Texas

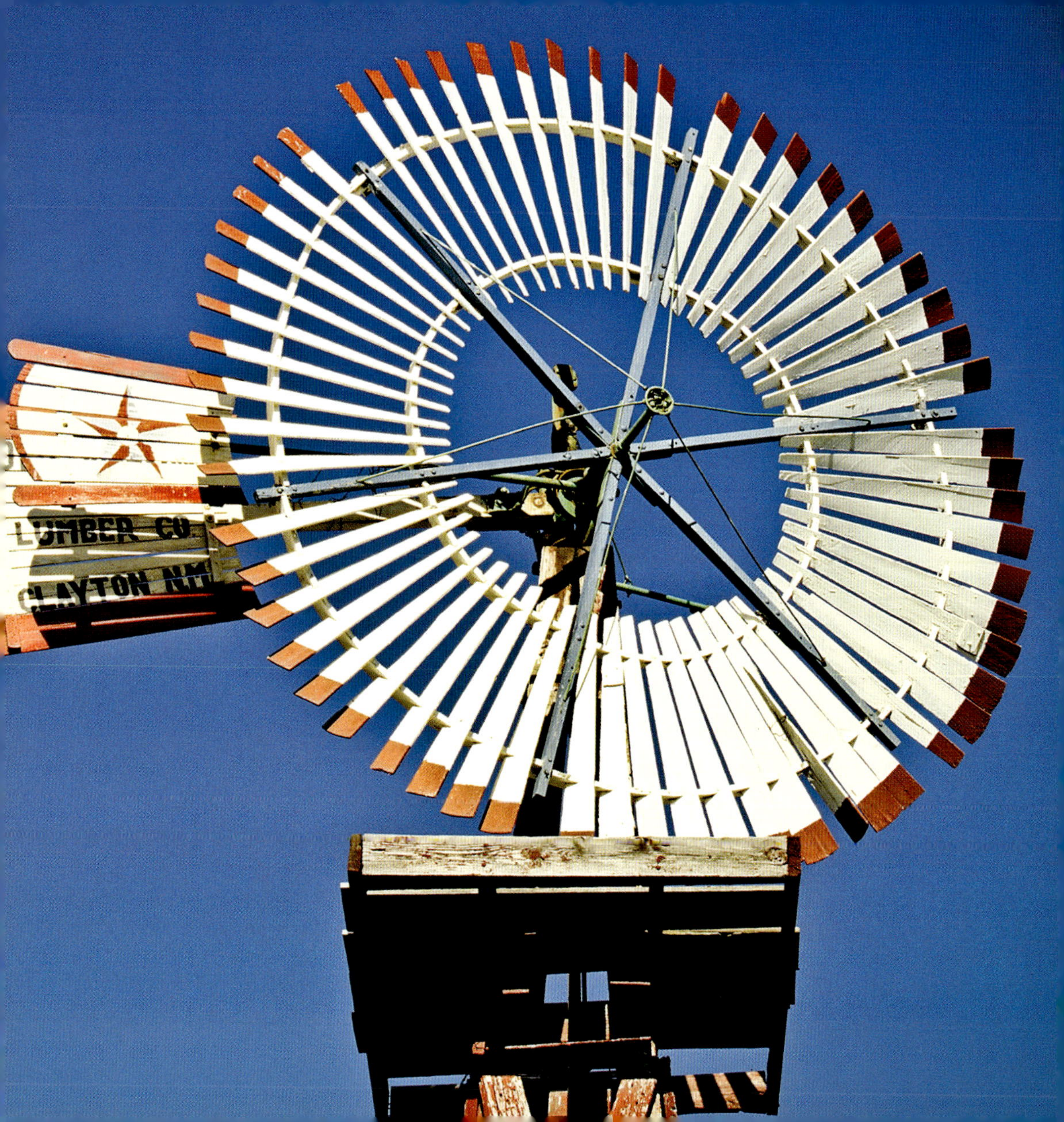
LUMBER CO.
CLAYTON NM

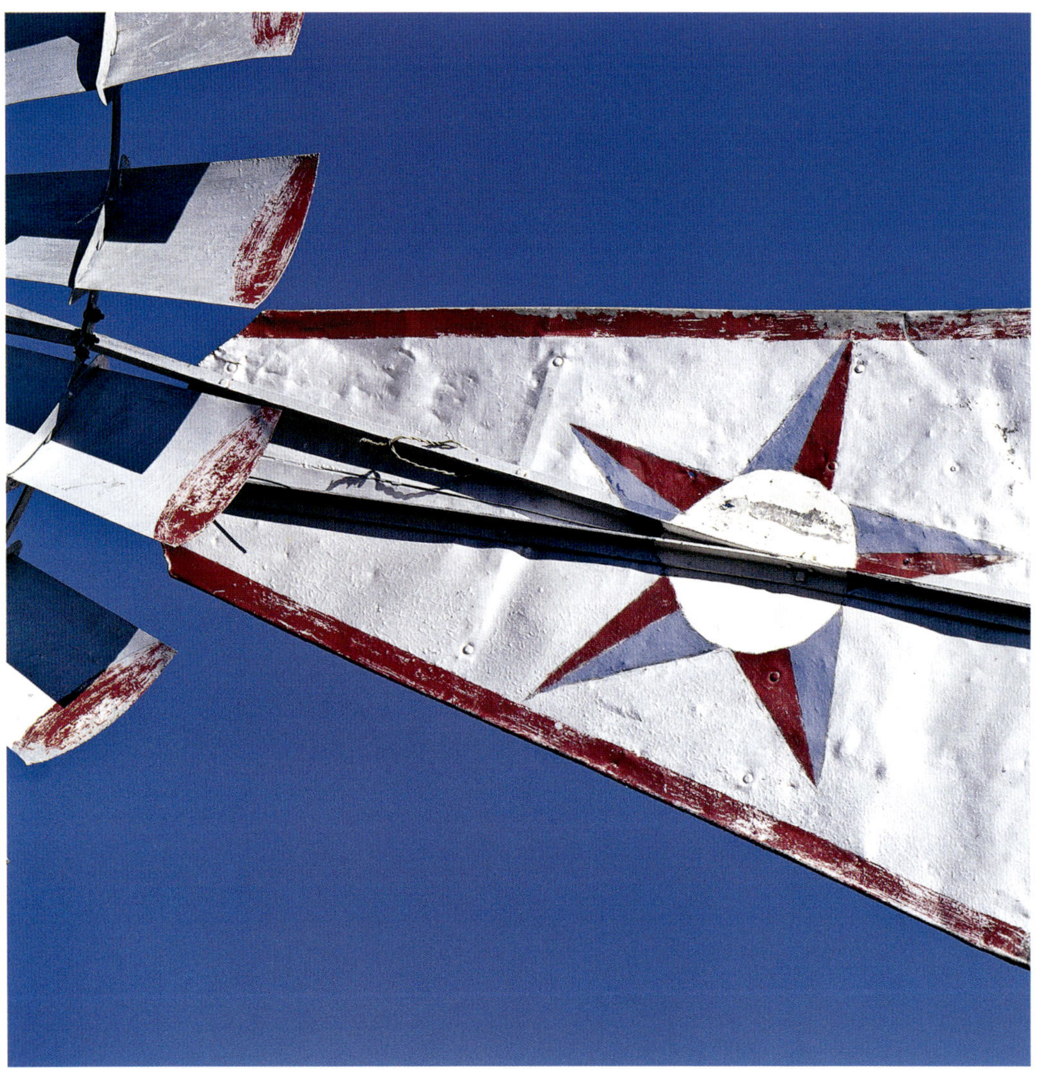

Introduction

Windmills exist in nearly every area of rural America. They are used to capture the continual power of wind and convert its energy to pump water from underground wells. These mills, made by a variety of manufacturers, feature a large number of blades so that they turn slowly with considerable torque in low winds and are self-regulating in high winds. A crankshaft converts the rotary motion into reciprocating strokes through a gearbox mounted on the tower and the power is carried downward through a rod to the pump cylinder below. Windmills are instantly recognizable and represent not only purpose and function, but are also icons of rural America's undaunting spirit of settlement and the expansion of this country's once untamed interior.

A windmill is a beautiful thing. It consists of a sturdy pyramid-shaped tower topped with graceful rotating blades and governed by a distinct horizontal vane that turns the blades into the wind. On other models, known as vane-less, the large fan has a long counterbalance arm with the maker's 'trademark' animal or symbol. The most popular weights were sand-cast iron images of horses, roosters, moons, stars, and others, including the iron-clad Civil War ship, the Monitor.

The mid-1800s were the beginning of the golden age of windmill technology. Those were times of growing pains for the country. Manifest Destiny was pushing the boundaries of development westward. Many forces were at work with the movement but the most defining issues were the building of the railroads, cattle ranching, and settlers taming the land and growing crops.

Antique Windmill
J.B. Buchanan Windmill Park
Spearman, Texas

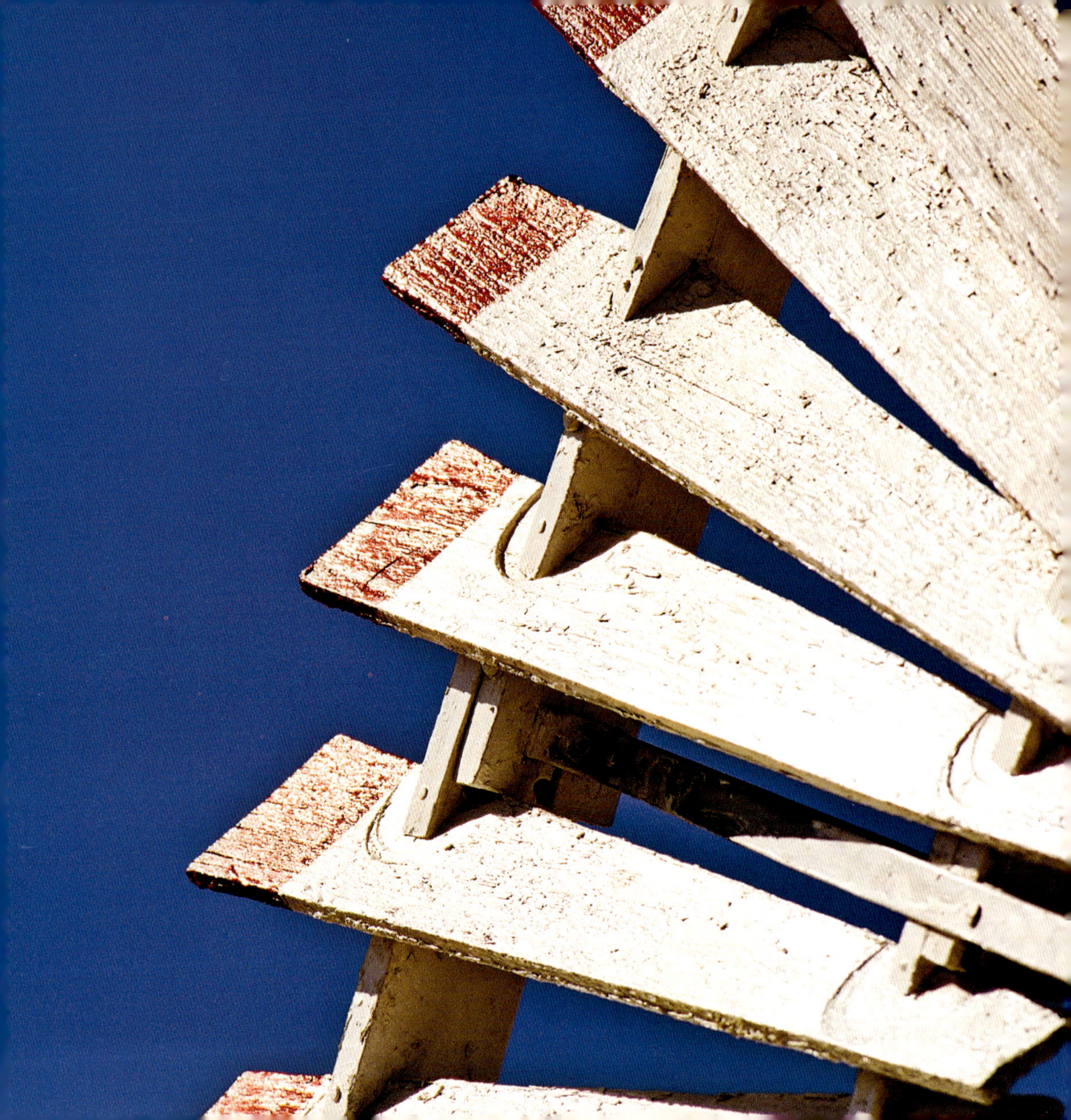

Railroads were connecting commerce and transportation from one coast to the other during that era. The power to drive the massive locomotive engines was produced by steam. Steam required huge amounts of water at close intervals. The need for water in vast barren wastelands was provided by massive windmills that lifted water from deep underground wells. Those windmills had enormous wooden towers of telescoping design topped with huge wooden fan wheels. Some of the wheels were as large as 35 feet in diameter. The large lumbering structures were needed to lift water from greater depths and to provide large volumes of water. With the completion of the railroads, the frontier became more open and accessible. Goods and materials could be shipped affordably. The nation was united and open for settlement and expansion of commerce.

The advent of the self-governing windmill provided power from the seemingly ceaseless wind that could be converted to pump or 'ratchet' water up a well casing to the surface in remote and harsh lands. The cattle and cowboys followed the windmills westward. In 1854, a Connecticut inventor named Daniel Halladay came up with the design for the first self-regulating windmill that was commercially successful. His firm was the U.S. Wind Engine and Pump Company of Batavia, Illinois. The first designs were made of wooden blades that could be assembled at the site of the well and mounted on top of a wooden tower. Demand and expansion grew in the late 1860s and by the 1880s there were over 400 companies producing windmills. By 1935 over 6.5 million windmills had been made and sold. They were, by then, made of lightweight metal components erected on metal towers and very affordable.

Windmills opened the range for large-scale ranching enterprises. Where no surface water was available, the windmill pumped water from far below the ground into tanks for cattle, horses, and the humans who tended them. The American Industrial Revolution was at its peak during the early 1800s. Europeans swarmed into the country by the hundreds of thousands to work in the factories. Higher cattle numbers were needed to feed the swelling immigrant populations of the eastern industrial mills and factories. In addition, more grasslands were needed to feed the expanding herds. The frontier plains were vast land expanses, rich in grass and fertile soil, but devoid of the one essential ingredient needed to settle and raise cattle in those harsh conditions—water. Windmills provided the technology to supply water for the cattle and the ranches starting to move across America's interior.

Antique Blades
J.B. Buchanan Windmill Park
Spearman, Texas

Looking Up
J.B. Buchanan Windmill Park
Spearman, Texas

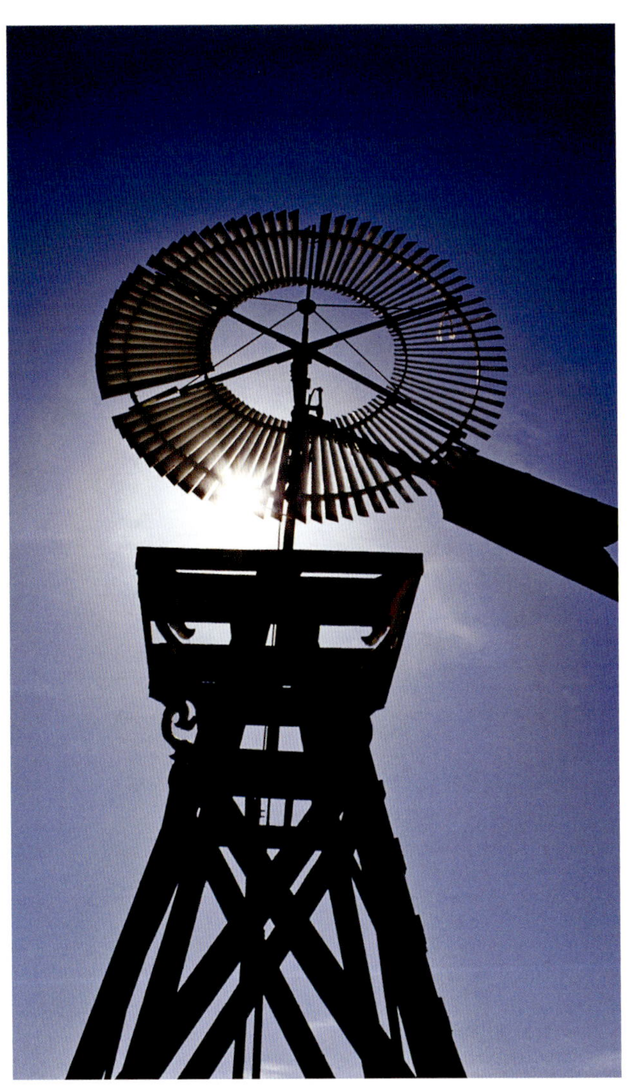

Antique Blades
J.B. Buchanan Windmill Park
Spearman, Texas

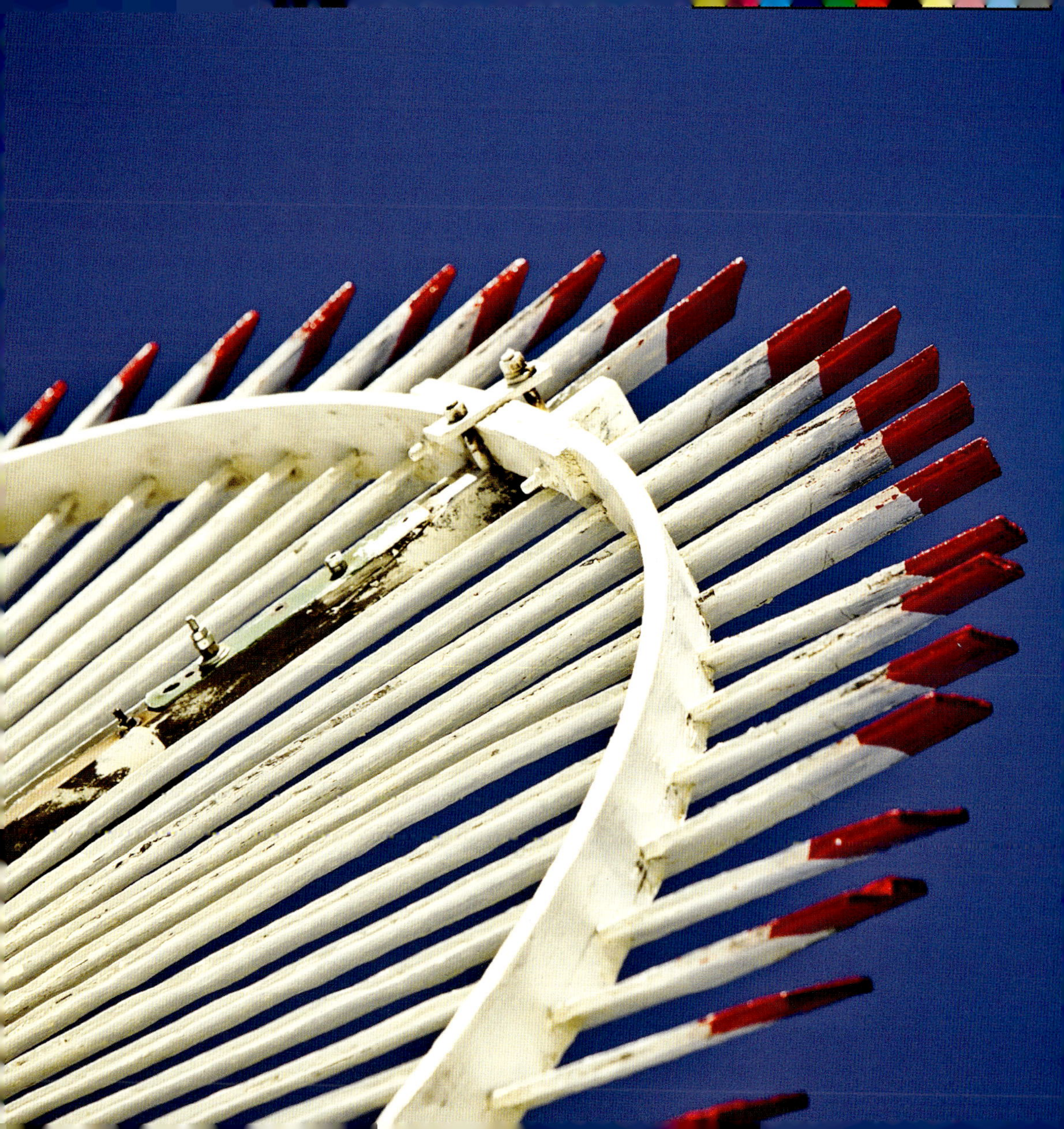

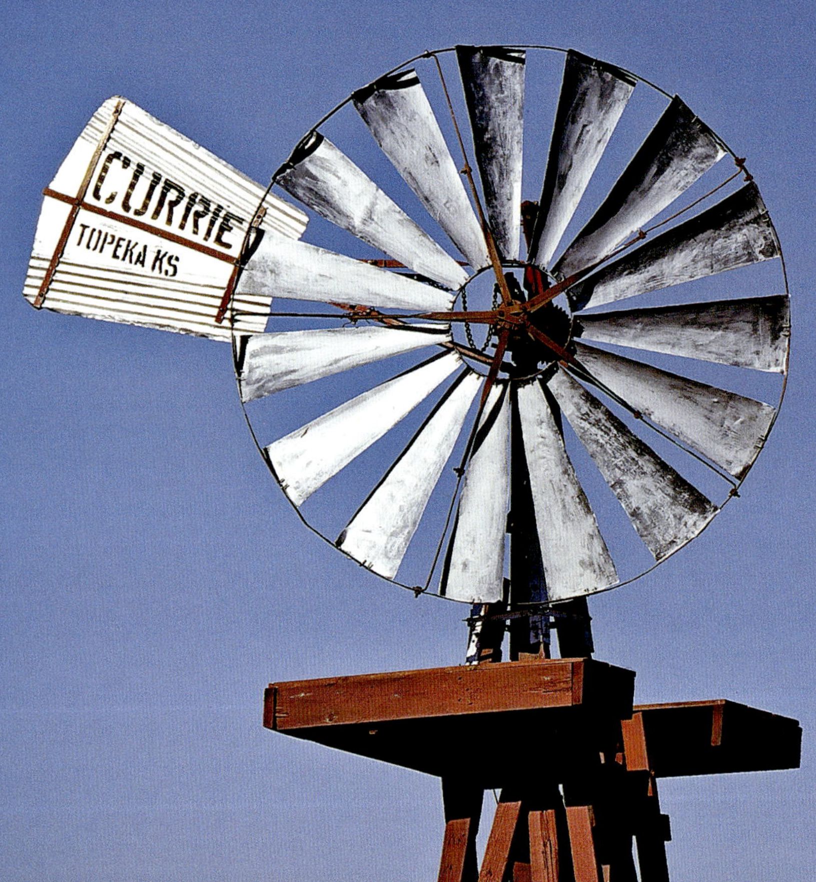
CURRIE
TOPEKA KS

One of the most famous early cattle ranches to use the windmill to expand and support its enterprise was the XIT Ranch. The newly annexed state of Texas was cash-poor but land-rich. A group of Chicago investors struck a deal to trade three million acres of what was seemingly worthless land in West Texas in exchange for building the capital buildings in Austin. The savvy investors knew that the land would eventually become productive farmland. In the meantime they needed to maximize their return. The owners used two new inventions: barbed wire to fence in the ranch lands and windmills to provide water in various enclosed management units. At intervals of about every five miles a well was dug and a windmill was erected to pump the water up to storage tanks with troughs. They erected nearly 400 windmills. With the new windmills and seemingly endless miles of barbed wire fence, the cowboy's job changed from one of just cow-punching to being a fencer and a 'windmiller.' A windmiller was a mechanic, of sorts, whose job it was to grease and tend the gear box on the top of the tower. It was never a job for anyone afraid of heights.

Antique Windmill
J.B. Buchanan Windmill Park
Spearman, Texas

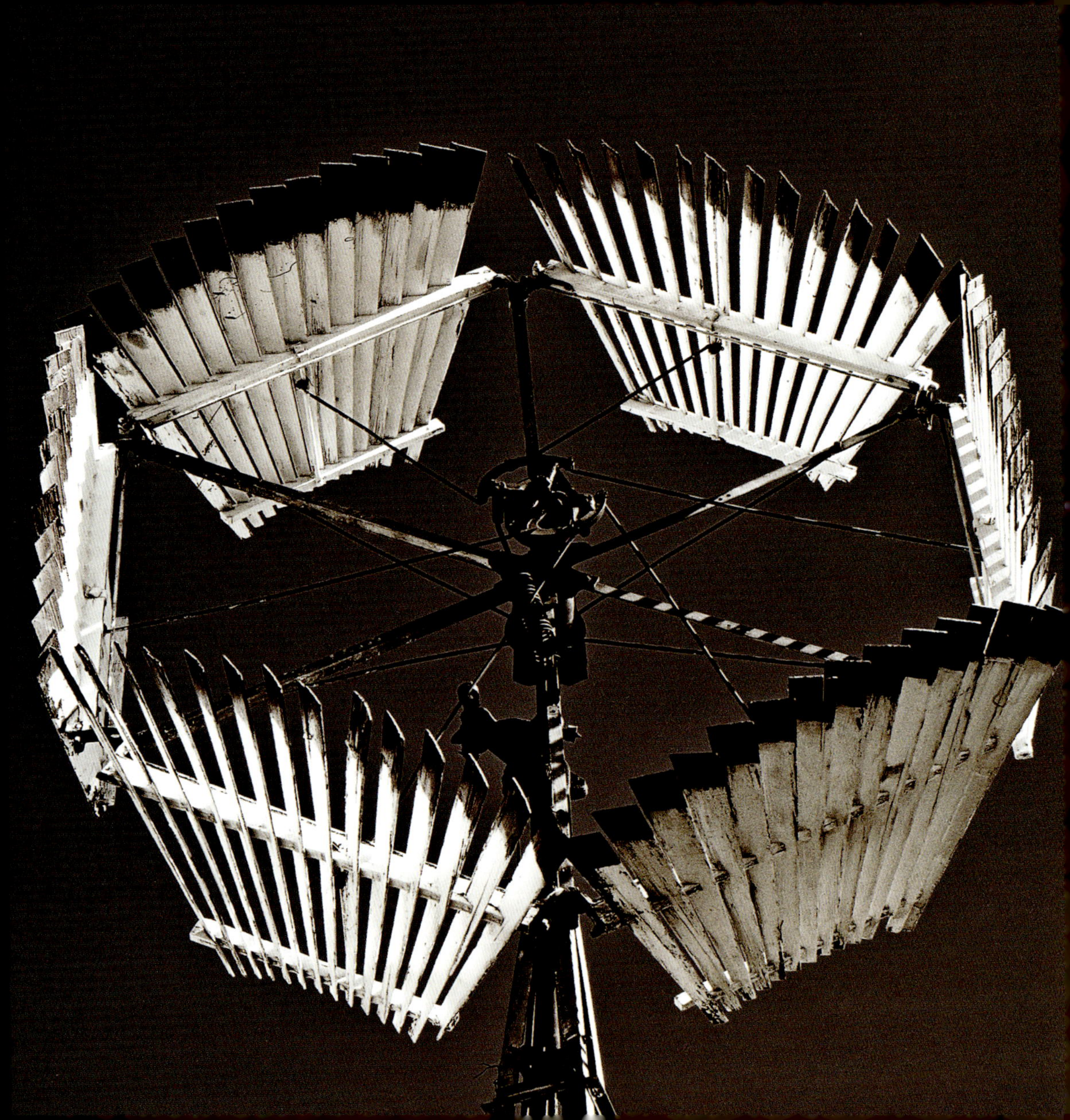

Up until 1862 the government controlled or had jurisdiction over much of the area between the Mississippi River and the Rocky Mountains. This prairie land was treeless—dry in summer and brutally cold in winter. The relentless wind never seemed to quit. After the Civil War, thousands of veterans needed land to survive and provide for their families. President Lincoln signed into law The Homestead Act, providing 160 acres of free land to settlers who could "prove up" on the claim by making the land productive. The windmills provided water, the most demanding restrictive component of settlement up until this invention.

With the railroads making delivery possible, windmill kits were soon mass-produced. The first ones were made of lightweight wood and could be assembled easily at a well site. The Eclipse, one of the first commercially successful windmills, was made of various woods. The arms were from oak and the rims and blades were from cypress or poplar. All the wooden parts were dipped in olive green paint at the factory and the tips on the blades and vane were trimmed in maroon or blood red. The castings and inscription on the vane were painted in black. Basically, one style of regular pattern Eclipse was made from 1869 through 1888, when several casting and wooden parts were modified. The mill was produced virtually without change for the next 35 years, and all parts on the mills are interchangeable. Other successful windmill makers were Aermotor, Challenger, Fairbanks-Morse, Elgin, Dempster, Monitor, Star, U.S. Wind Engine, and Currie. There were about 400 manufacturers producing the machines during the last decade of the 1800s.

The Currie windmill, one of the most common and easily identified mills on the central Great Plains, was manufactured in Kansas from the 1890s through WWII by the Currie Windmill Company. Due to its economical prices, the Currie for many years was known as "the poor man's windmill." It could be purchased for fewer than twenty dollars. Despite this reputation, however, it proved to be one of the most durable American windmills.

Beauty is certainly in the eye of the beholder, but there is something about a windmill that makes a sunset more spectacular and an evening silhouette more dramatic. The hypnotic rotating of the fans on the turning wheel is somehow very soothing and peaceful. Even the rhythmic moaning and creaking sounds are comforting. Windmills continue to be a defining image of the landscape of the American West.

Antique Boss Vaneless Windmill
J.B. Buchanan Windmill Park
Spearman, Texas

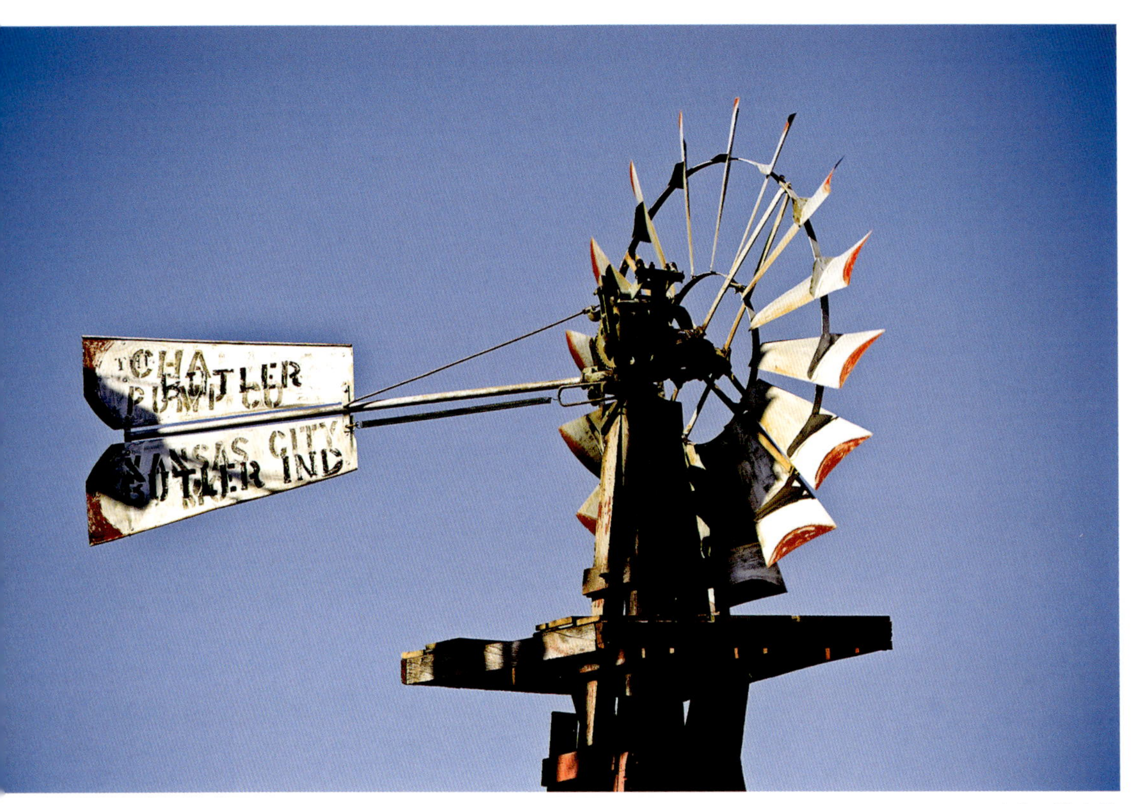

Antique Windmill
J.B. Buchanan Windmill Park
Spearman, Texas

Antique Windmill
J.B. Buchanan Windmill Park
Spearman, Texas

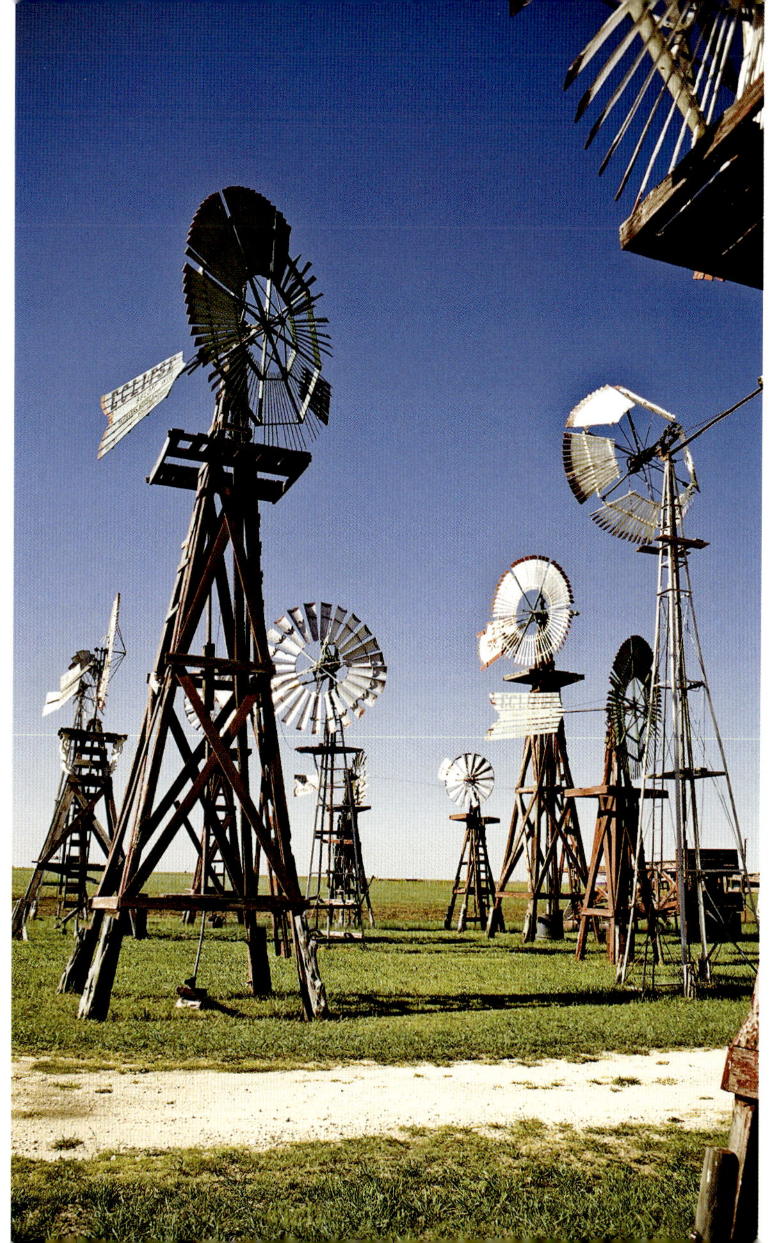
ECLIPSE

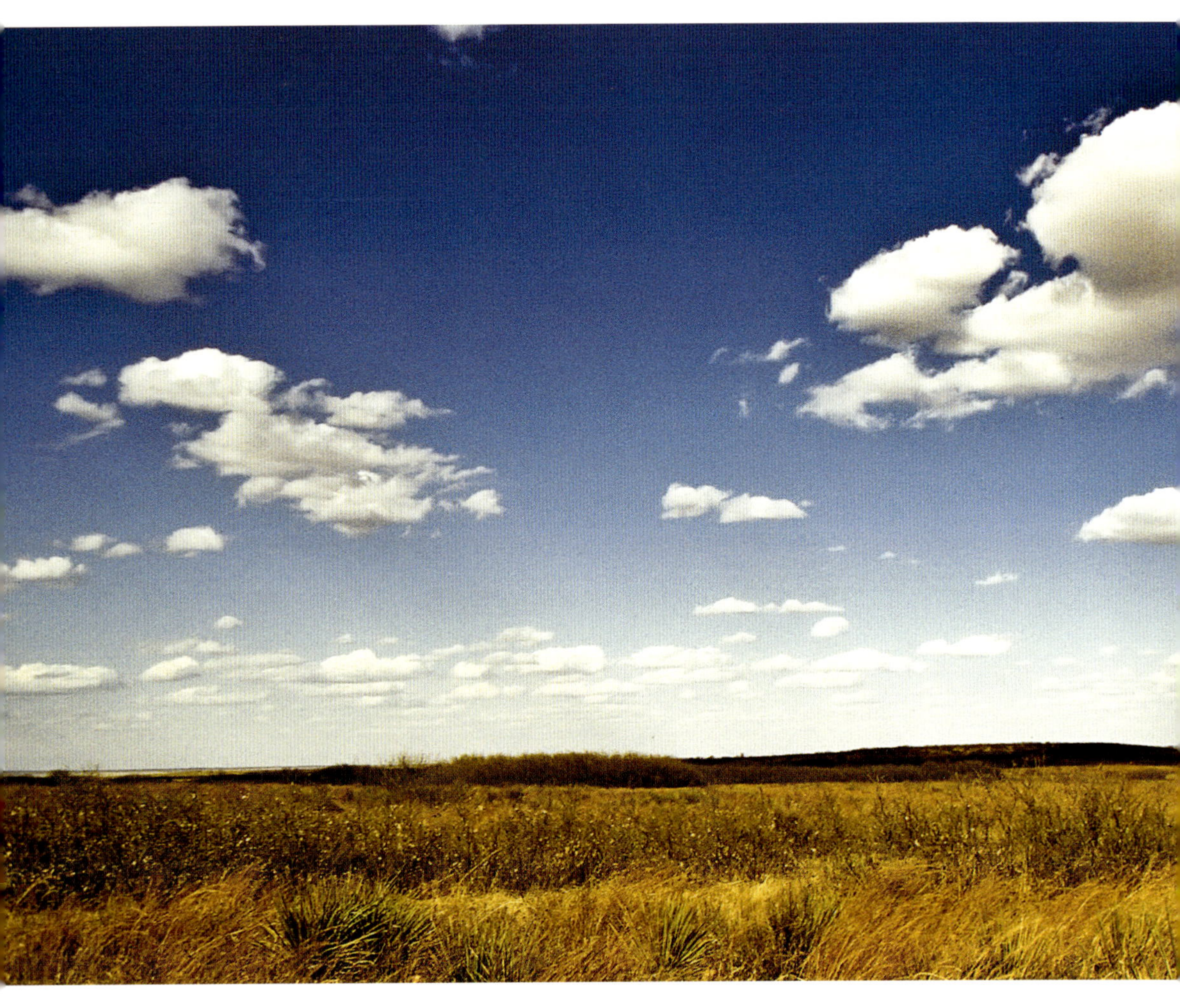

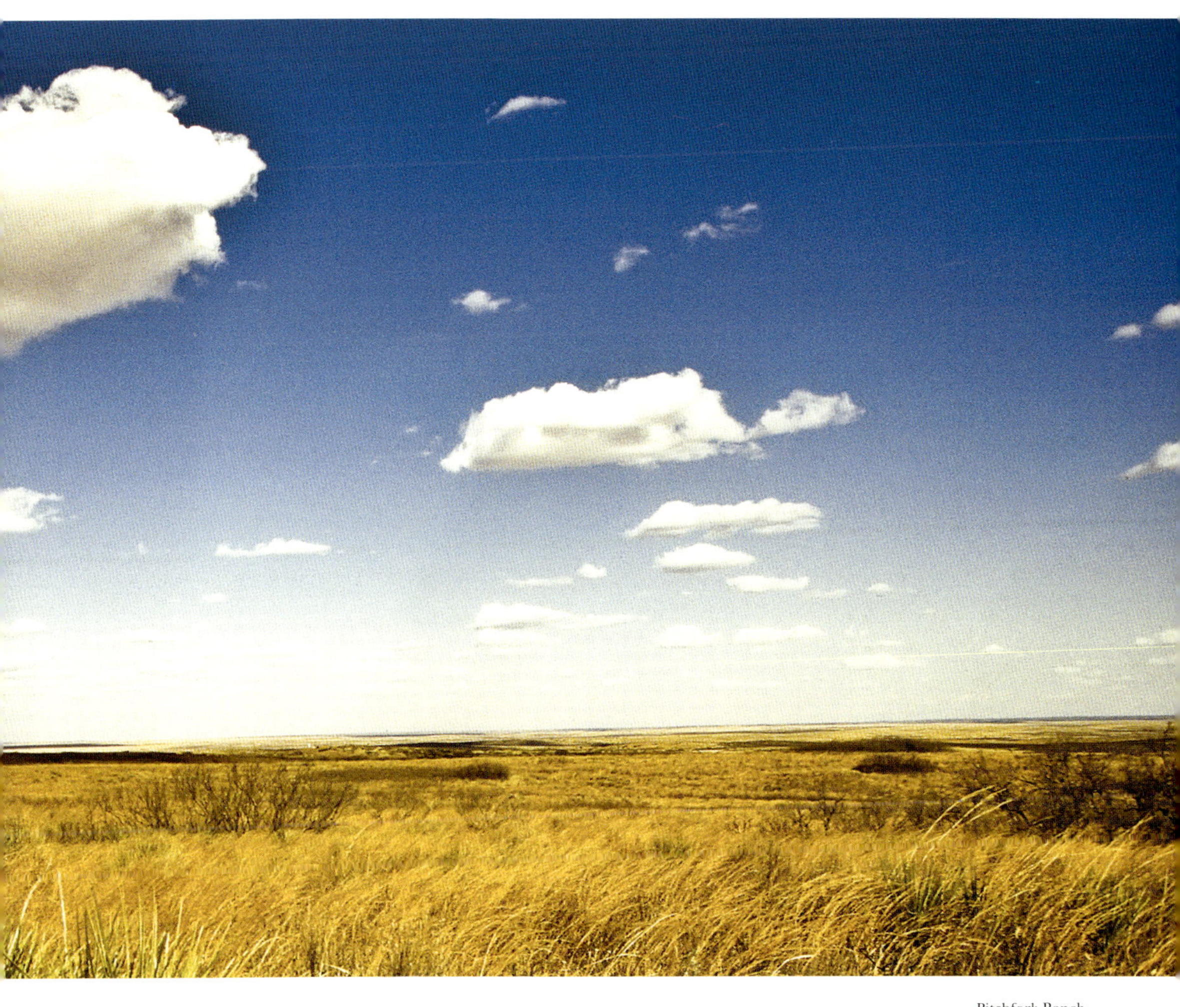

Pitchfork Ranch
Guthrie, Texas

What Windmills Can Teach Us About Life

Be reliable and steady.
Keep going even though no one is watching.
Don't let your head spin out of control.
Bring forth water from beneath your own tower.
To weather a storm, always face into the wind.
Fear not the raging of a storm but the idleness of a dead calm.
Don't hide from a storm but embrace its power.
Provide an oasis for your fellow man.
The bigger the wheel, the deeper the water.
It takes a broad base to support a tall tower.
The higher you go, the stronger the wind, but keep going.
The more wind, the more water.
The wind cannot be seen but the results can be tasted.
Let the vane of your soul keep you pointed in the right direction.
Point into the wind only if you have the right counterbalance.
The higher the view, the smaller problems appear.
A tank full of water is filled one drop at a time.
The gentlest breeze can produce the greatest results.
The outcome of life is not always the product of what is seen, but
rather, the result of what is not seen.
Even though you creak and groan, get the job done anyway.
Stand tall against the sky.

Fresh Water
LX Ranch
Amarillo, Texas

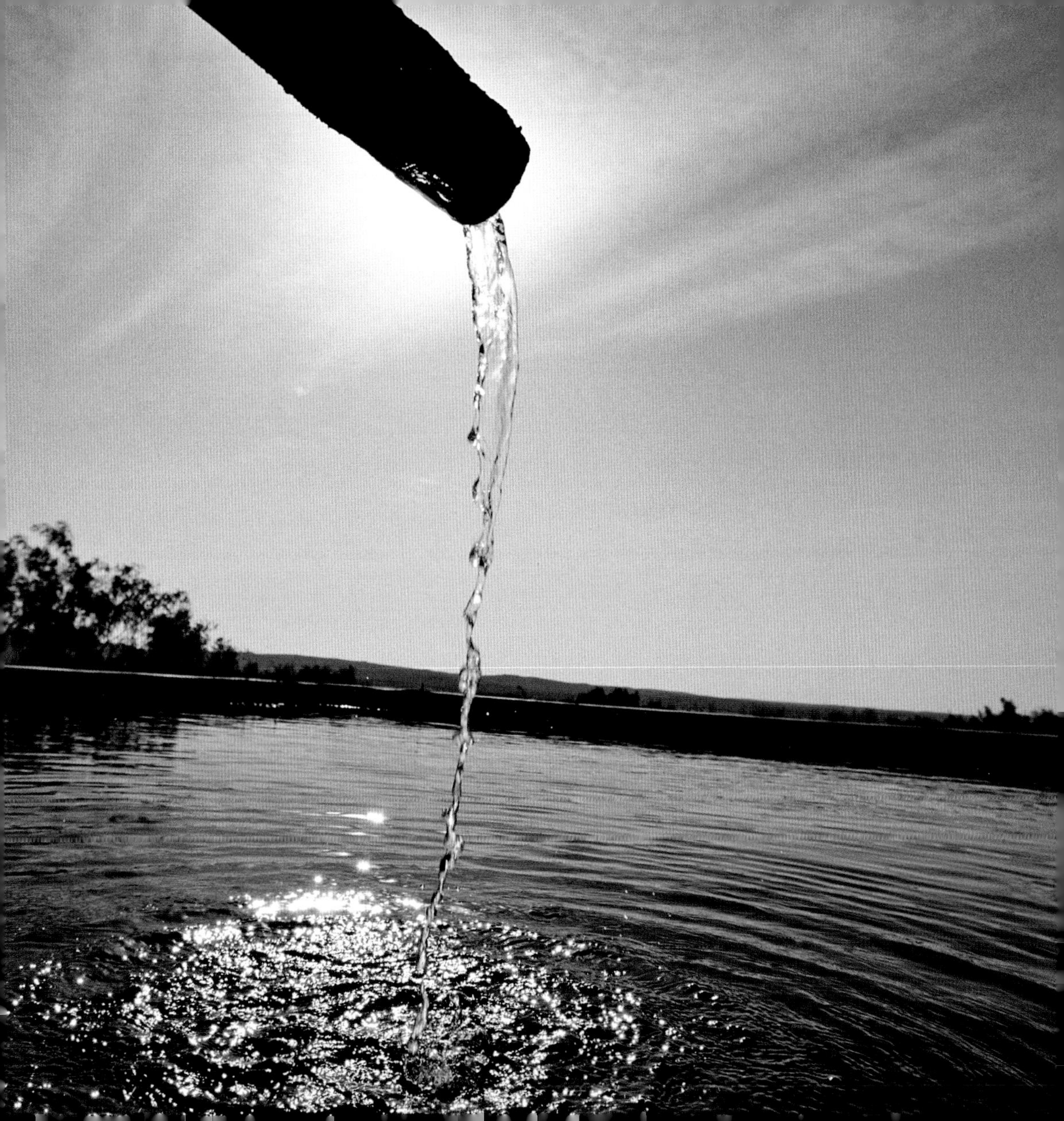

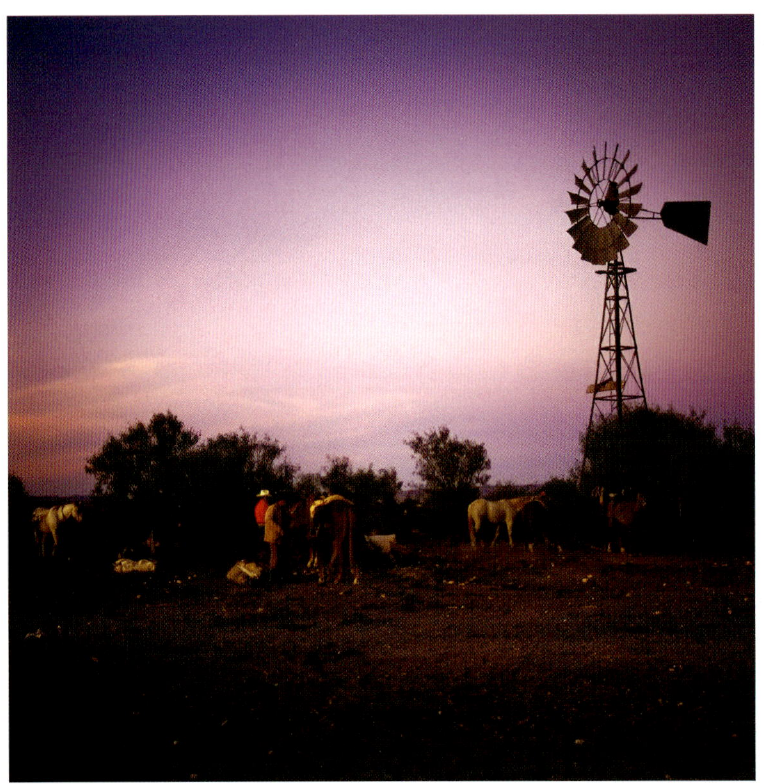

Hold-up at the Mill
Eppenauer Ranch
Toyah, Texas

Blue Morning
Rancho El Fortin
Old Mexico

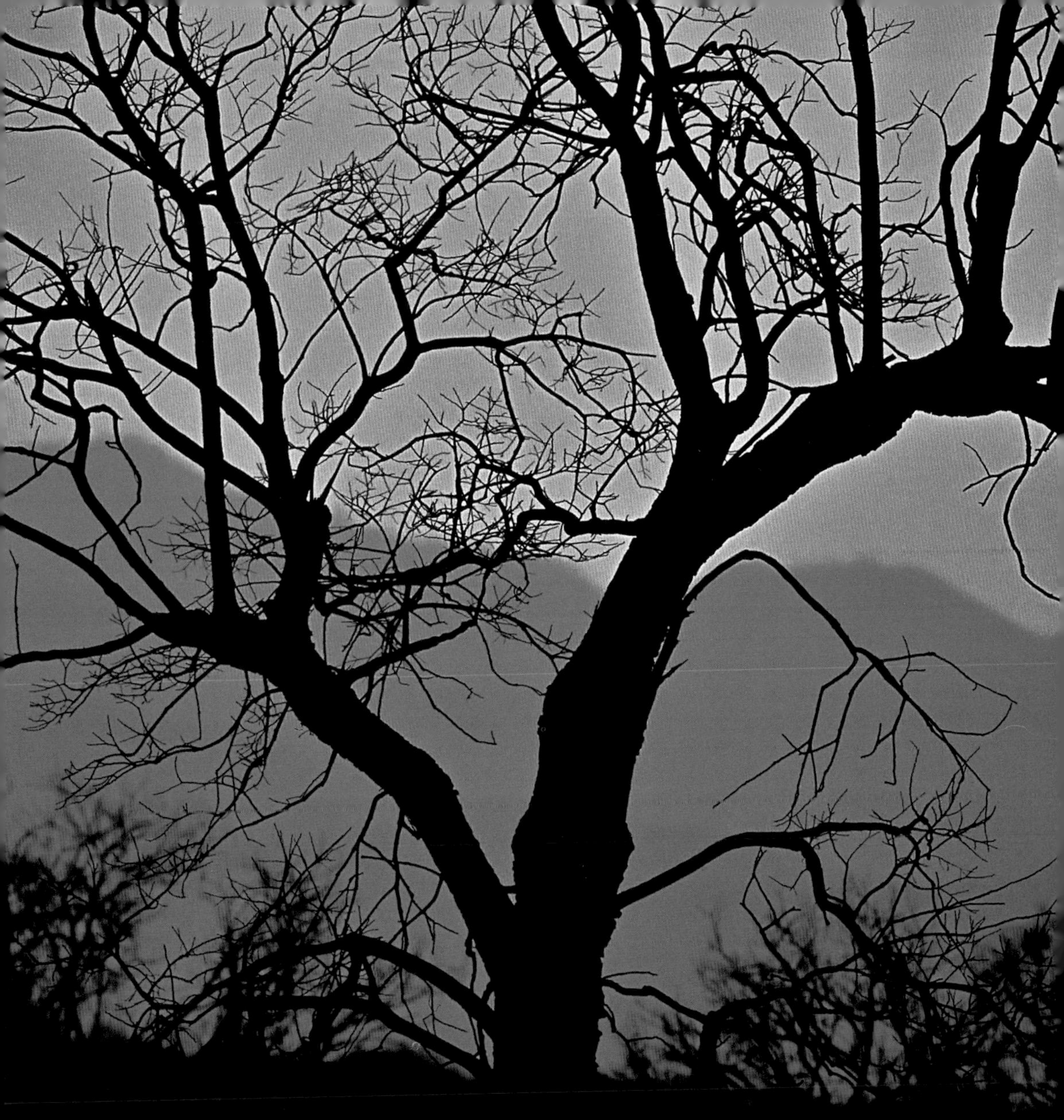

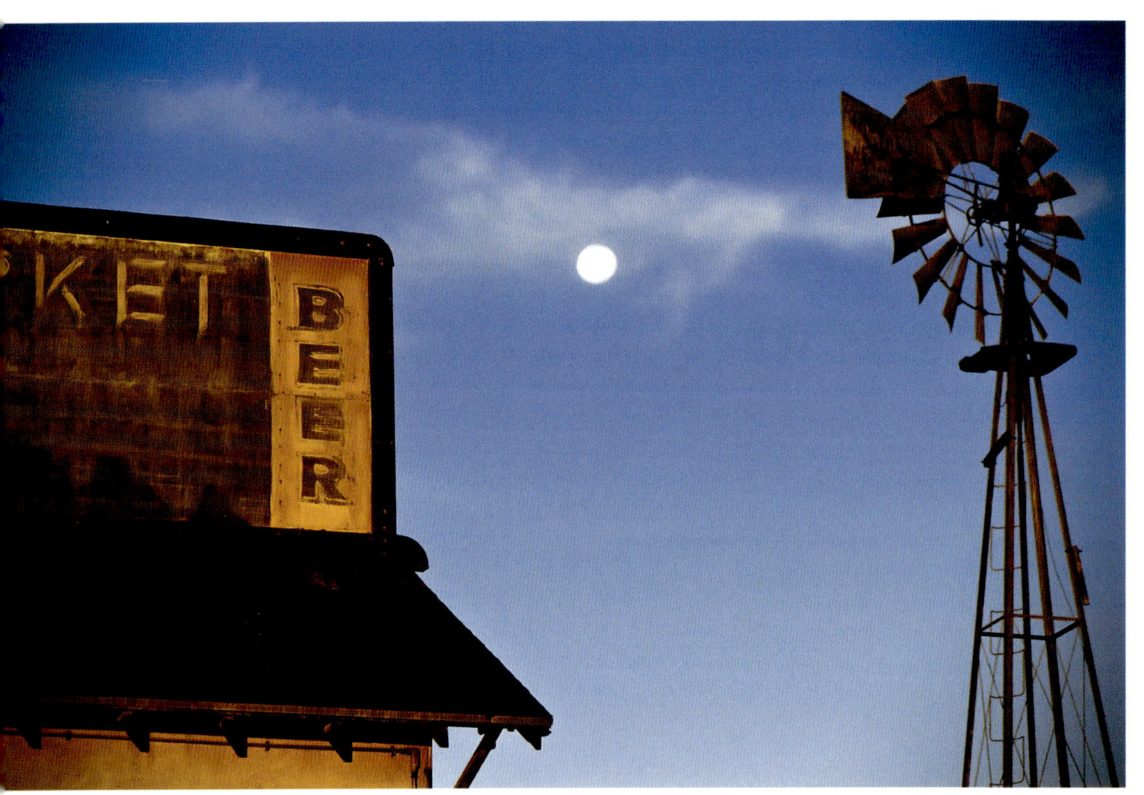

Moonrise at the Old Montanaro Market
Los Olivos, California

Adobe Water Tank
Pitchfork Ranch
Guthrie, Texas

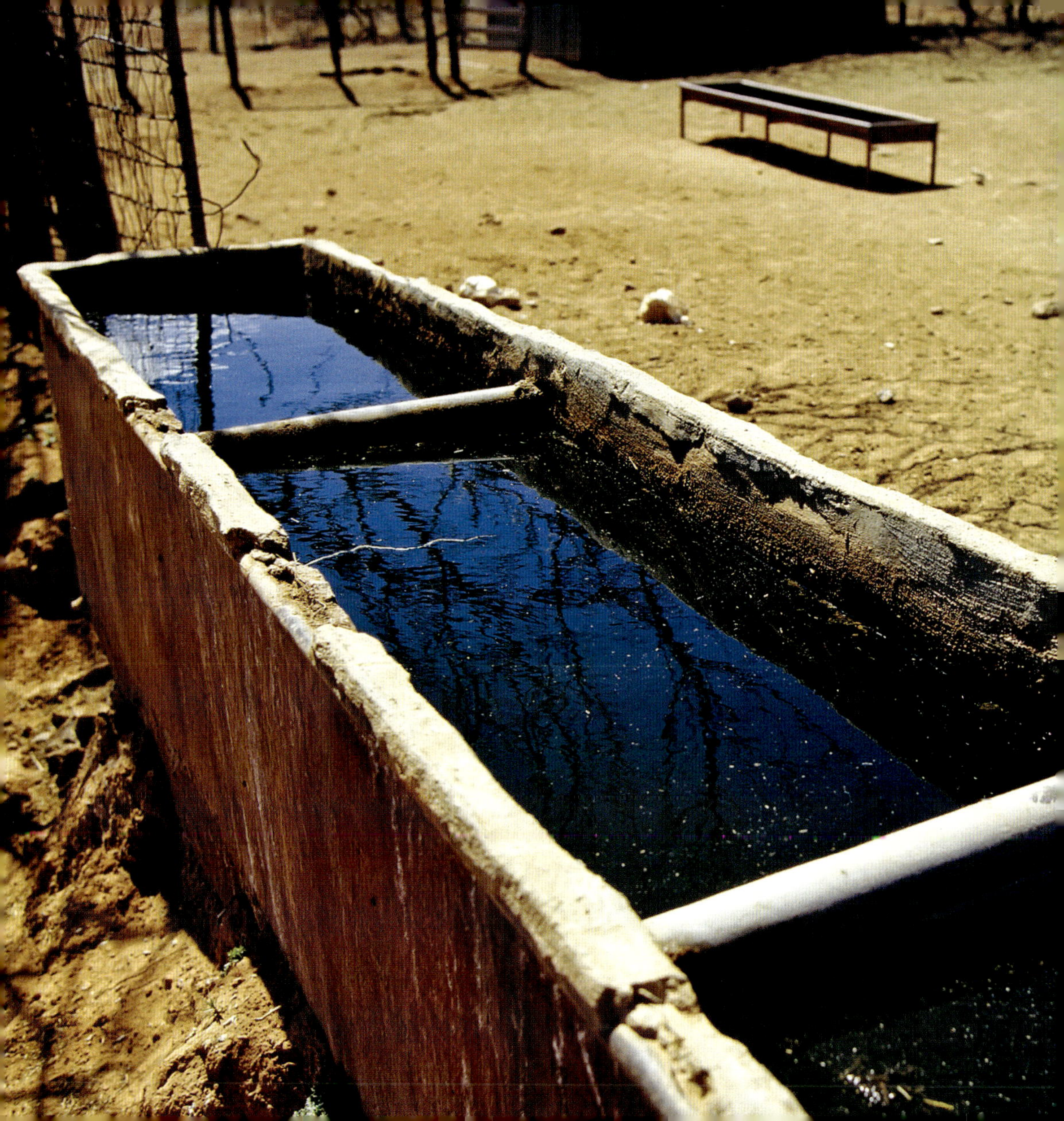

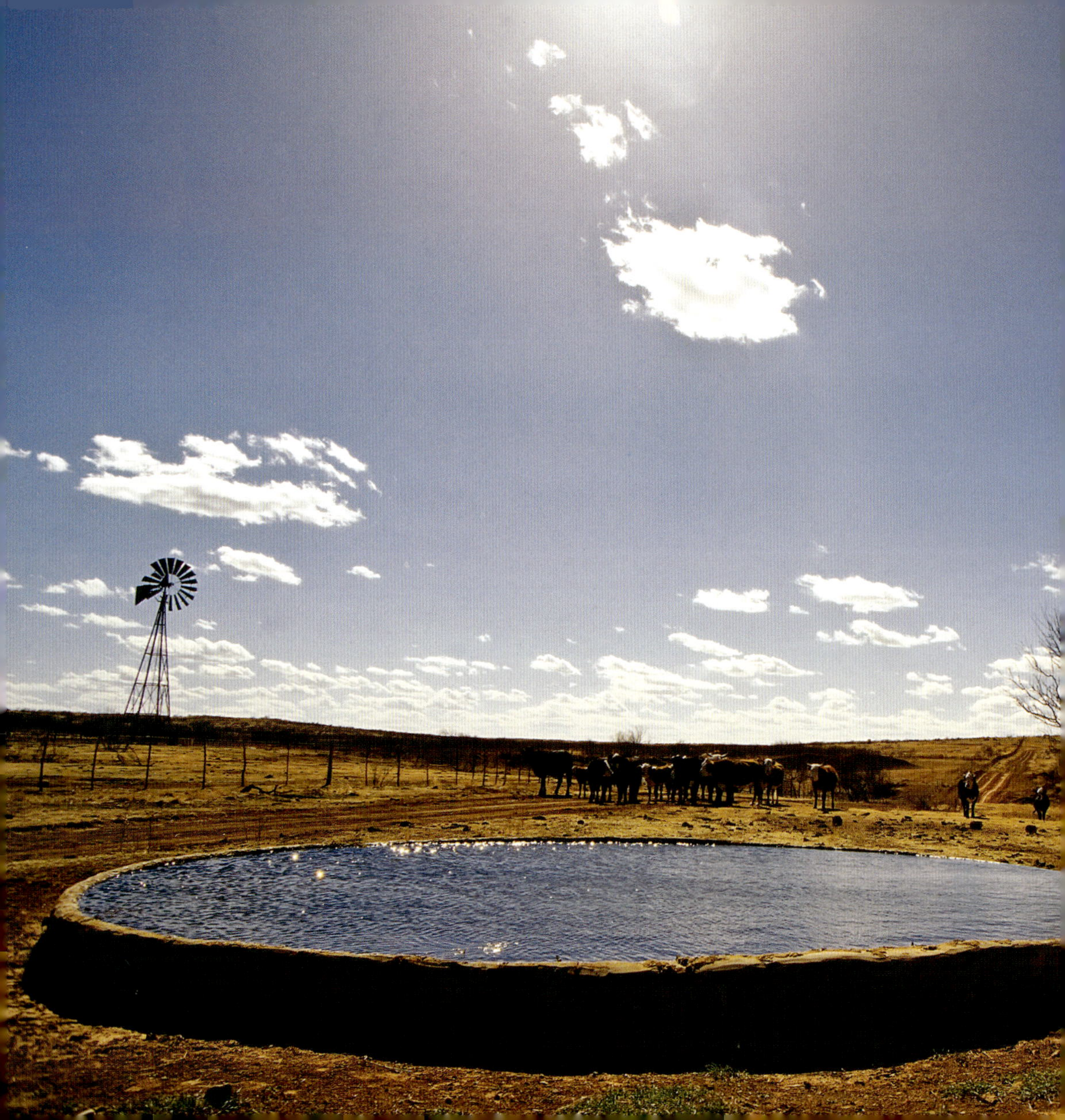

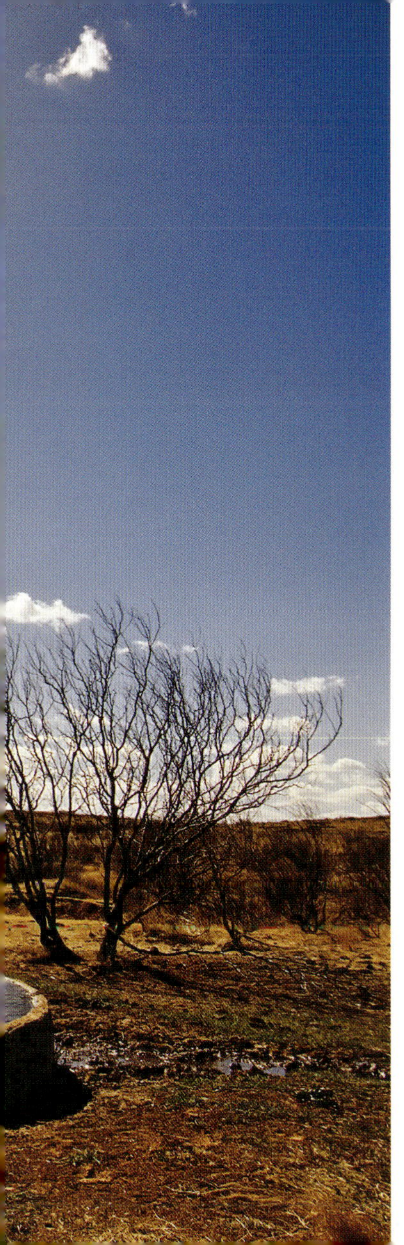

You cannot operate a ranch without water for the livestock. The Pitchfork Ranch in Texas has 120 windmills on the property and a full-time windmill crew to keep them all running.

Hot and Dry
Pitchfork Ranch
Guthrie, Texas

Big 'Ole Wheel

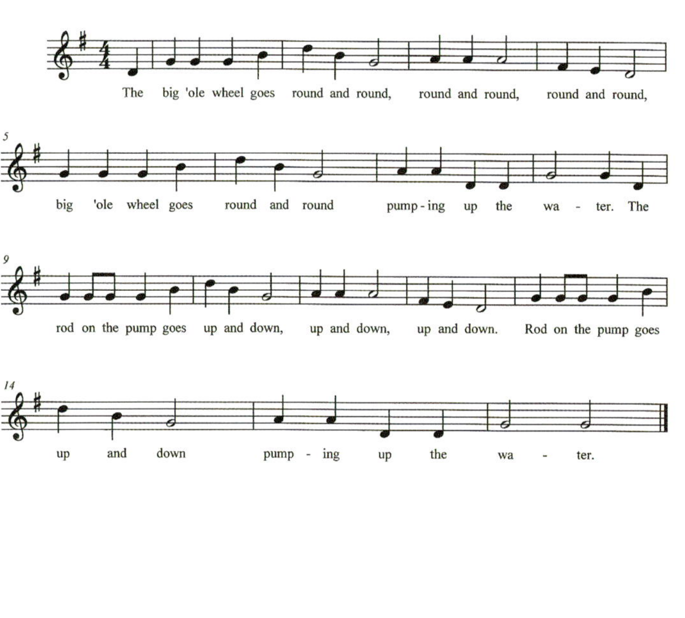

Deep, Dark, and Dangerous But No Rain in Sight
Cluck Ranches
Gruver, Texas

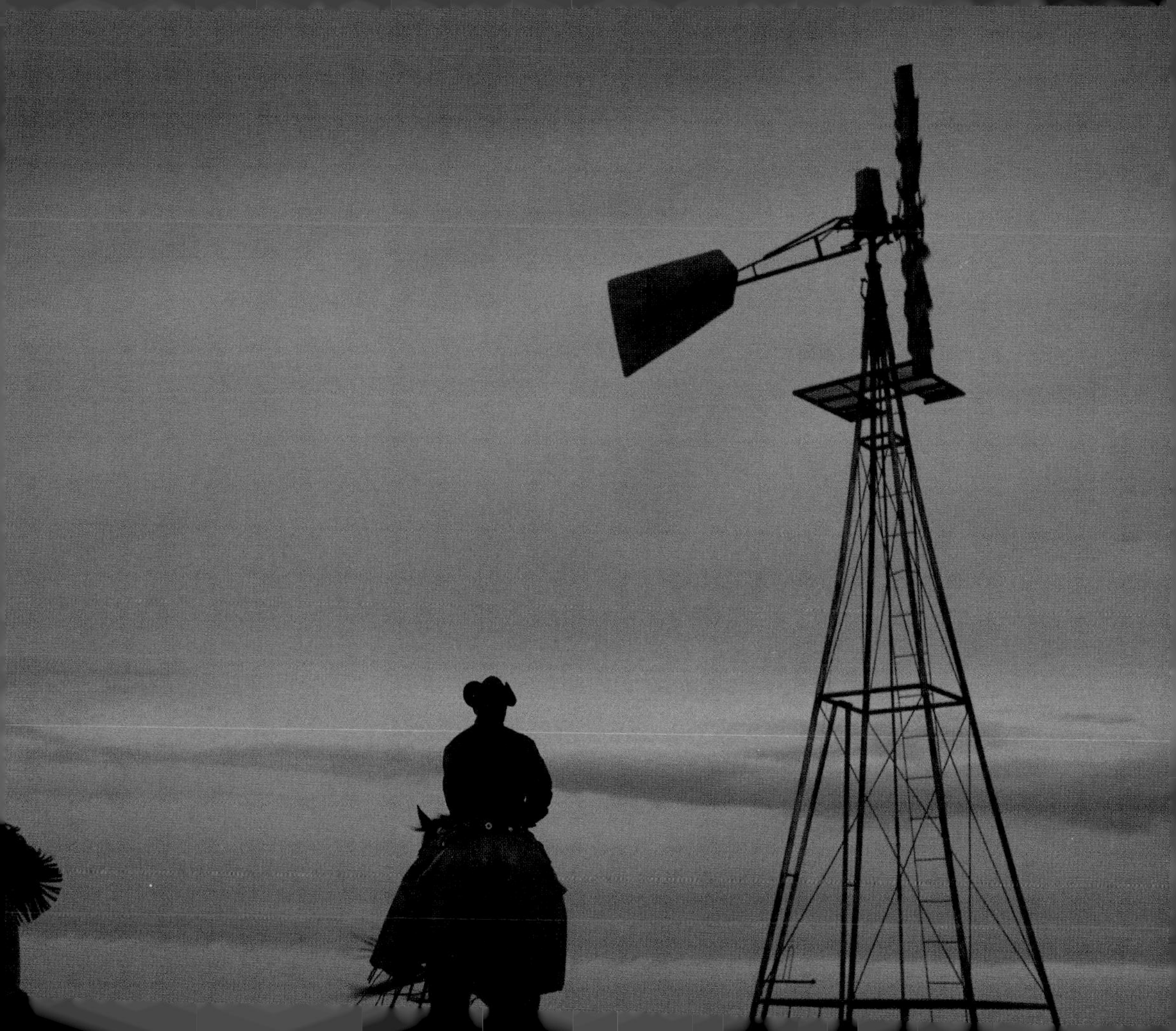

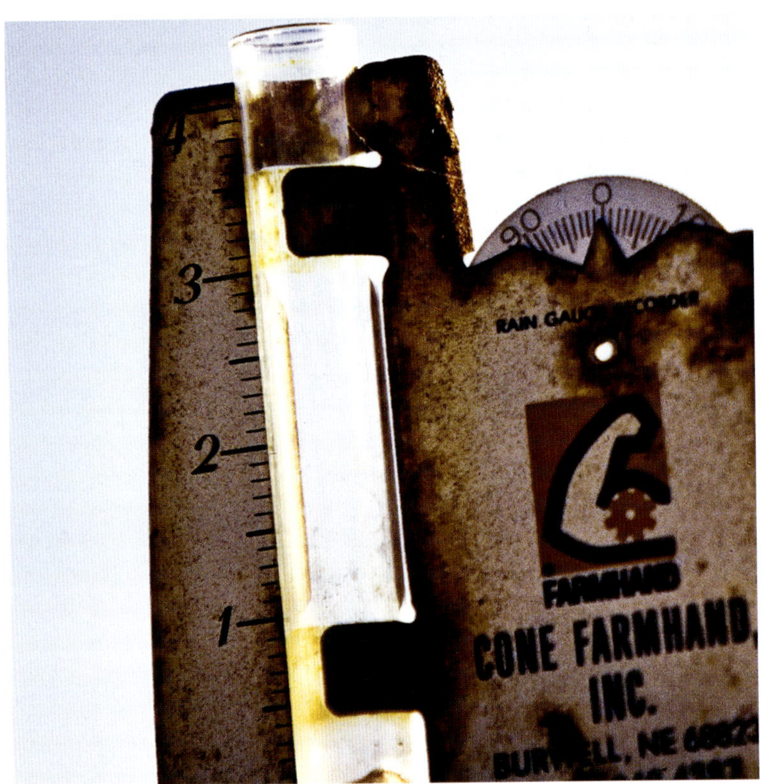

Rain Gauge
Saunders Ranch
Weatherford, Texas

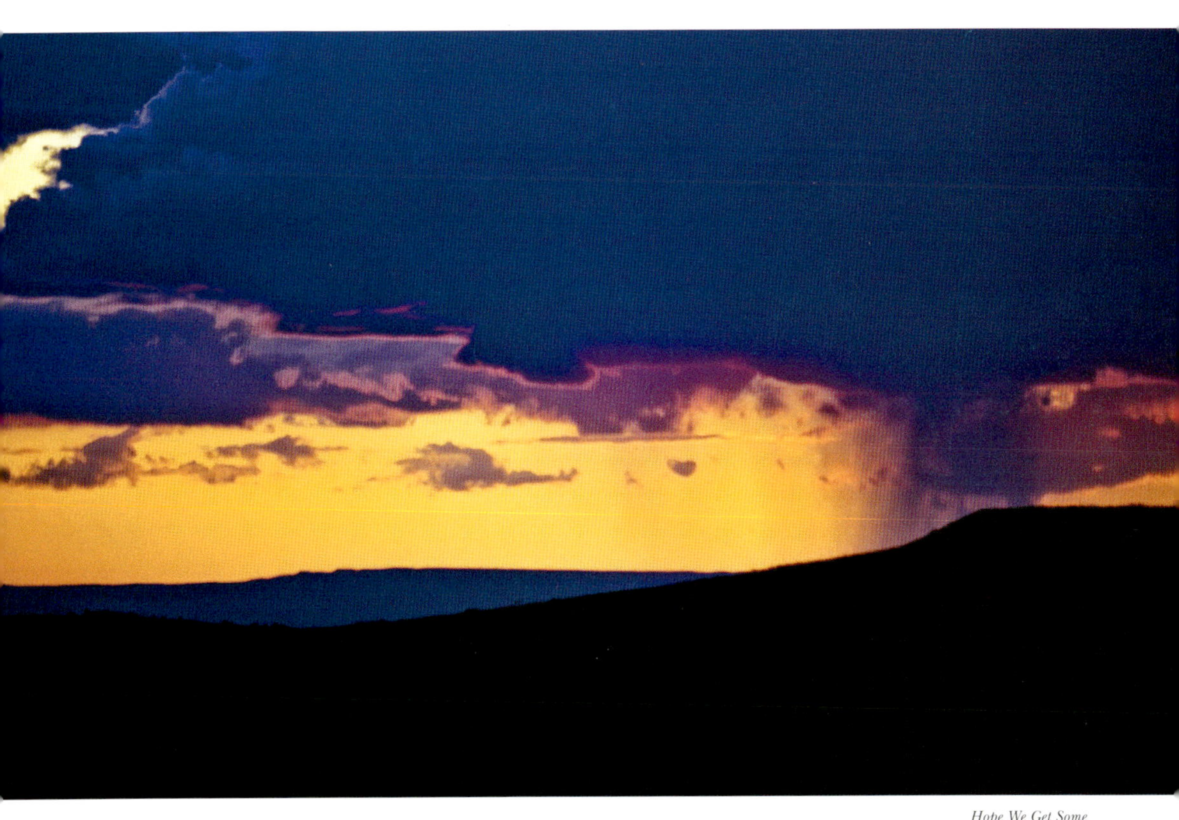

Hope We Get Some
Western Montana

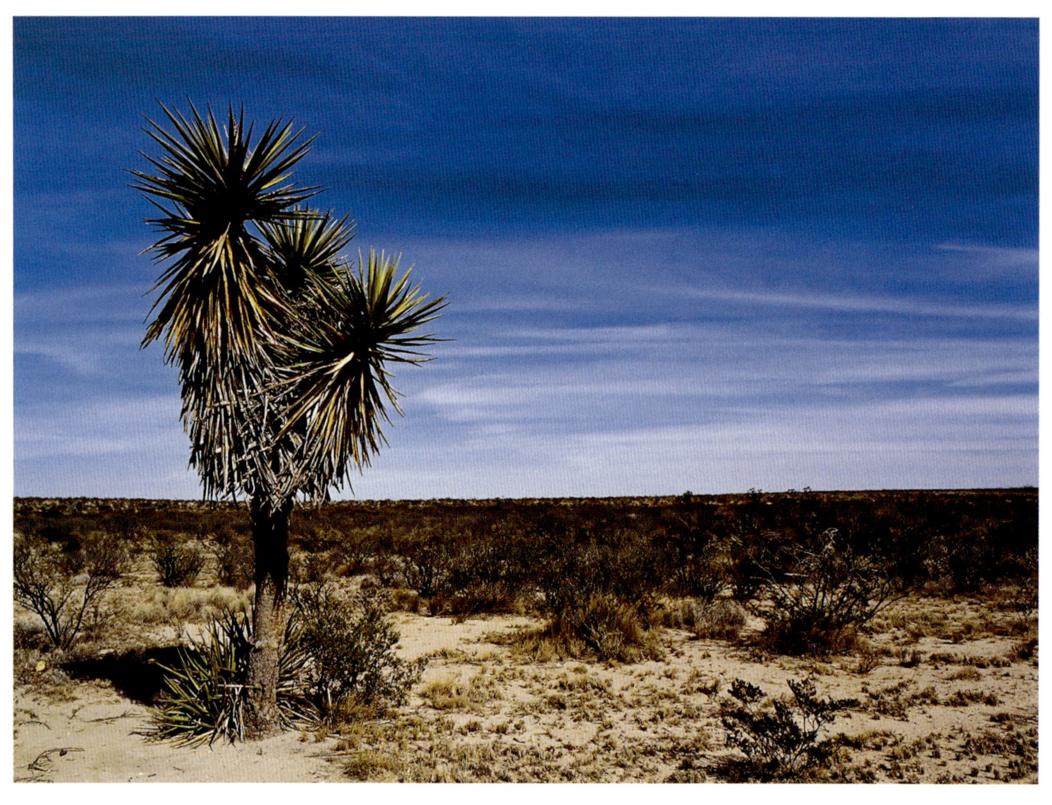

Absence of available water was the biggest problem on the prairie. Said one newcomer to the Plains, "This would be a fine country if it just had water." "Yes," replied a disgruntled settler heading back East, "so would Hell."

Not Much Grows That Does Not Bite, Sting, or Stab
West Texas

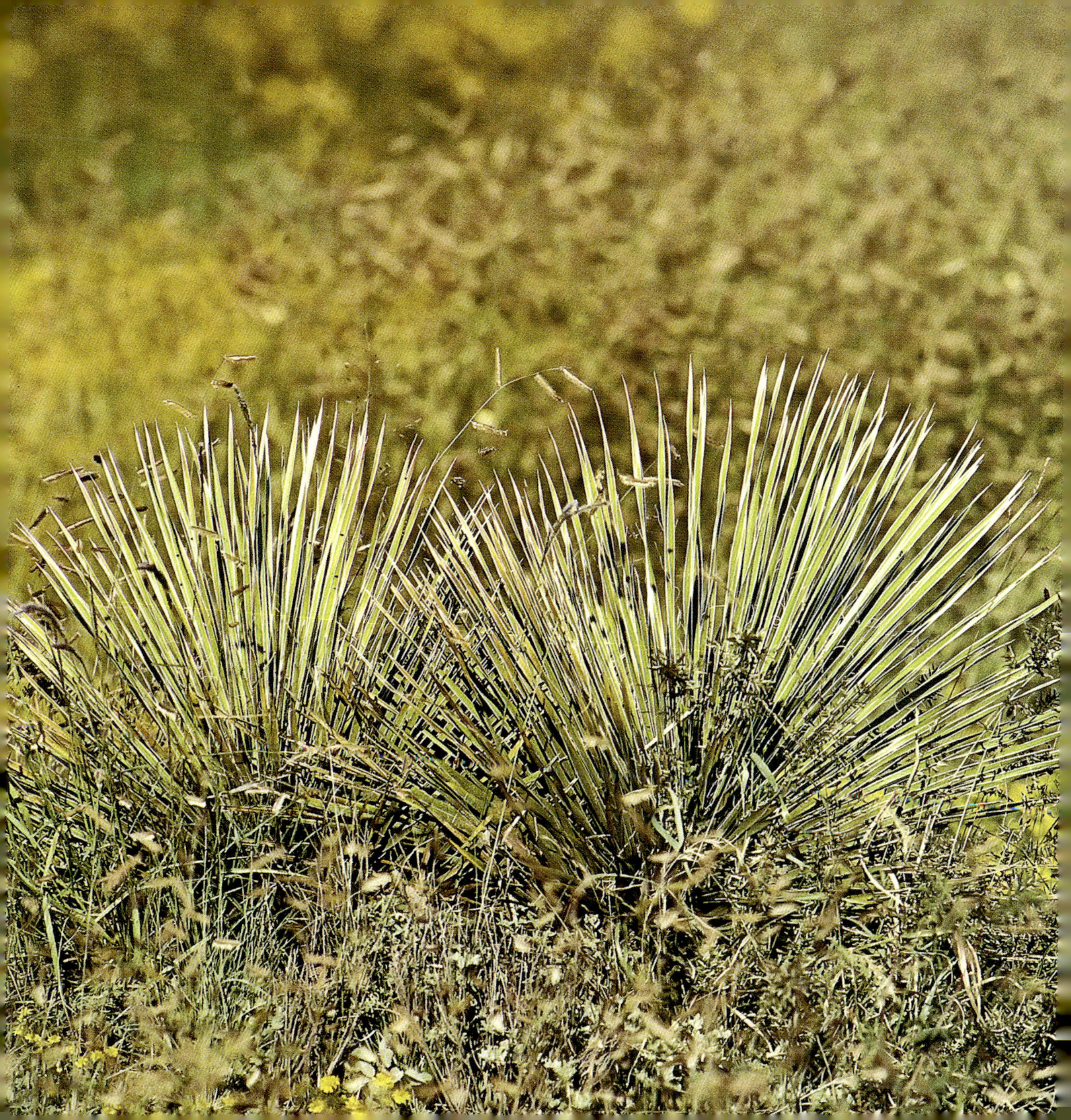

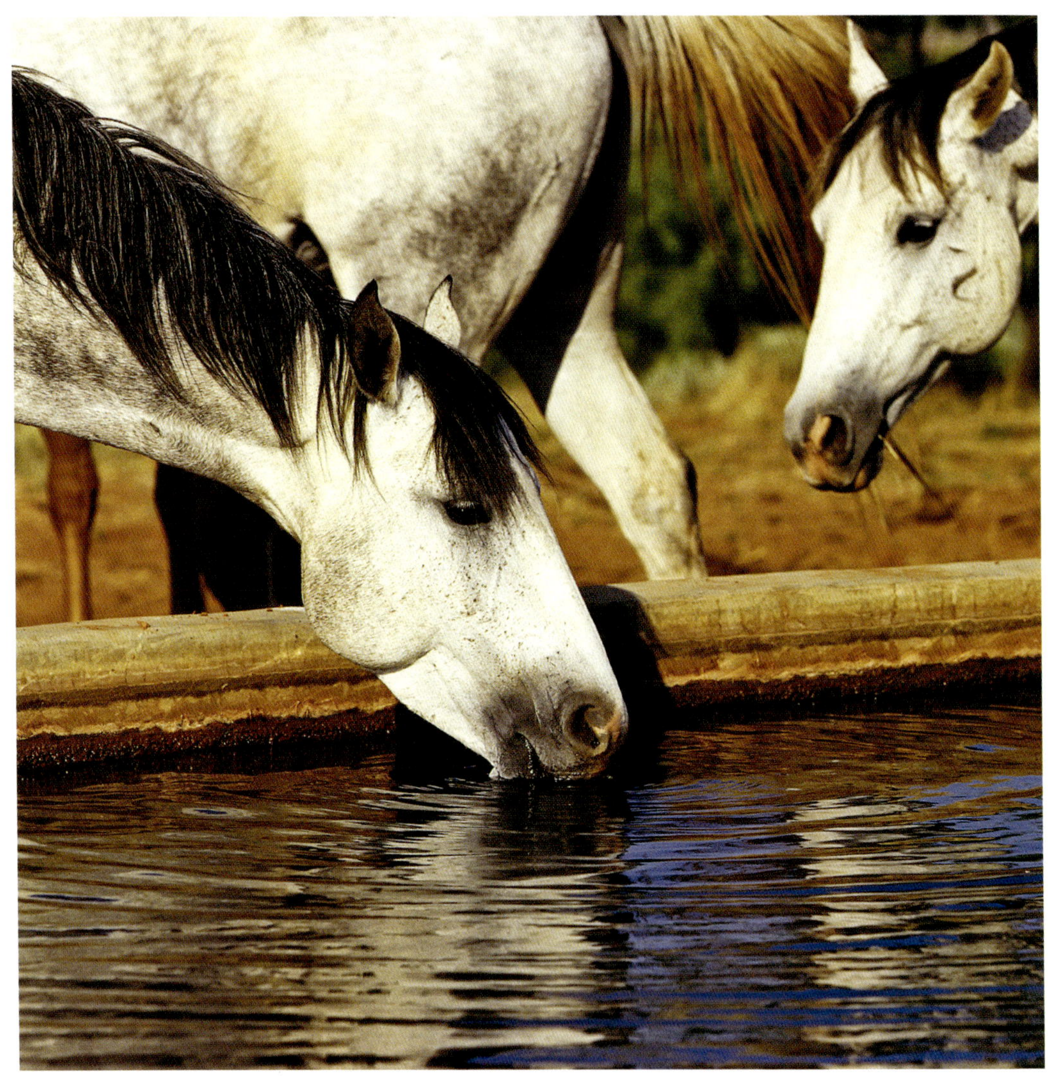

Cool Sip
Beggs Ranch, Post, Texas

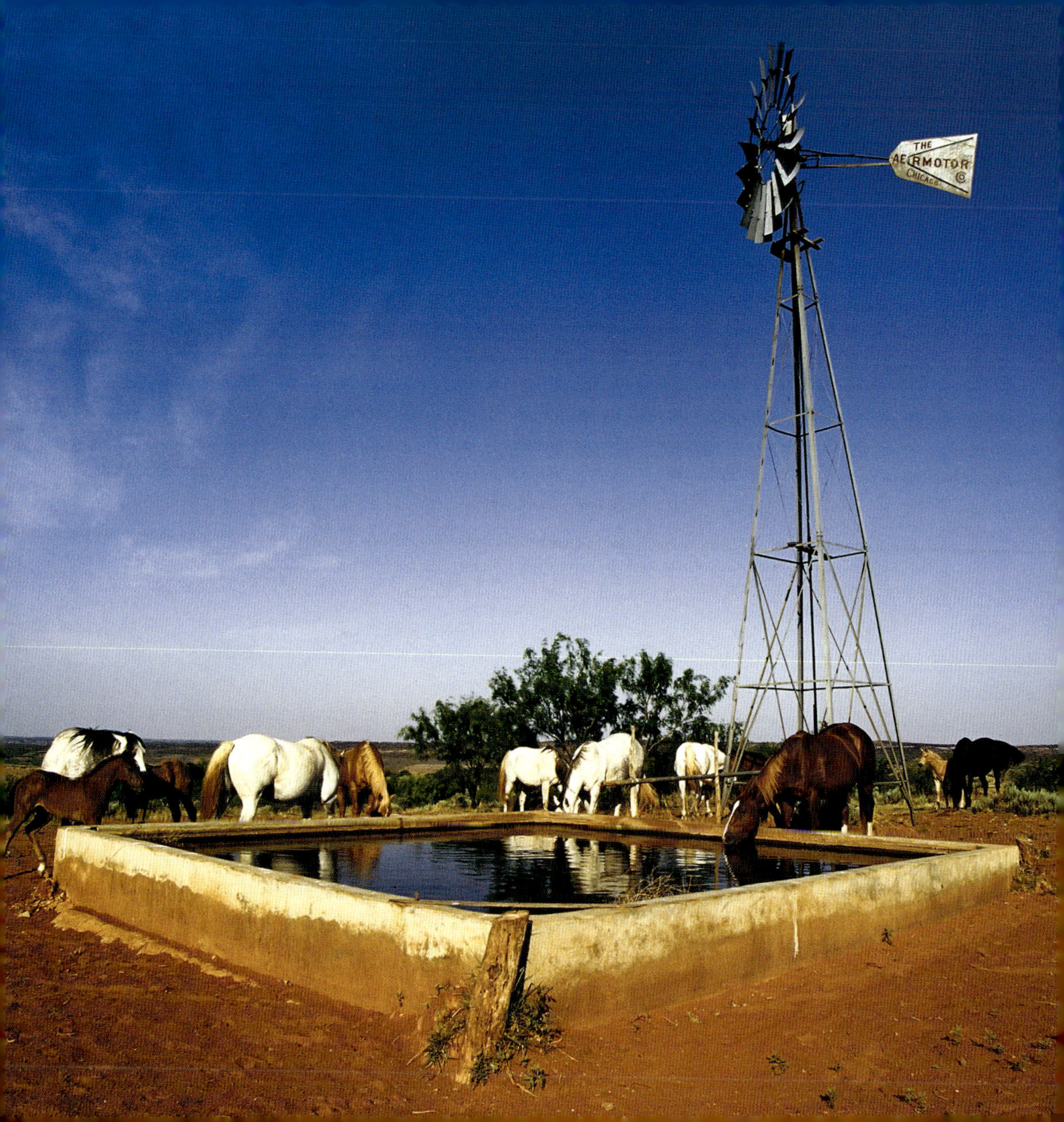
THE
AERMOTOR
CHICAGO

Broken Dreams

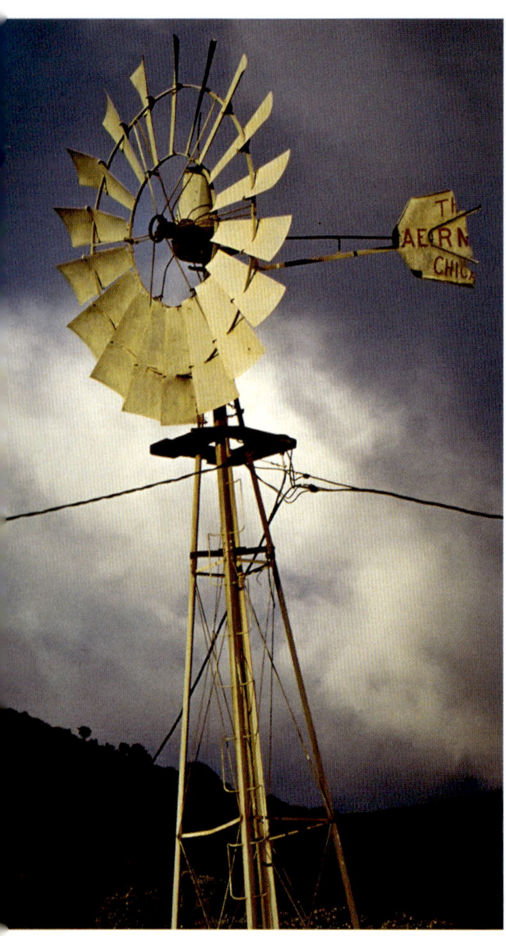

A young Yankee lieutenant, drifting west after the Civil War, rode up to some abandoned ranch buildings and stopped at the water trough at the base of an old creaking windmill. He looked around slowly at the ghostly weather-beaten structures as his horse began to pull in long draws of water. He noticed a flat Prince Albert tobacco can wired to the leg of the wooden base next to him. As his horse continued to drink, he flipped open the lid and pulled out a yellowed, wrinkly piece of paper. Unfolding it gently, he began to read the fading words written in pencil:

"This once was a homestead of love and hope, but now it's just a monument to our broken dreams. The dreaded 'pox' came and took my sweet Sarah and our precious little ones. I buried them one by one, yonder past the one-room sodder. I've been here by myself for so long now that I can no longer stand it. The ranch is yours for the taking. The land gave me the wind, Sears & Roebuck gave me the windmill, and God gave me the water. All I ask is that you water the wildflowers growing on their little graves beyond the house."

Corralitos Ranch
Guadalupe, California

At Long Last
Texas Panhandle

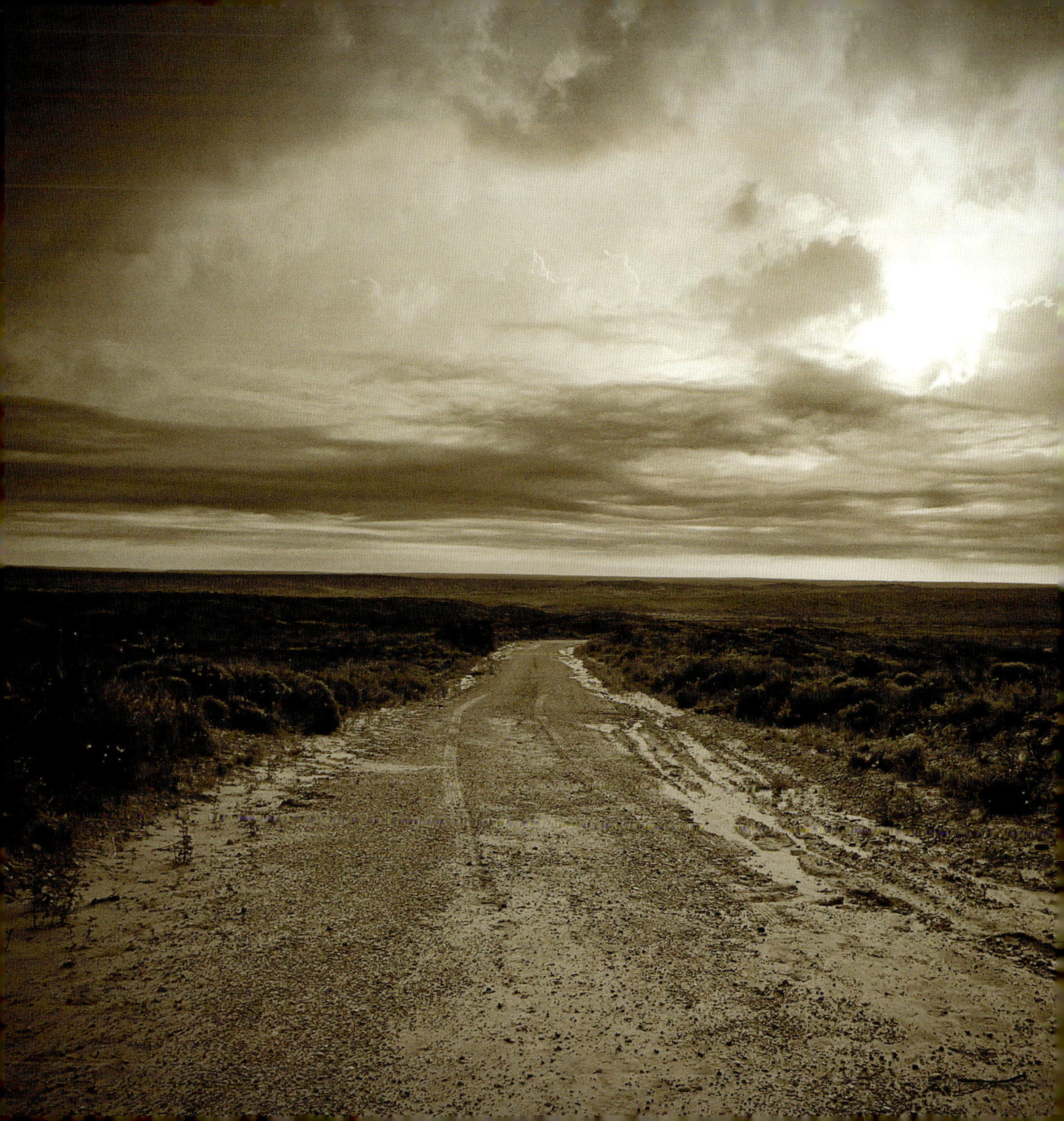

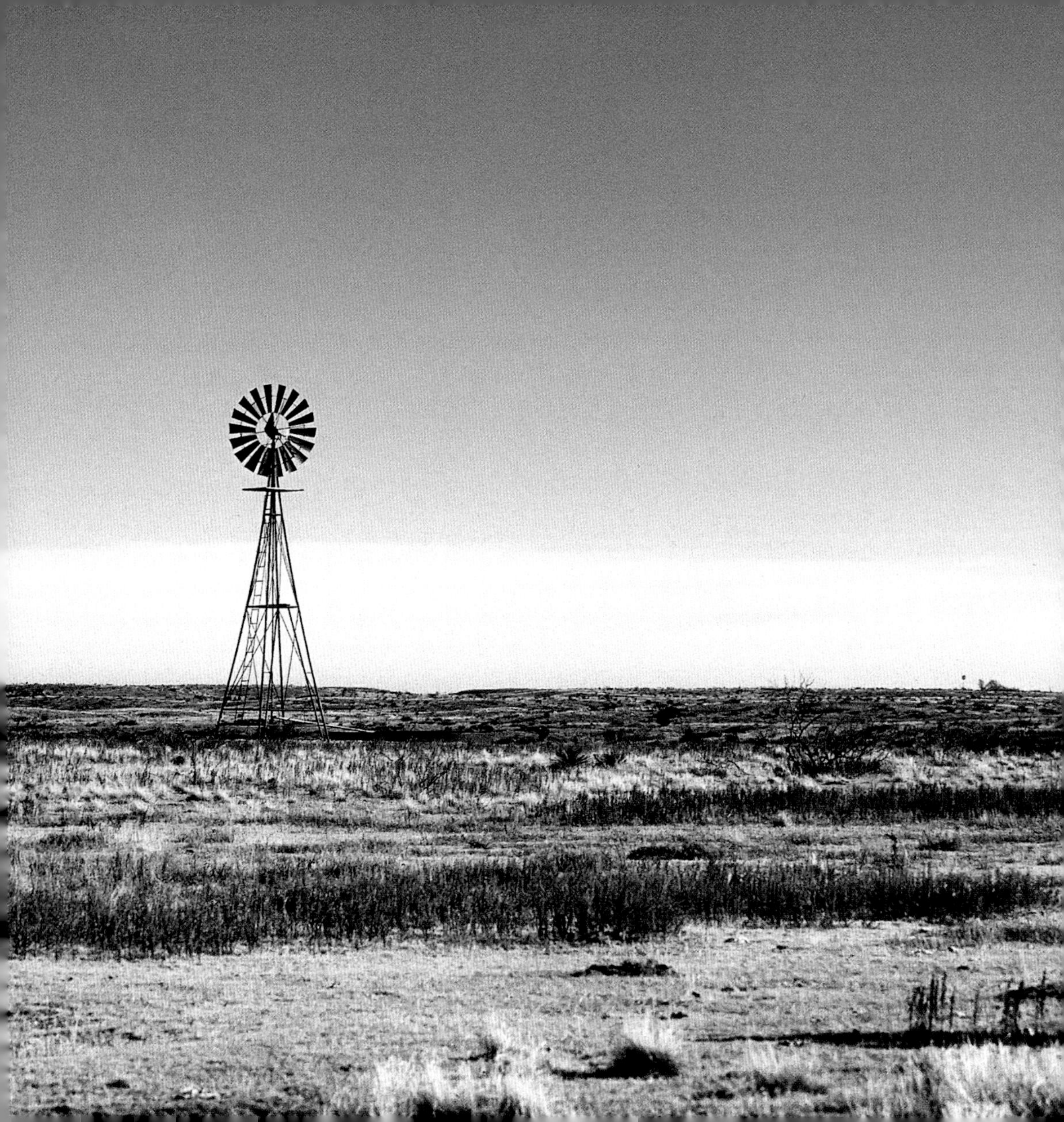

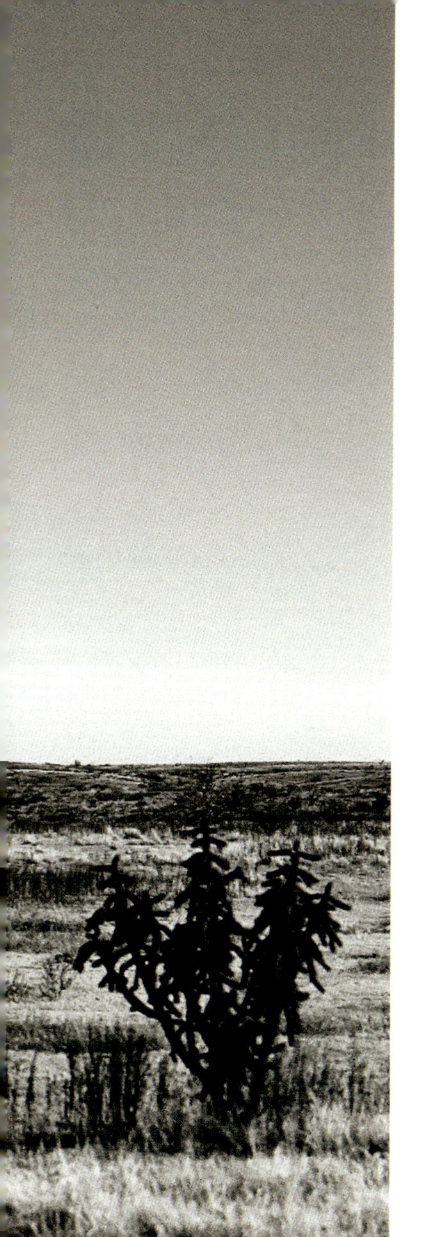

A census taker once asked a remote Kansas settler when his son had been born. He simply answered, "That summer it rained!"

Only Water for Miles Around
Toyah, Texas

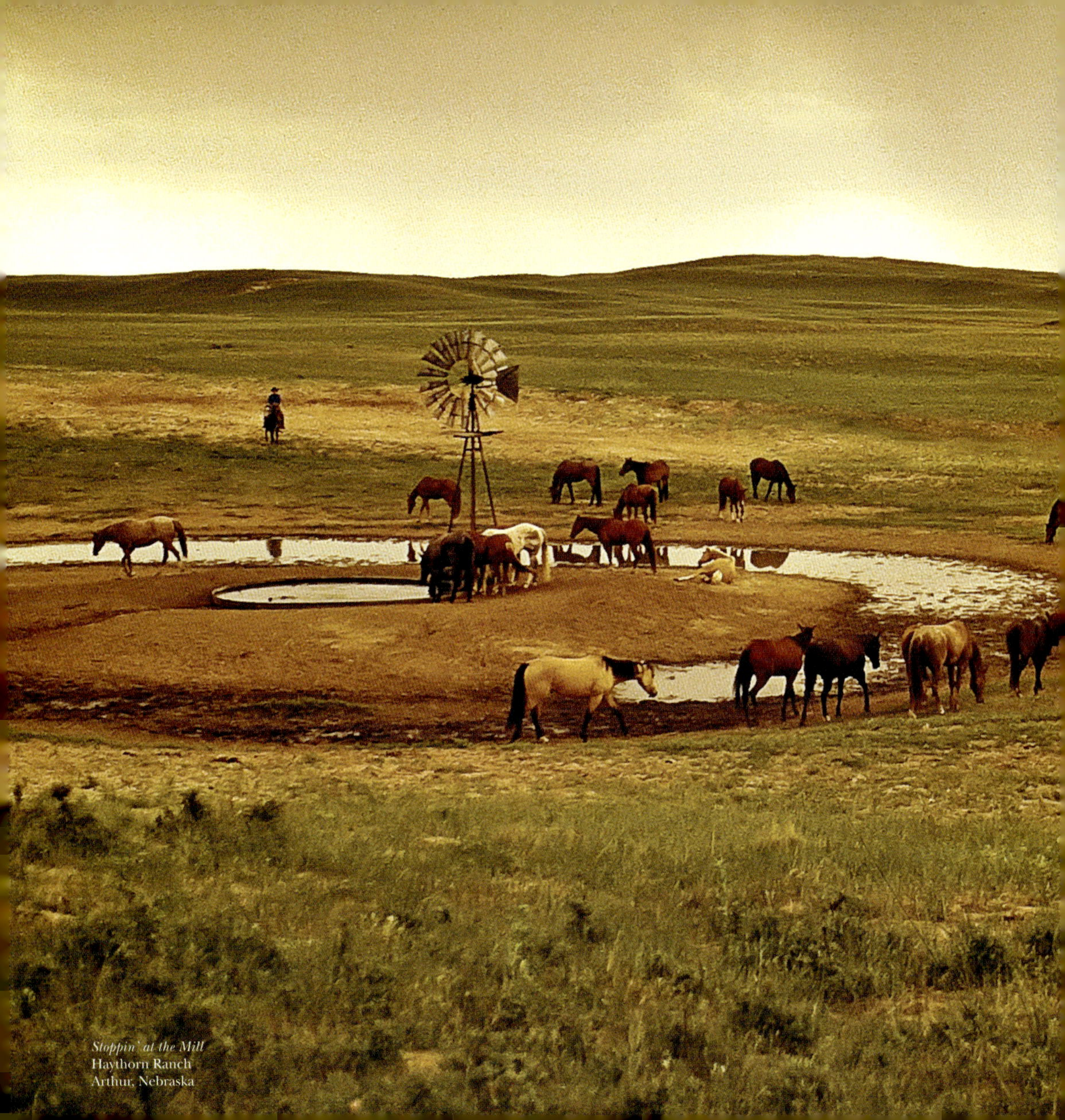

Stoppin' at the Mill
Haythorn Ranch
Arthur, Nebraska

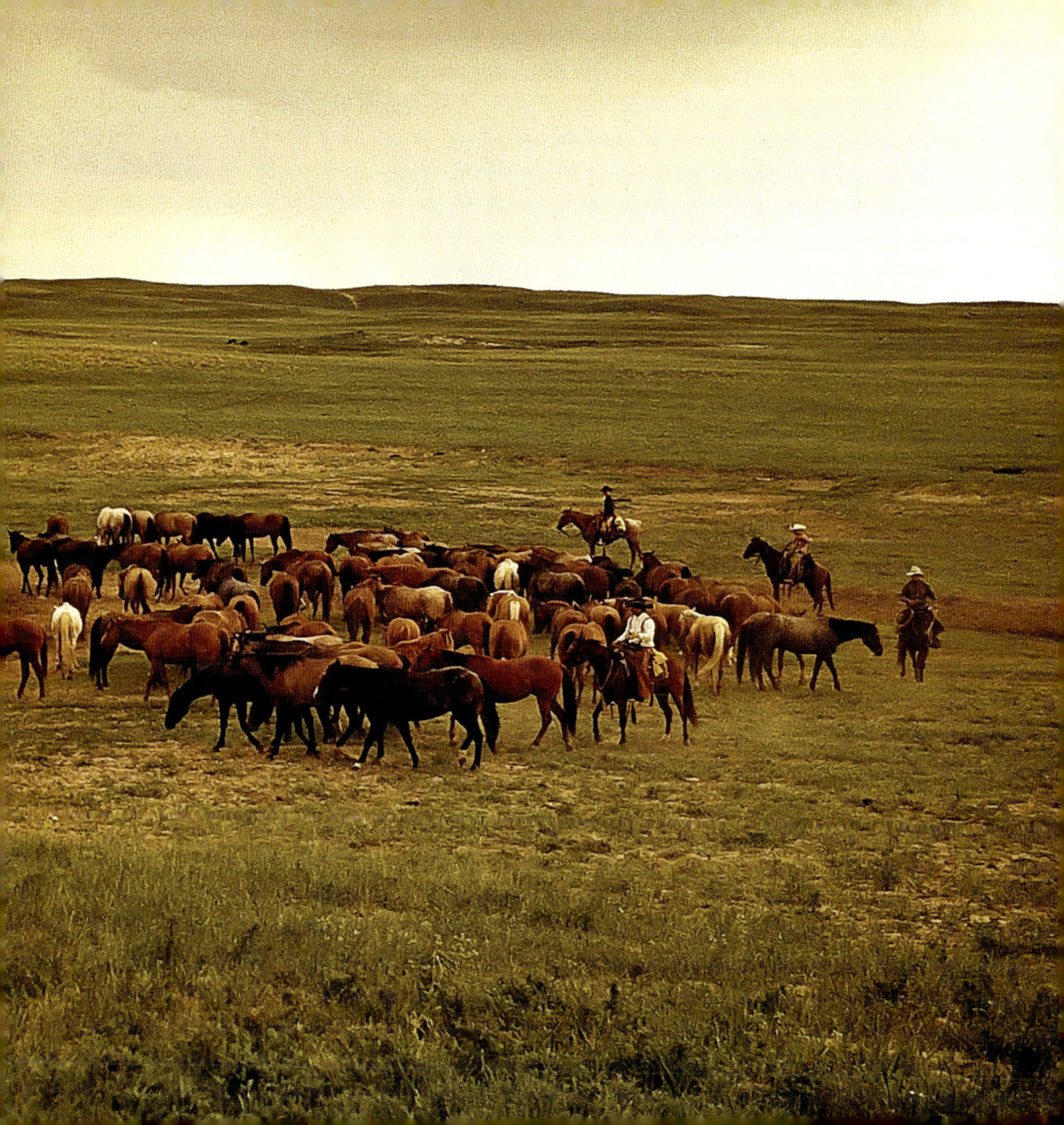

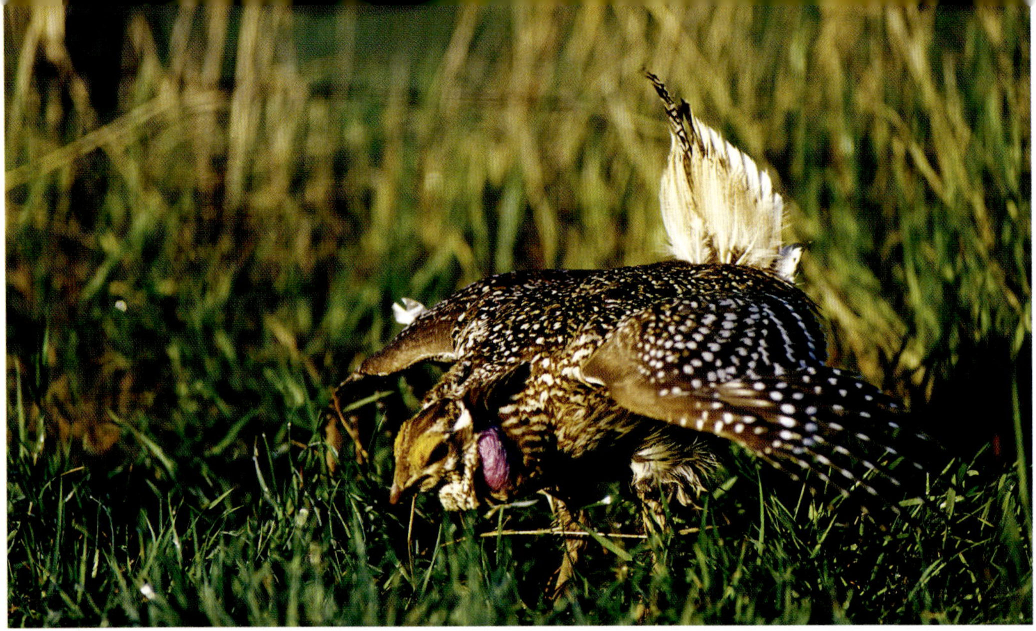

Sharp-tailed Grouse
IO Ranch
Montana

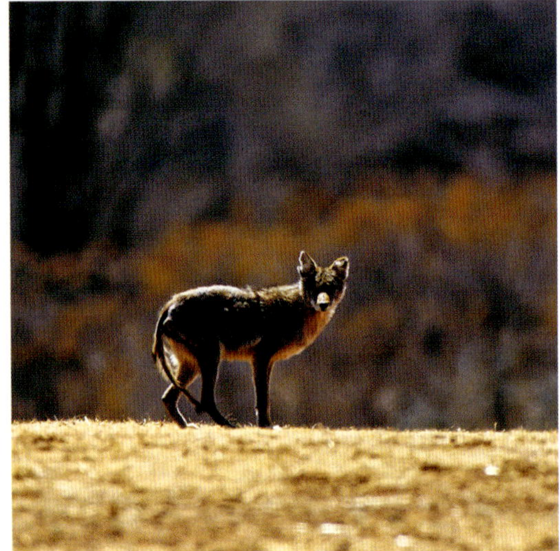

All creatures great and small depend on the windmill's bounty for survival.

Coyote
Pitchfork Ranch
Guthrie, Texas

Antelope
Granby, Colorado

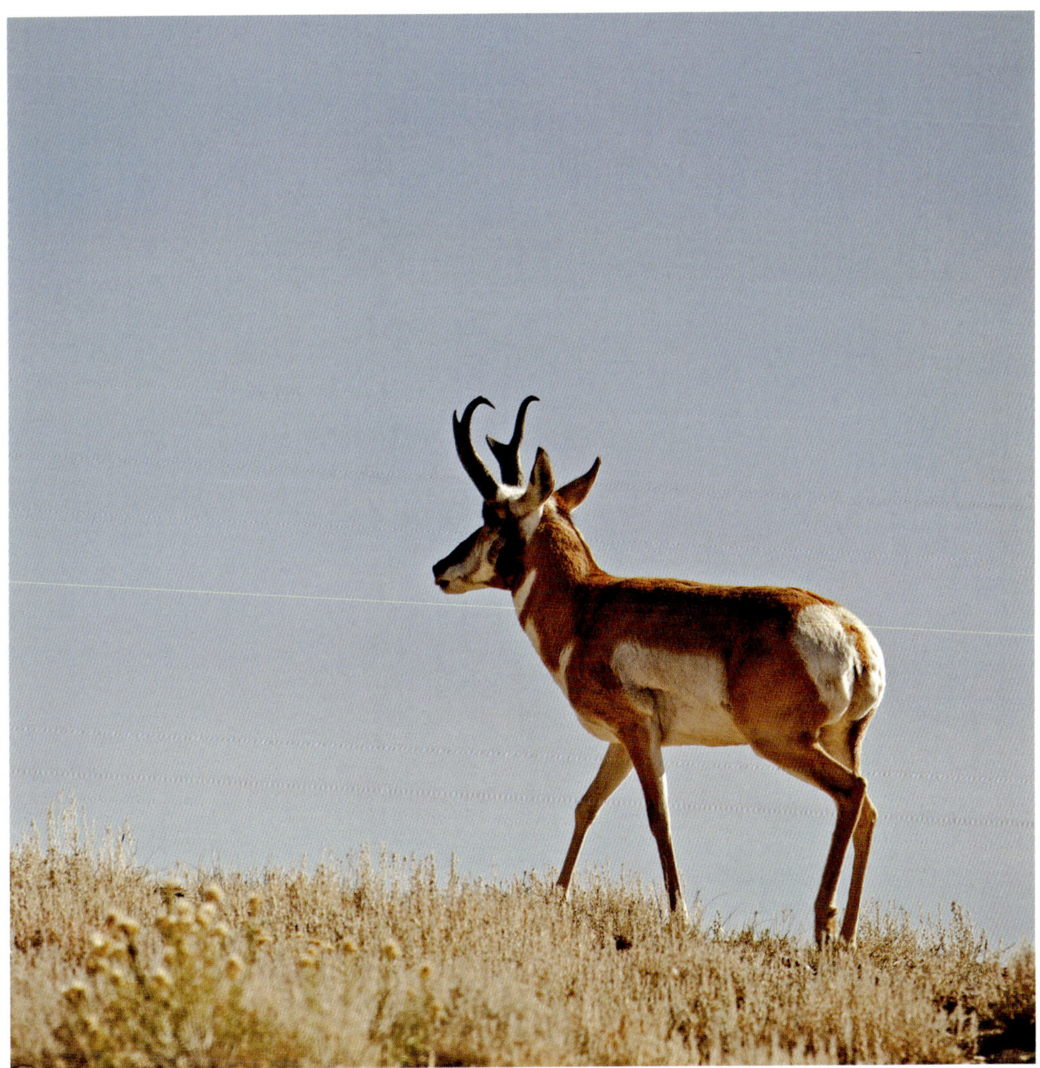

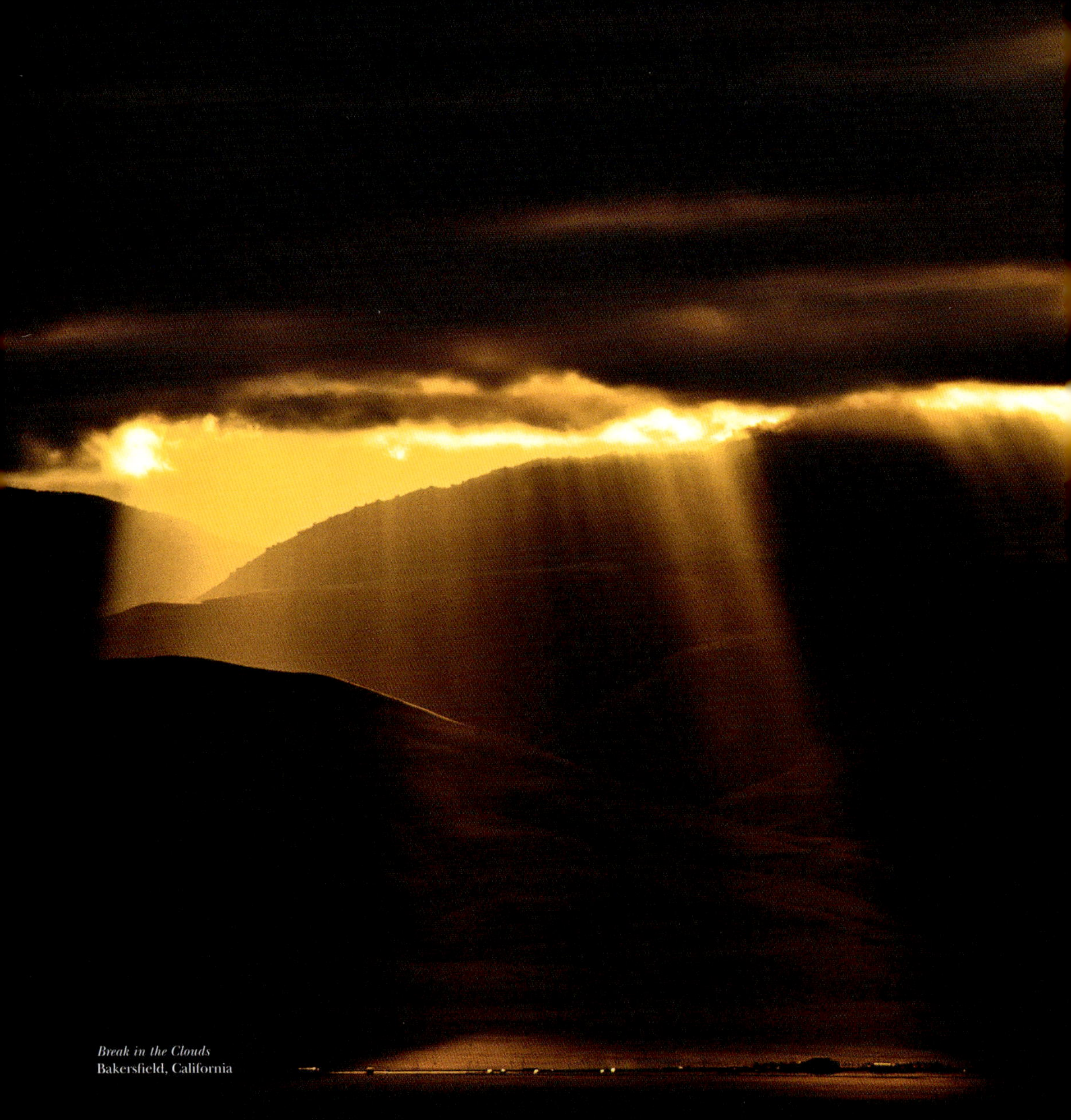

Break in the Clouds
Bakersfield, California

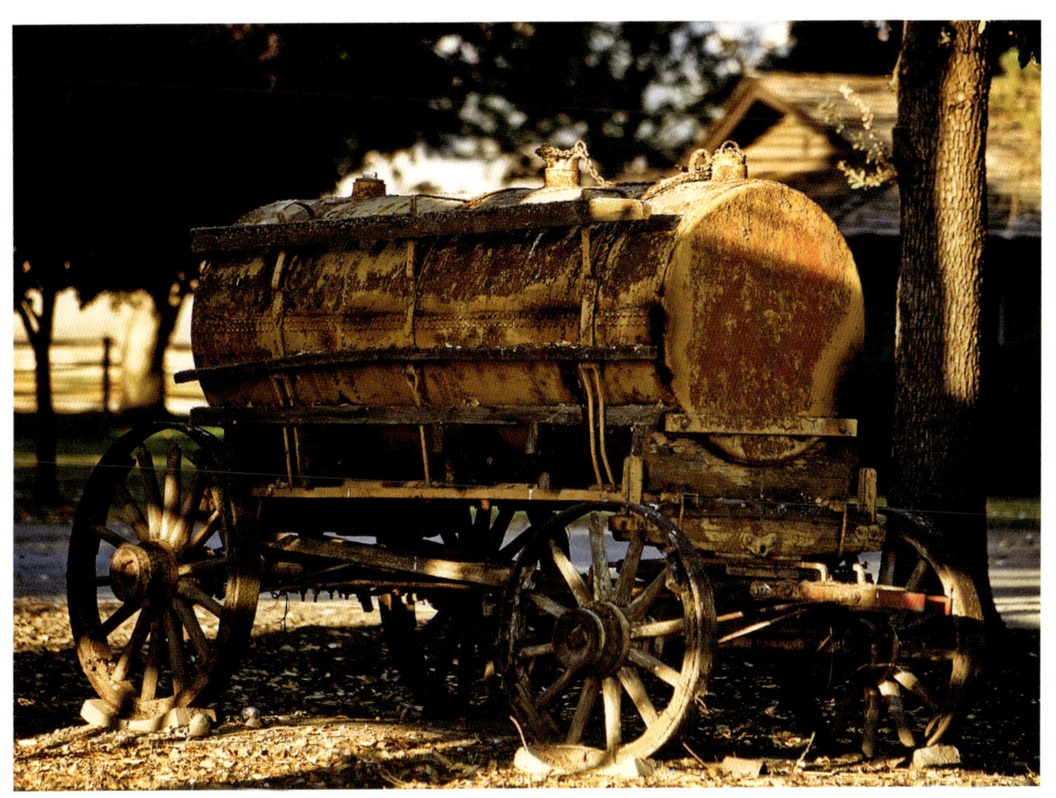

Water Wagon
Jack Ranch
Parkville, California

Hallelujah, grace fell down like rain
And washed away my sins and pain.
Spreading out like a blue ink stain
Spreading forth across the plain.

—lyrics from an old New Mexico hymnal

The Short Mill

Windmills don't always have to be up high in the sky. This is a short, stubby Nebraska windmill designed to catch the wind as it blows across the sand hills close to the ground.

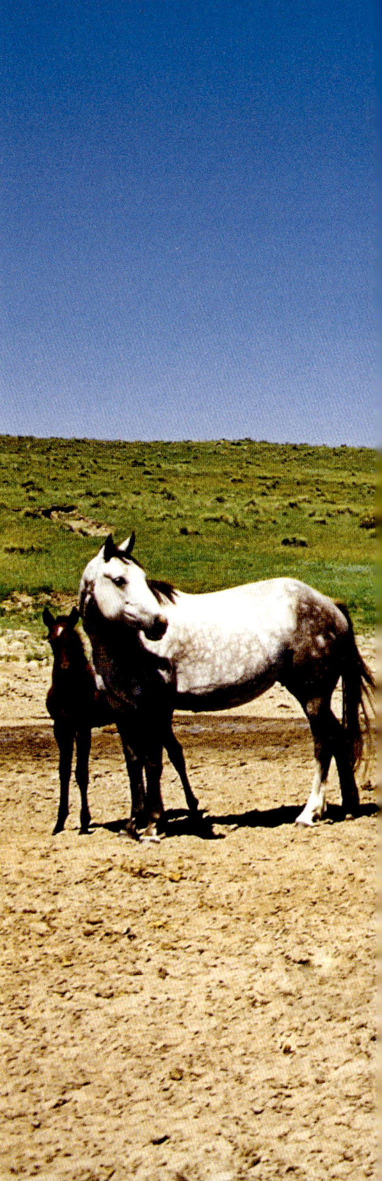

Low to the Ground
Haythorn Ranch
Arthur, Nebraska

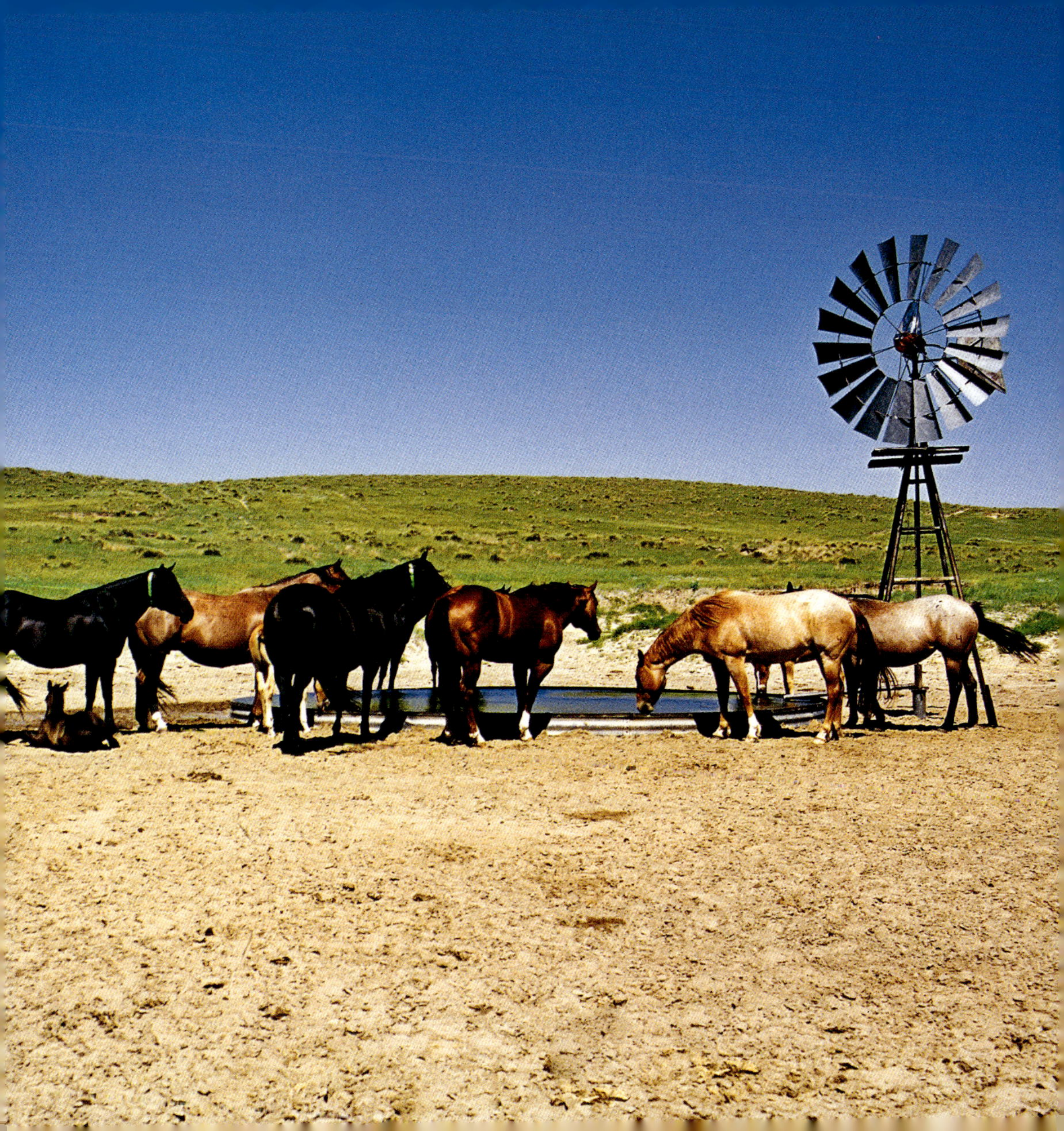

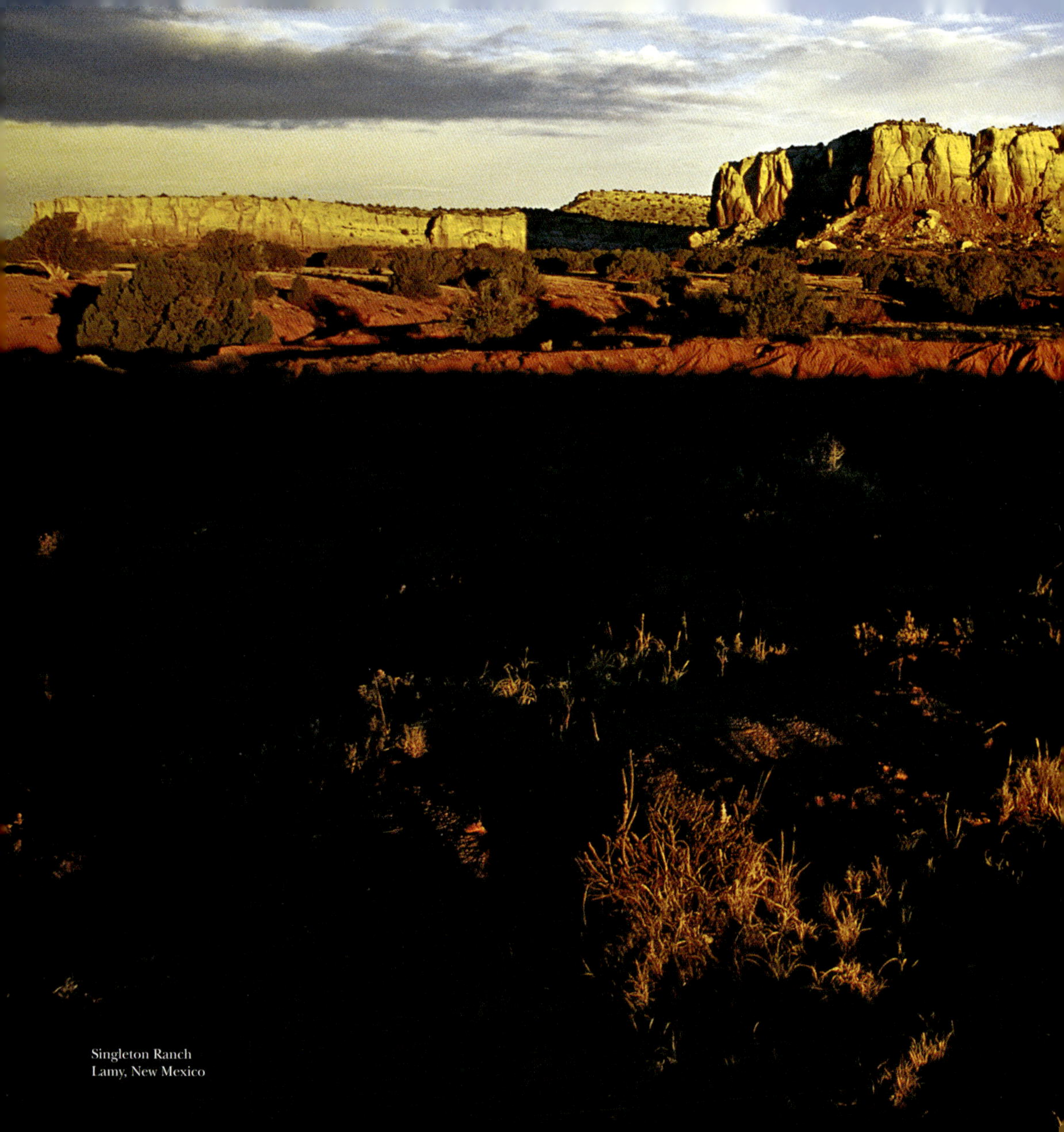

Singleton Ranch
Lamy, New Mexico

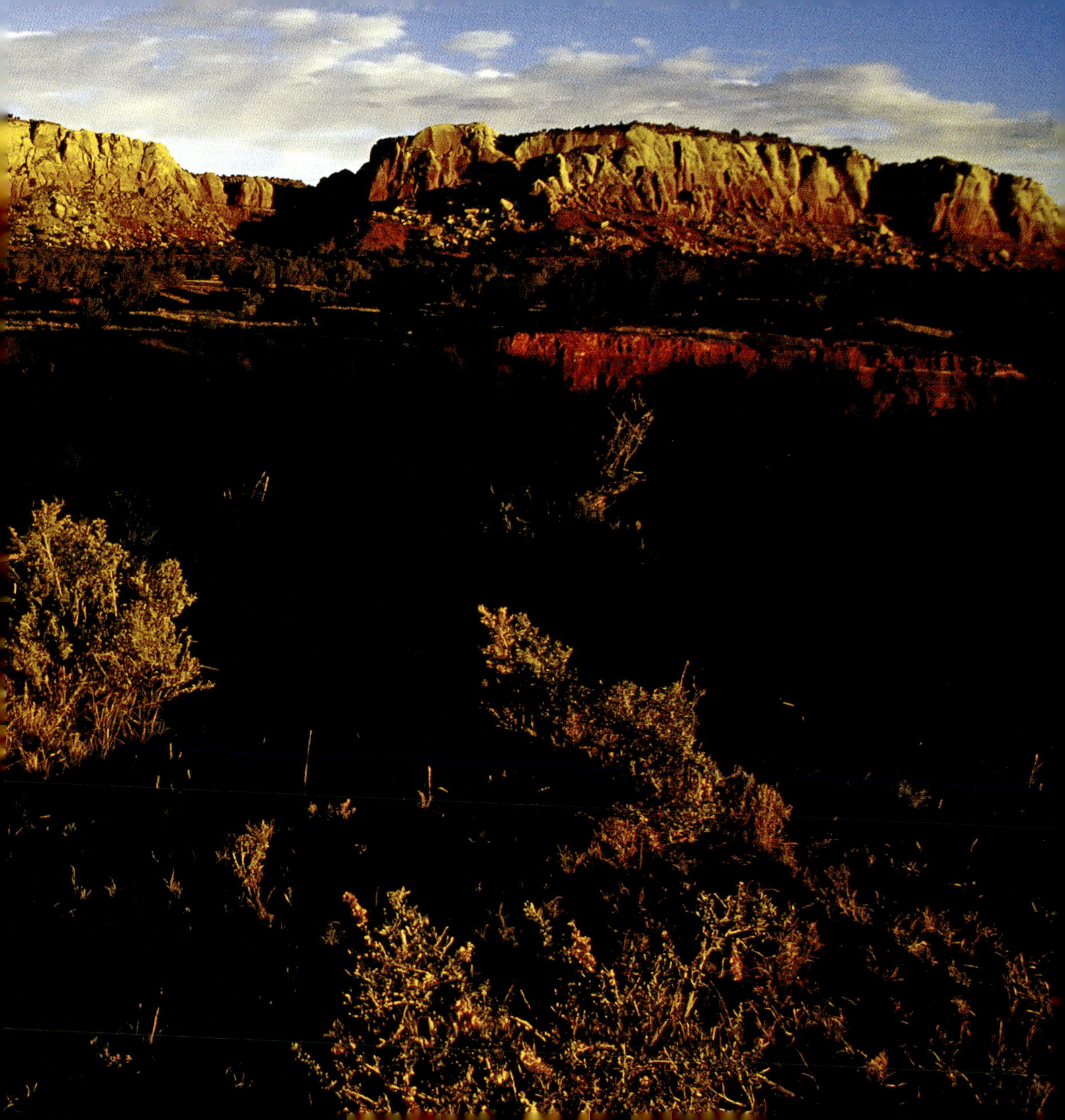

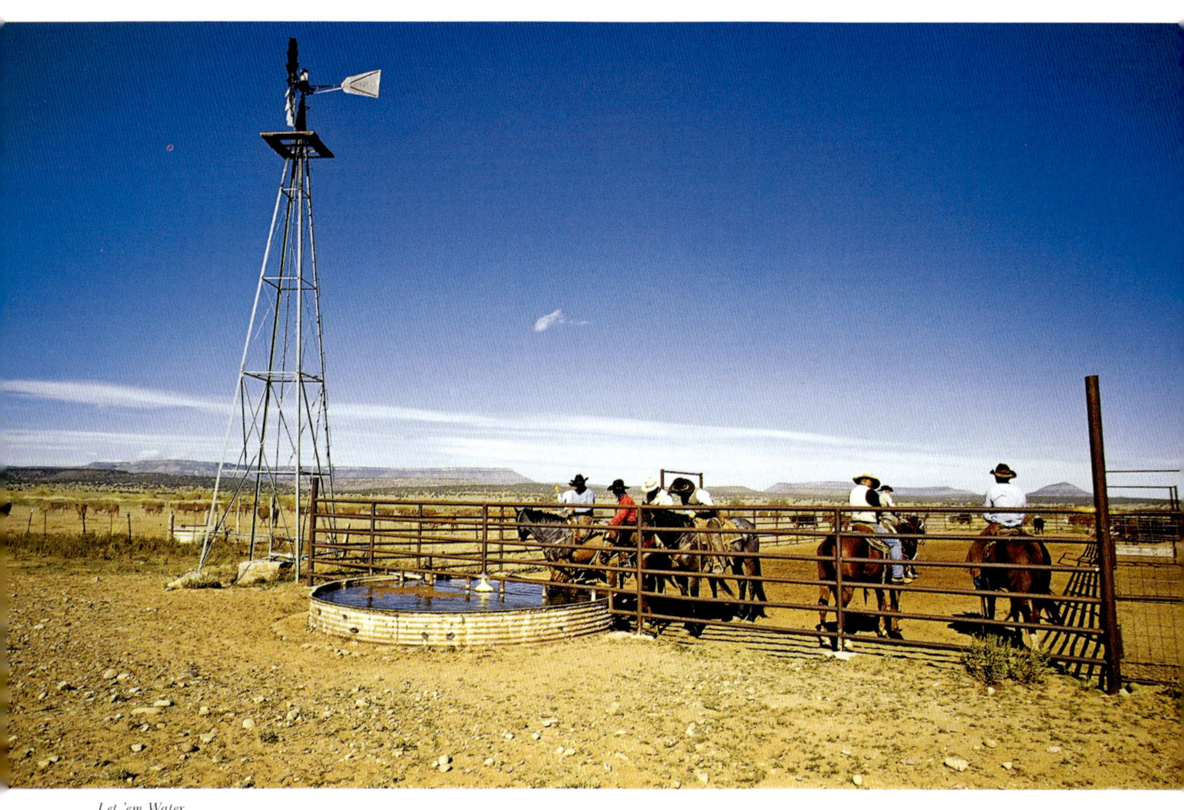

Let 'em Water
Singleton Ranch
Lamy, New Mexico

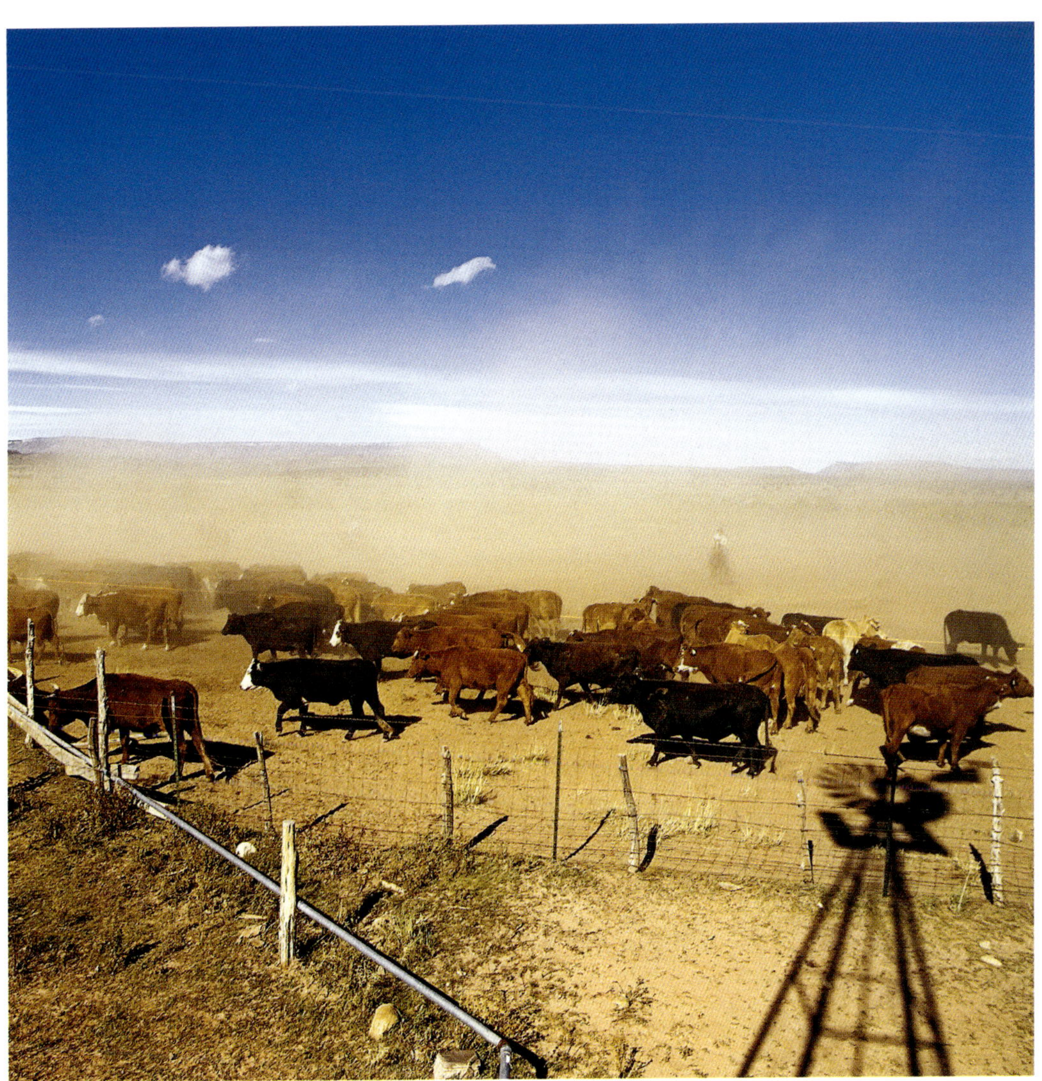

Singleton Ranch
Lamy, New Mexico

The Bully

Billy Carver was the neighbor kid who lived down the road. He had to walk past our house every day on the way to school. We had an old one-eyed dog we called Popcorn whom we really loved. We kept him inside the fenced yard in the front of the house so he wouldn't wander out on to the road and get hit by a car he couldn't see. Billy was as mean as a snake and cruel to animals. Dad said his ill temper probably came from his alcoholic father who would come home drunk and in a blind rage. That, and the fact his mother had run off with the Surge dairy supply salesman didn't contribute to a model kid. He had a badly chipped front tooth that made his sadistic smile even more vile when he tormented us. Billy liked to throw rocks at Popcorn every morning when he went by the house. After a while, the dog grew mean toward Billy. I know if he had gotten out of the yard after one of those peltings he would have eaten the pockets right off Billy's pants.

One late summer day Billy came over to the yard to play with my older brother, Danny. The two of them climbed up to the windmill to play on the platform. What my brother didn't know was that Billy had filled his pockets with rocks and began to throw them down at Popcorn from the tower. This made Danny furious and he quickly climbed down, ran over to the gate, and let the dog out. Popcorn was at the bottom of that windmill in a flash and would have climbed up the ladder after him if he could have. He just sat there at the bottom, baring his teeth and growling up at that surprised bully. We could still hear Billy bawling well after sunset. When my folks got home from town they wanted to know what was going on. After Dad heard the story he decided to leave that ornery kid up there a while longer. He sure wouldn't be missed at home. When Dad went out a short time later, the crying had stopped. Apparently, Billy had fallen asleep on the platform. Dad quietly put Popcorn back in the yard, shut the gate, and came back into the house. We weren't sure how or when Billy got down off the windmill tower, but in the morning he was gone. He never came around again and from then on he took the long way to school.

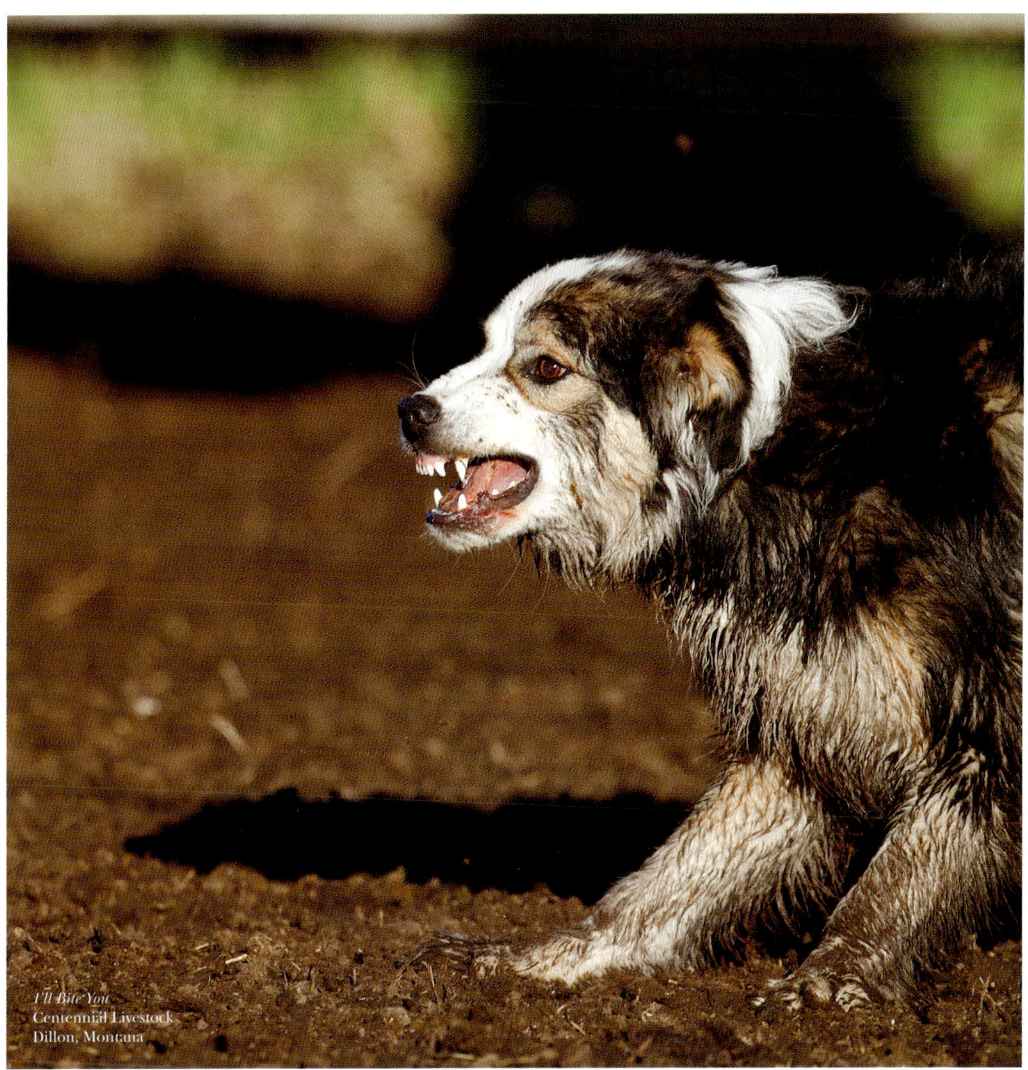

I'll Bite You
Centennial Livestock
Dillon, Montana

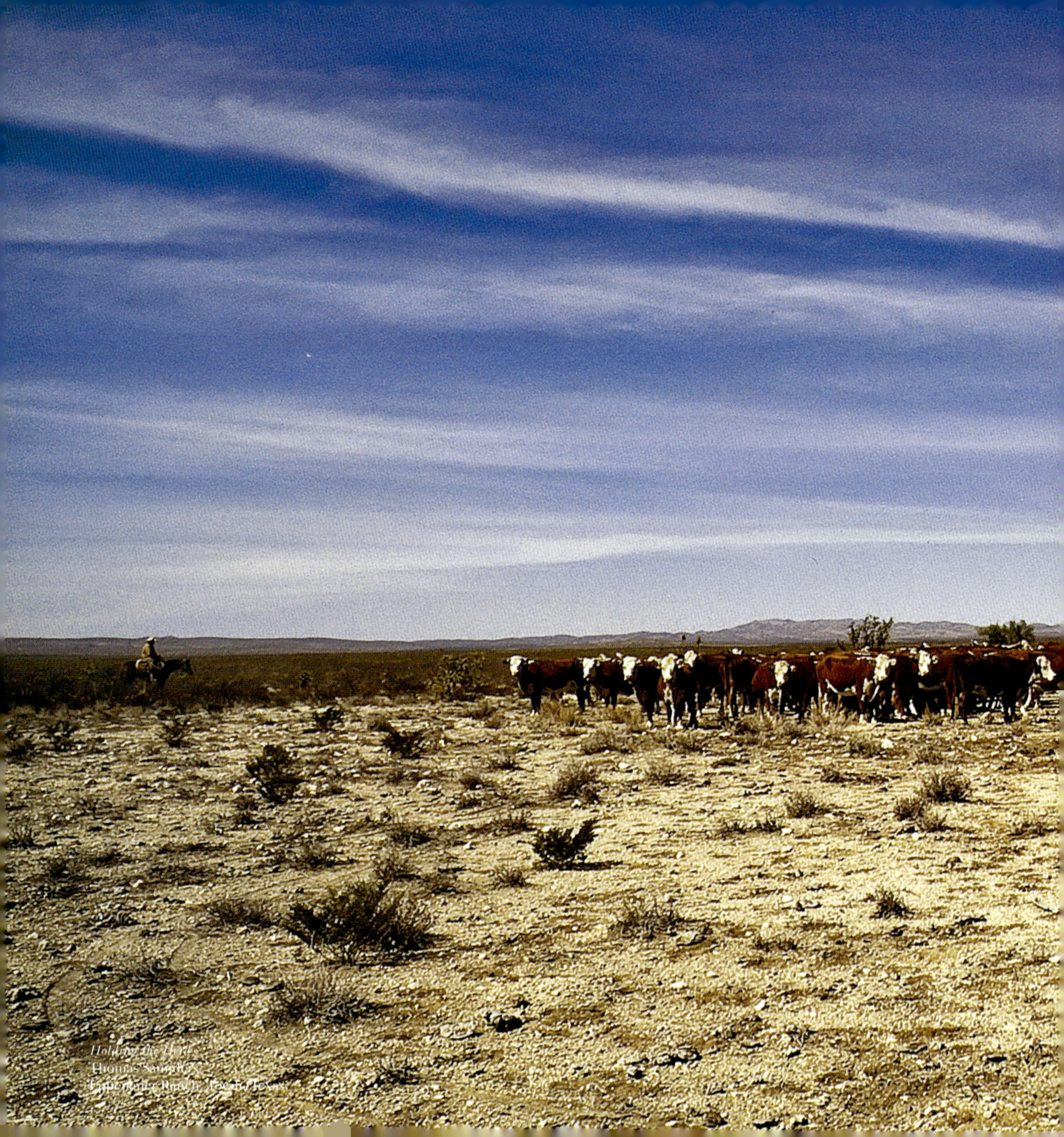

Holding the Herd
Thomas Saunders
[illegible] Ranch, [illegible] Texas

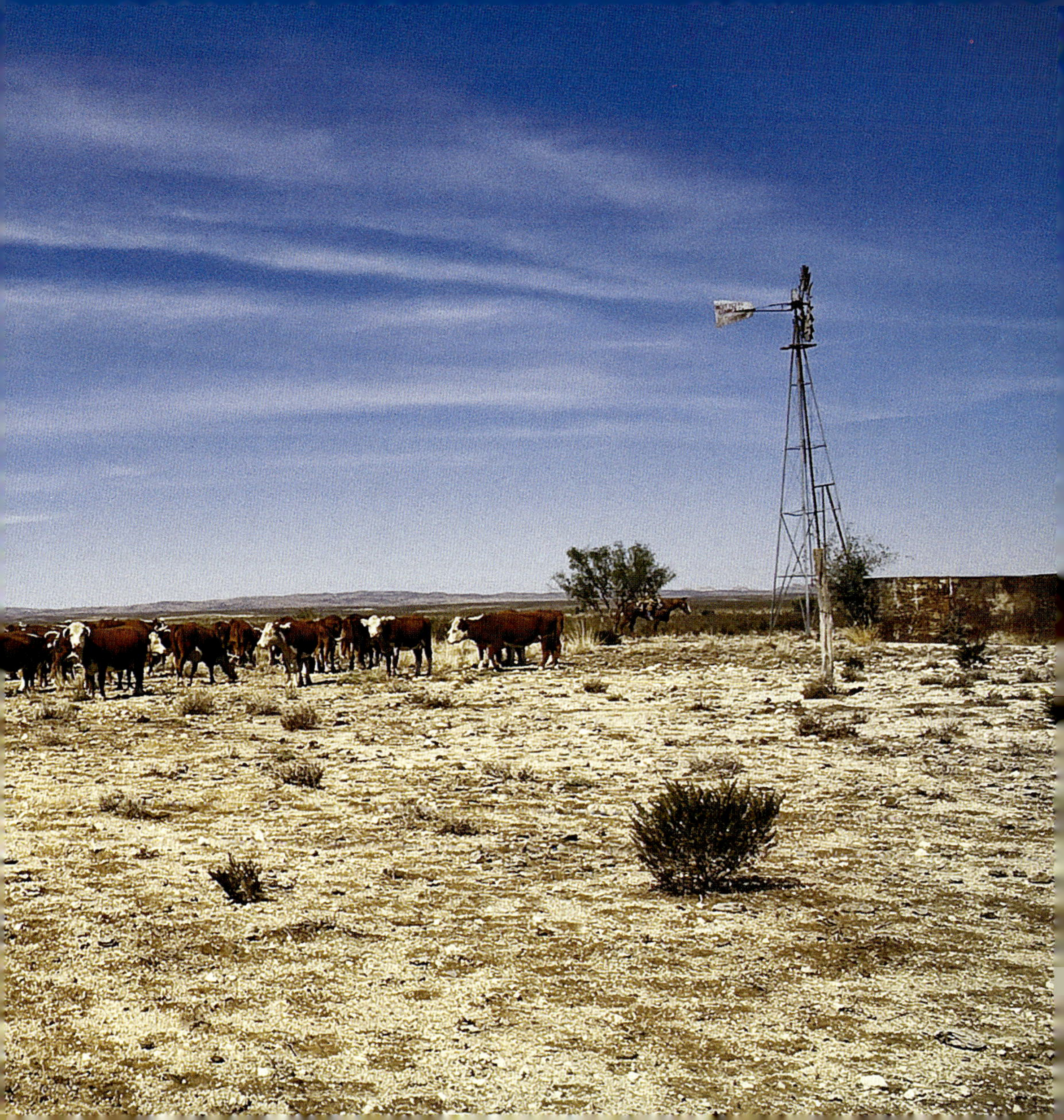

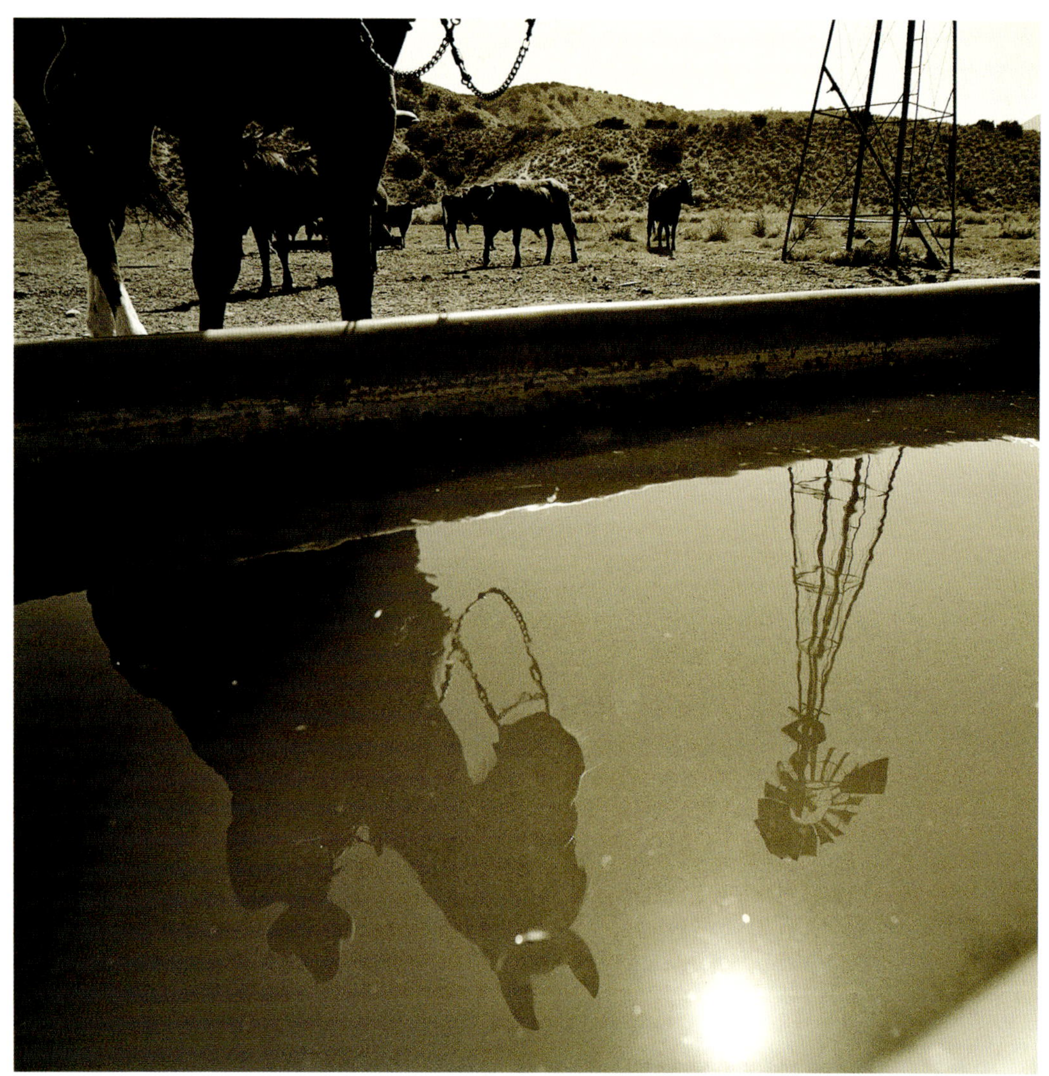

A Hard Country
Fred Reyes
Walking R Ranch, Cuyama, California

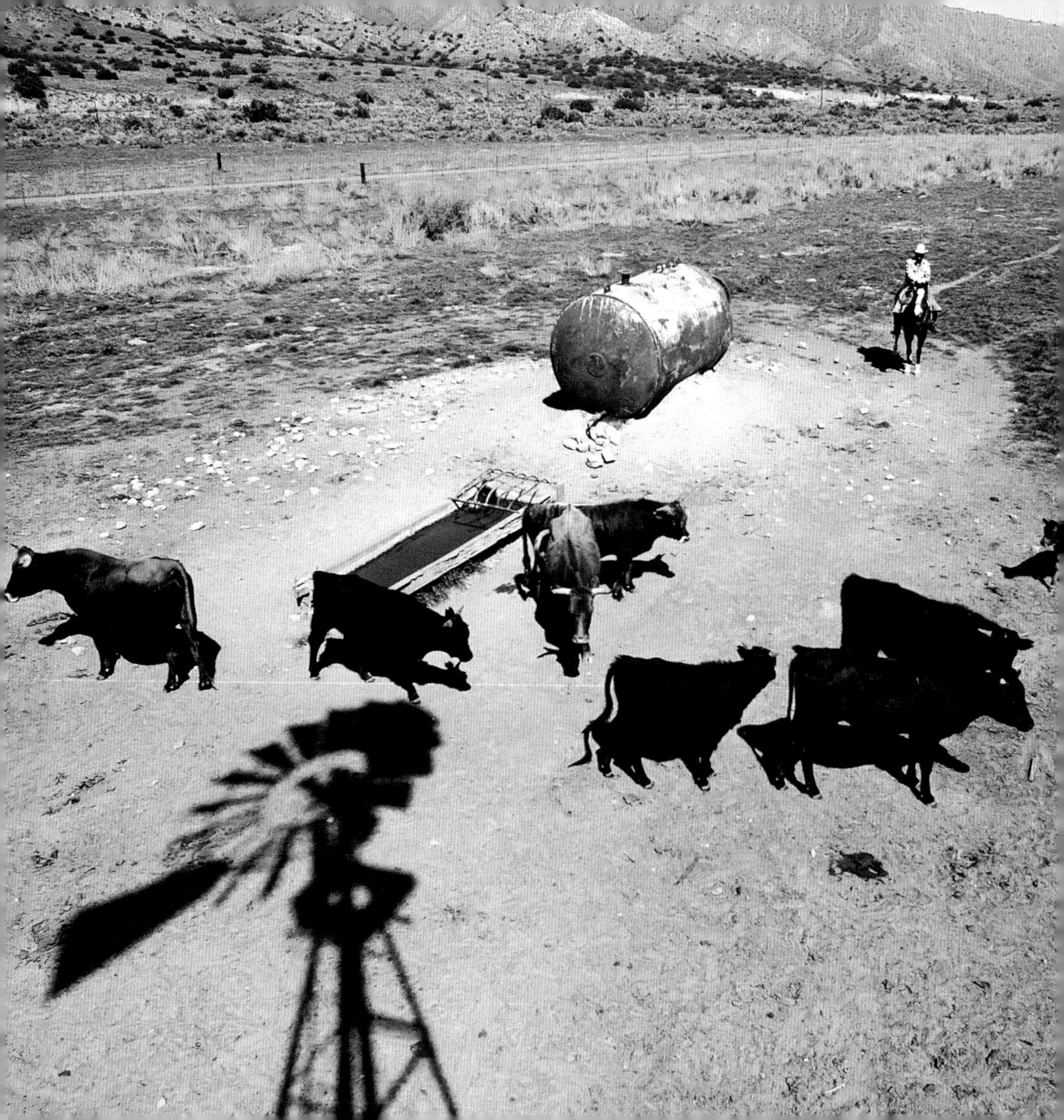

The Bare Necessities

An exhausted dockhand at Fort Benton on the banks of the Missouri took a break from unloading the cargo of a big paddlewheel steamship. He noticed a young cowboy, from the looks of his attire, loading a wagon full of lumber, planking, kegs of nails, wire, food staples, and boxes of beautifully painted slats, notched for what seemed would become a large wheel pattern when put together.

He yelled out to him, “Hey Sonny, you goin’ out there on that God-forsaken prairie all bys yourself?”

“No, Sir,” he hollered back. “I've got my three friends, two men and a lady, riding with me.”

“Where the hell are they then? I don't see any other pilgrims,” shouted back the crude stevedore.

“Why sir,” the cowboy yelled back, now through cupped hands. “Open up your durned eyes and let me introduce them to you. Here’s Barb Whyre, Samuel Colt, and Winn Miller and were fixin’ to settle in.”

Checking the Mill
Ed Harrell and Jim Detten
Harrell Cattle Company, Claude, Texas

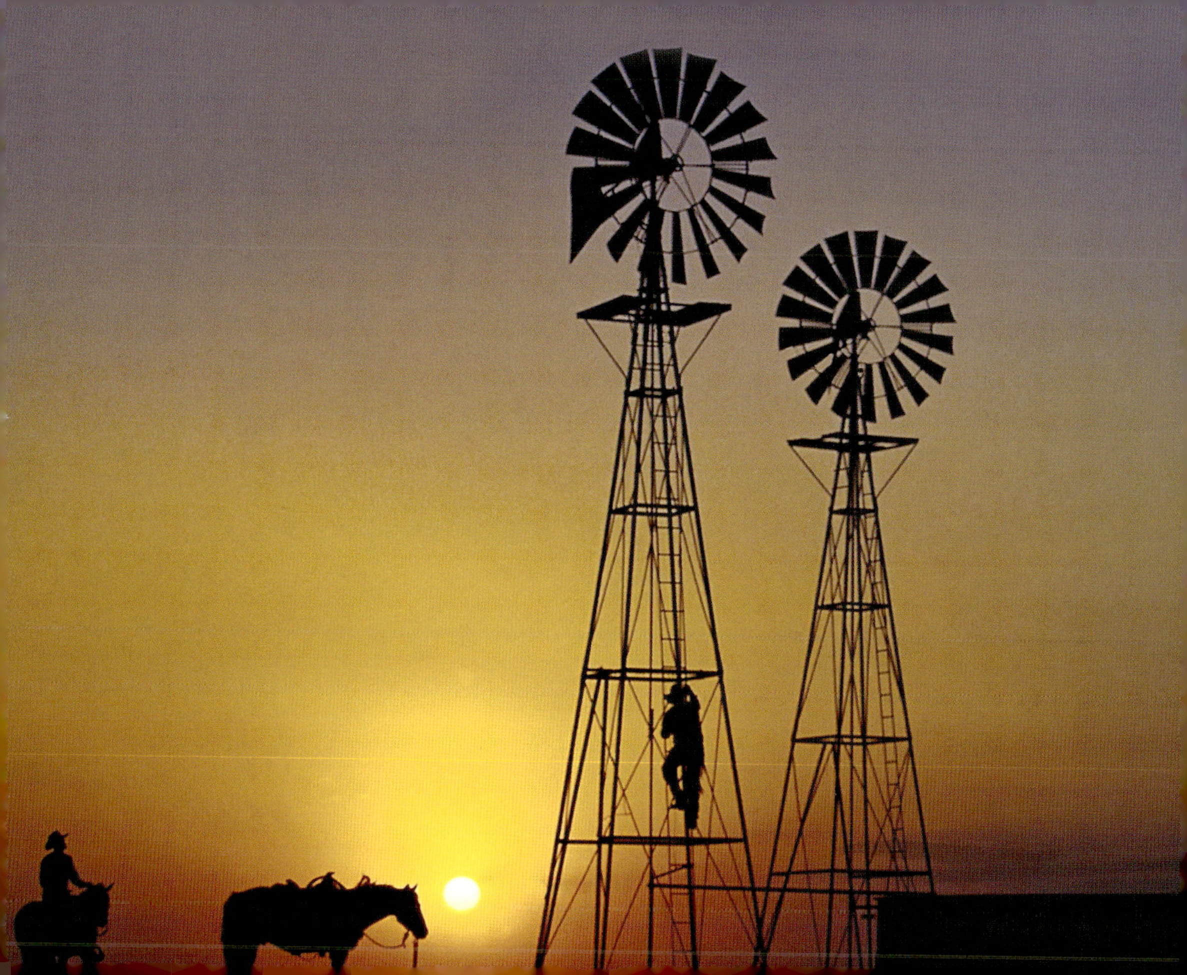

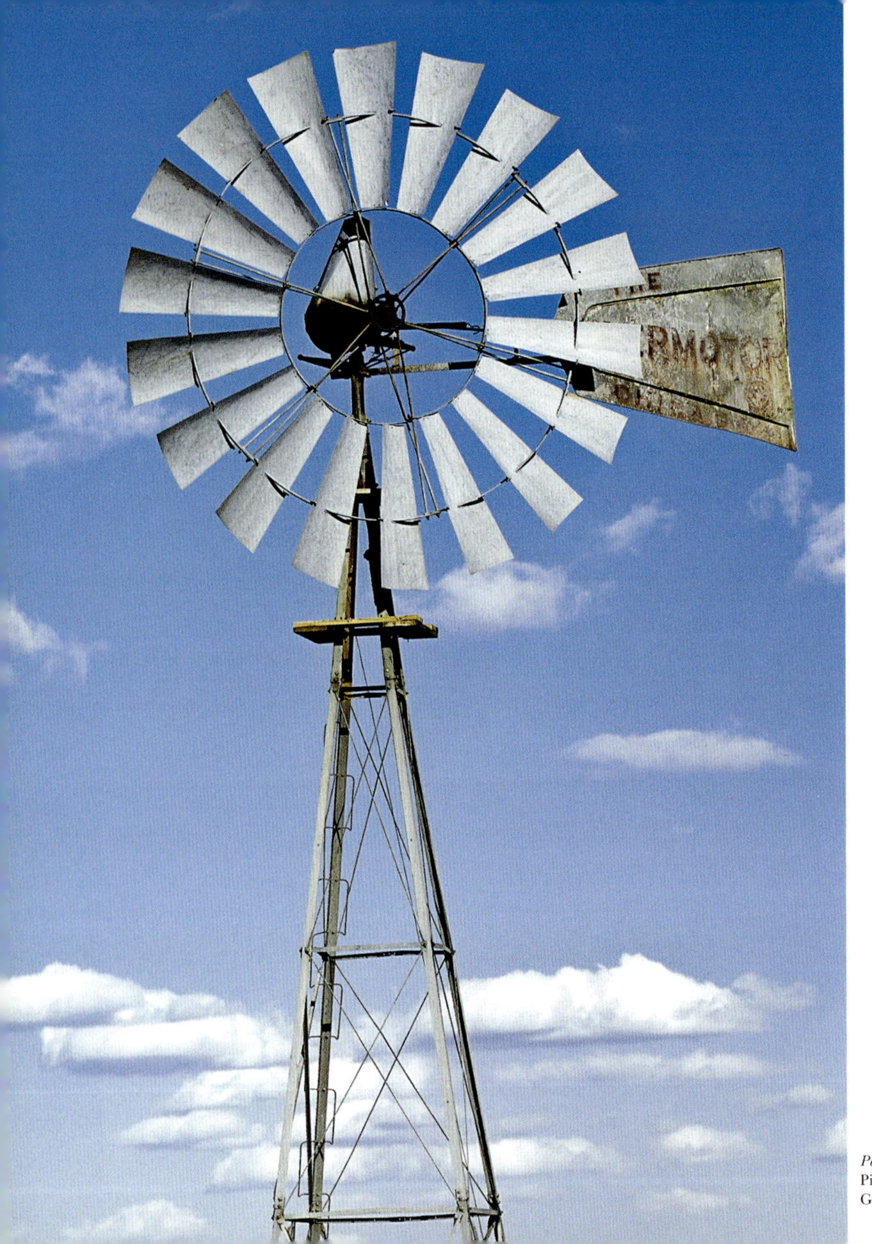

Perfect Day
Pitchfork Ranch
Guthrie, Texas

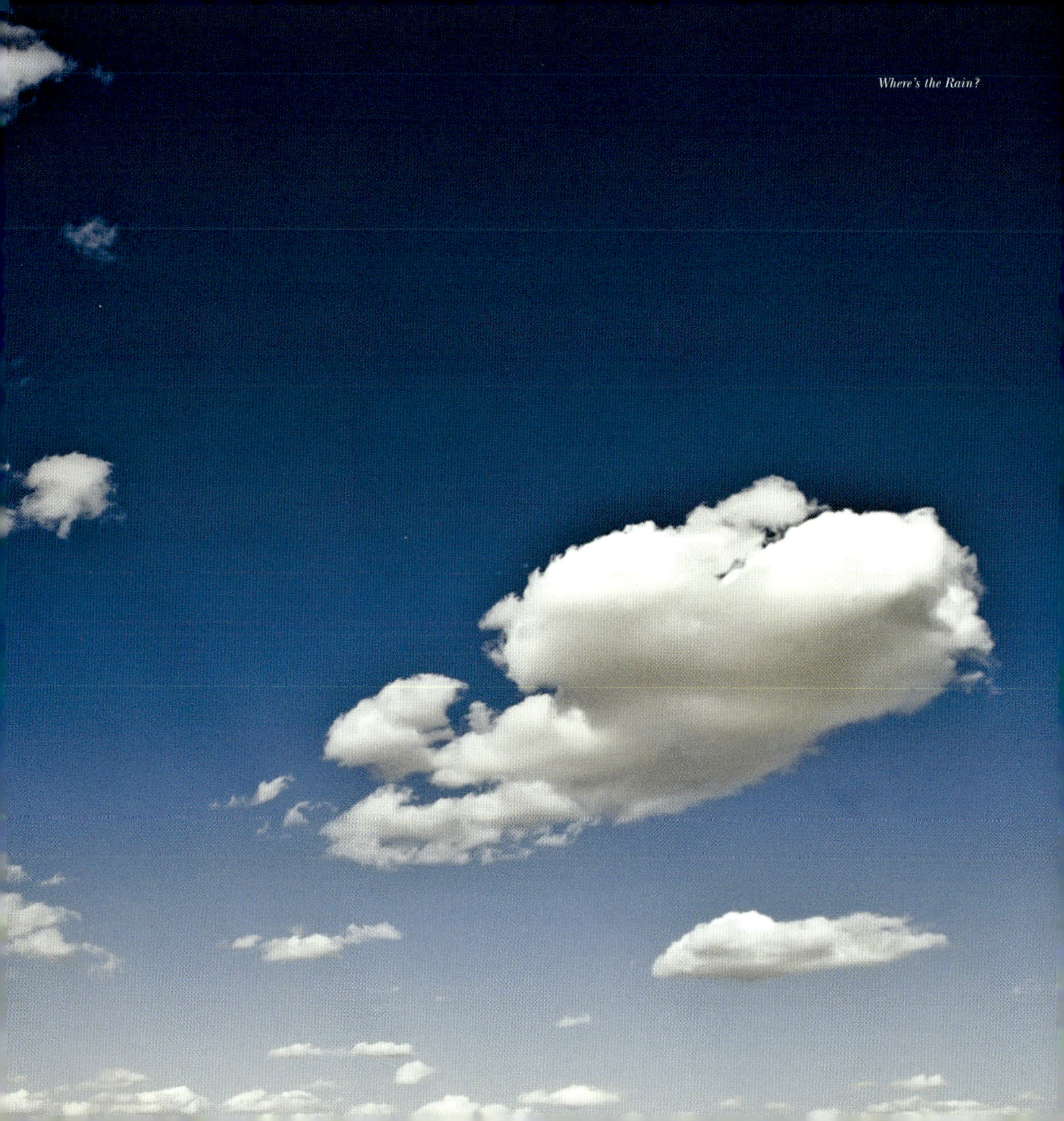

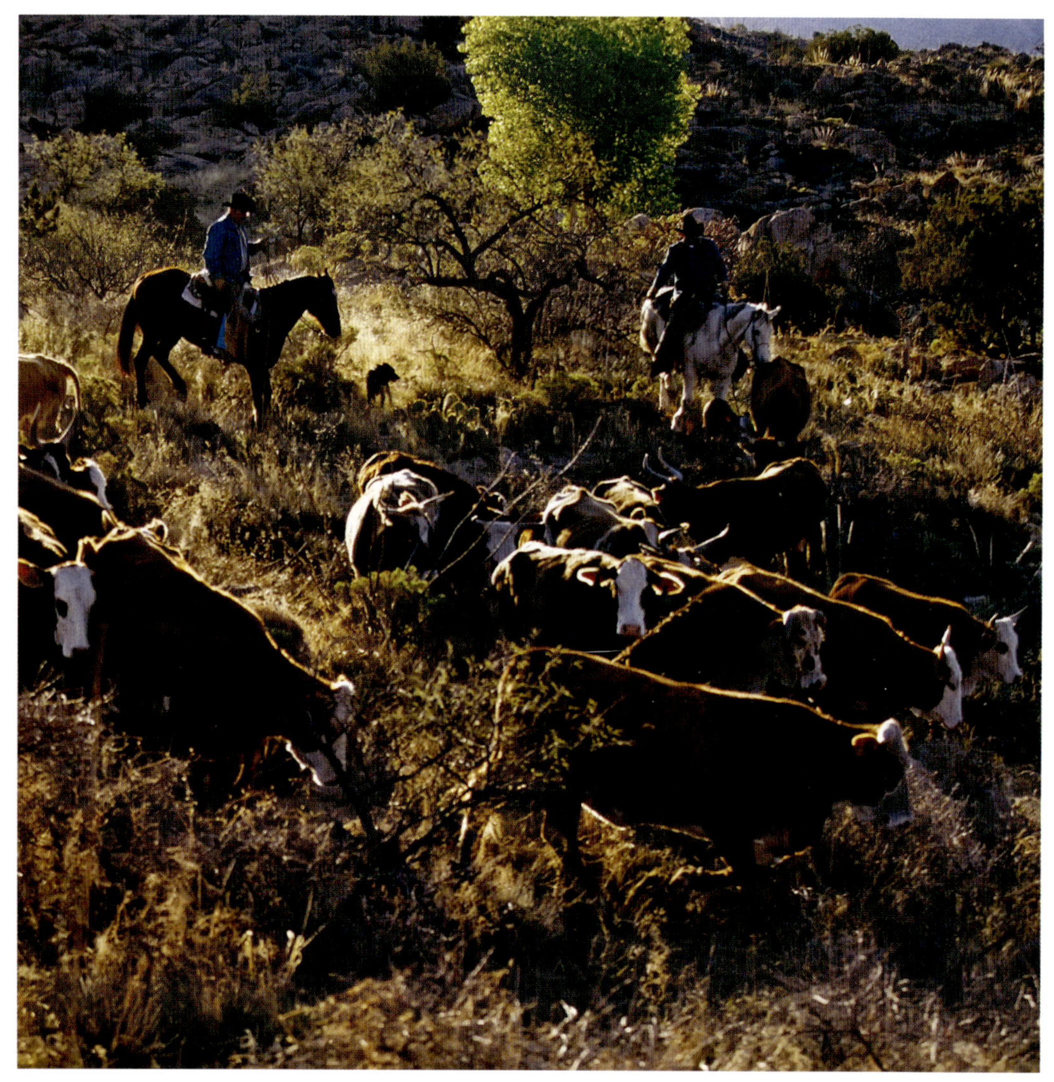

Arizona Gather
Bellota Ranch, Tucson, Arizona

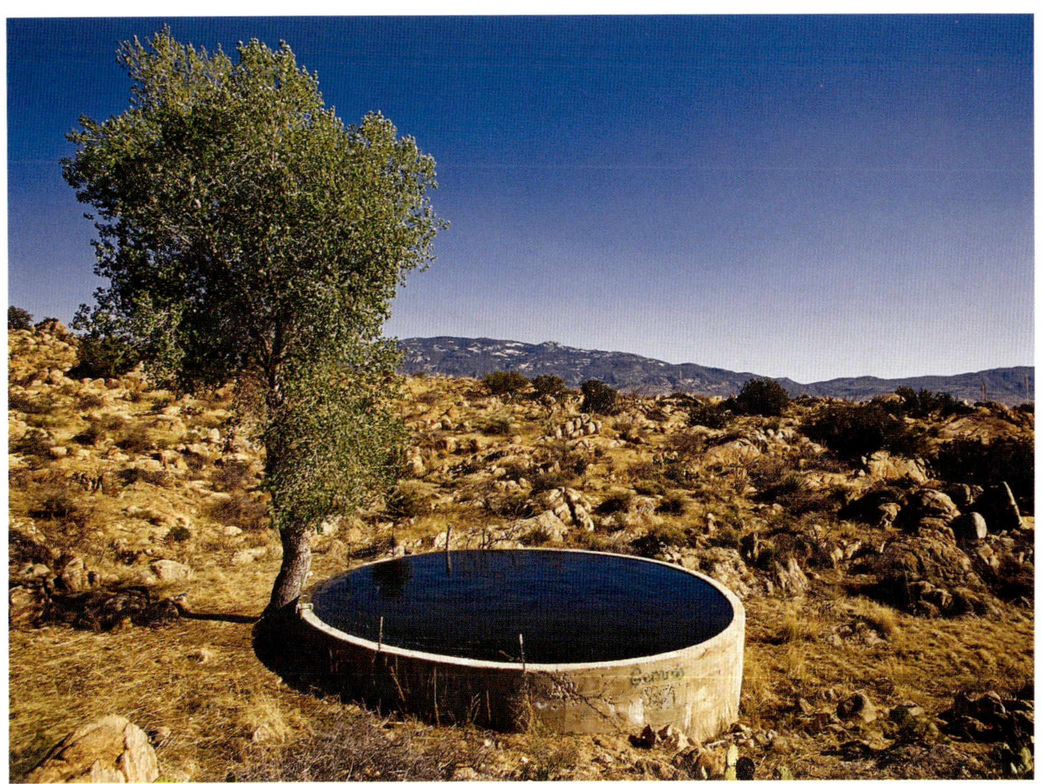

Stock Tank

The noted Plains historian, Walter Prescott Webb, once wrote, "The windmill was like a flag marking the spot where a small victory had been won in the fight for water in an arid land."

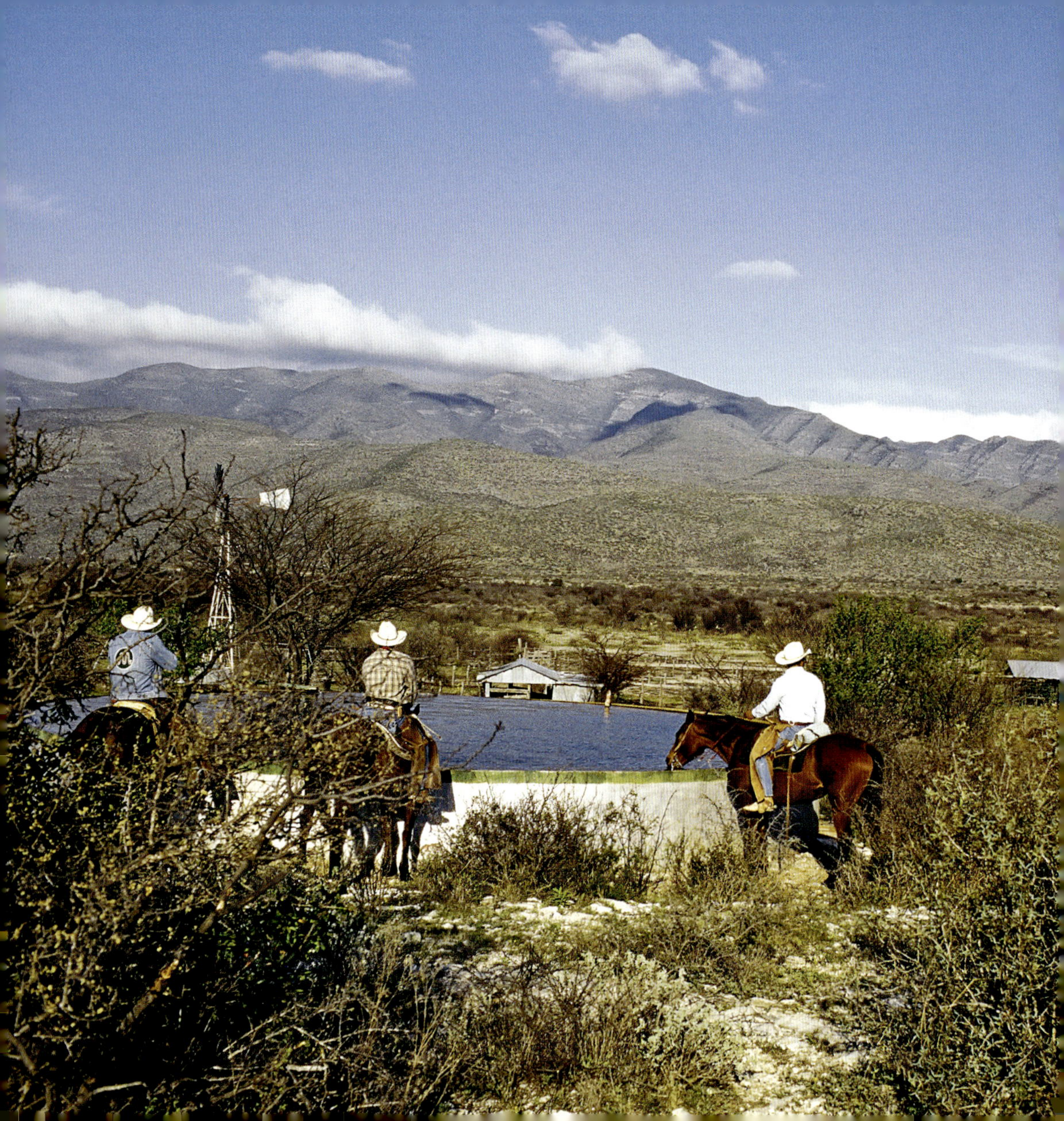

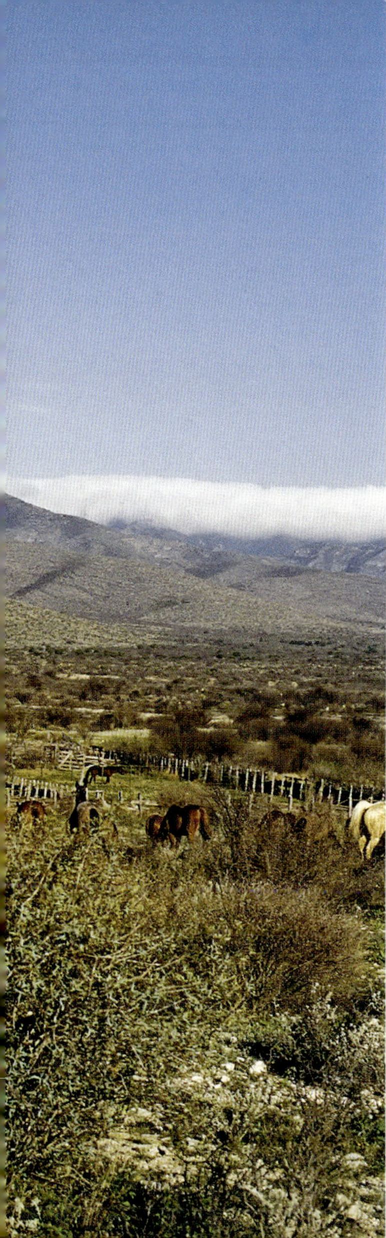

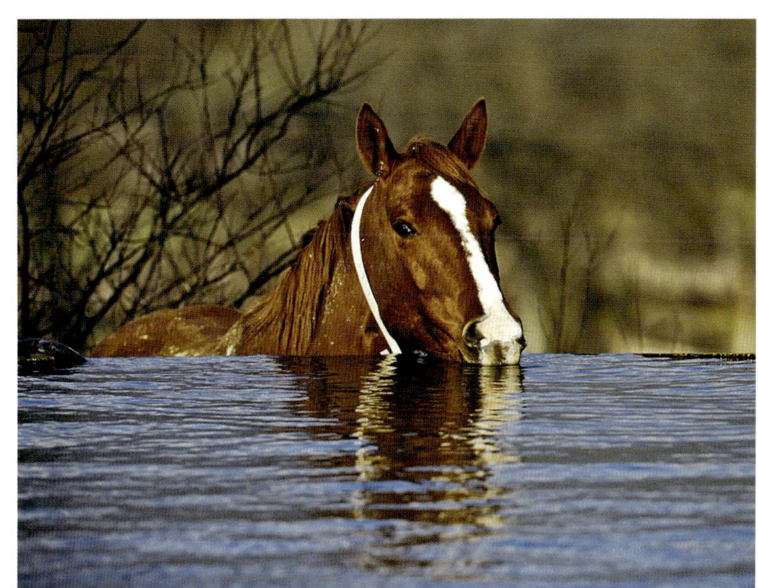

Getting a Drink

Tank and Mill
Rancho El Fortin
Old Mexico

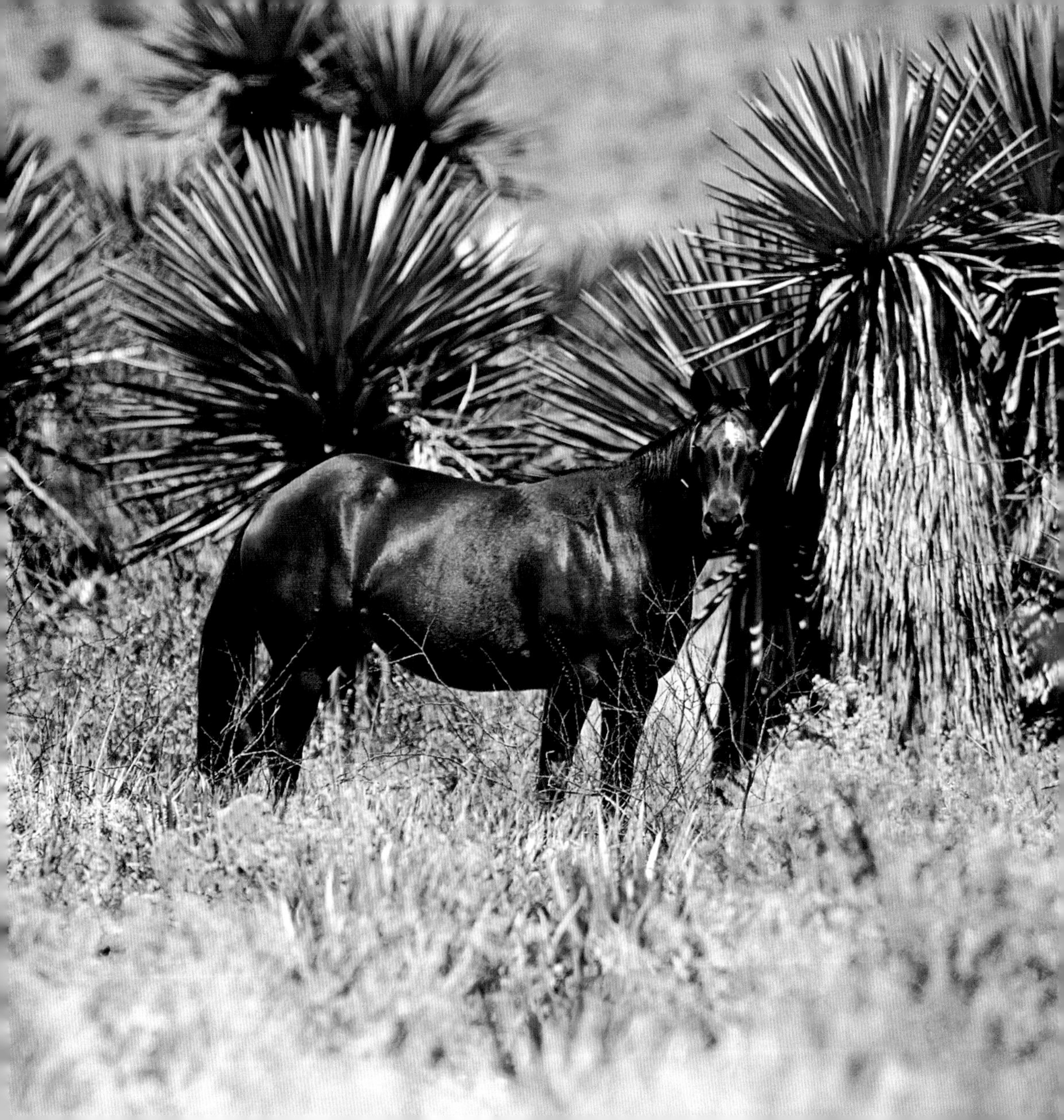

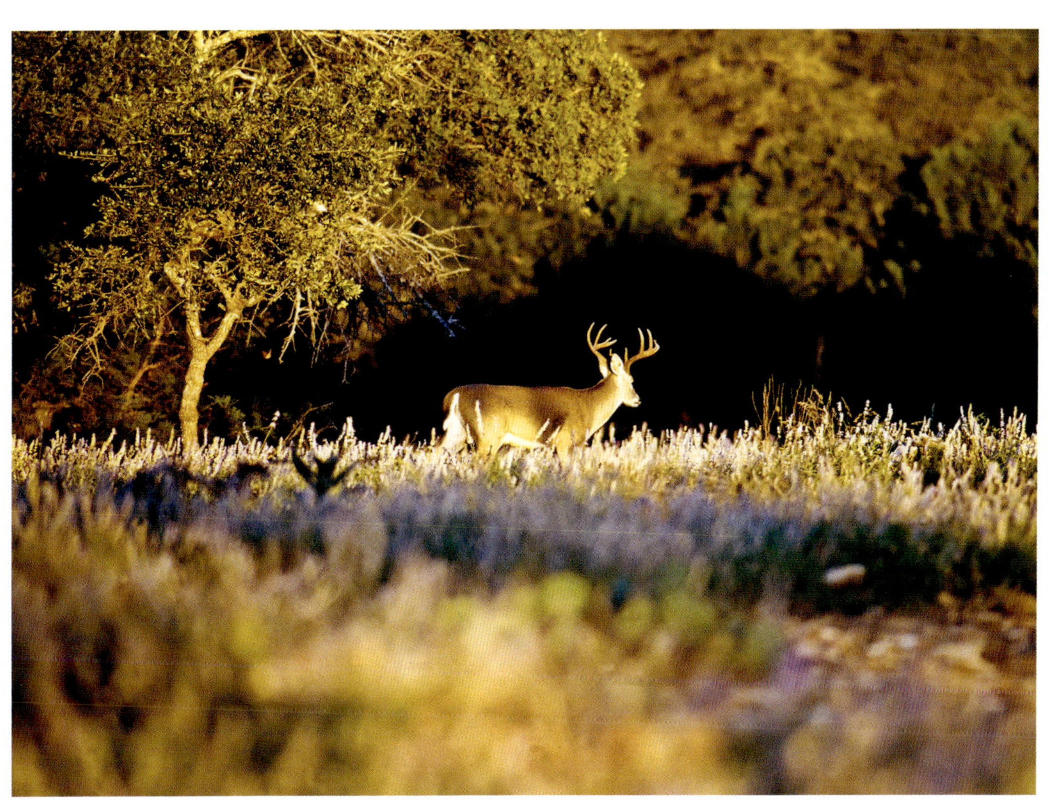

Whitetail Deer
YO Ranch
Mountain Home, Texas

Stallion in a Stark Landscape
Rancho El Fortin
Old Mexico

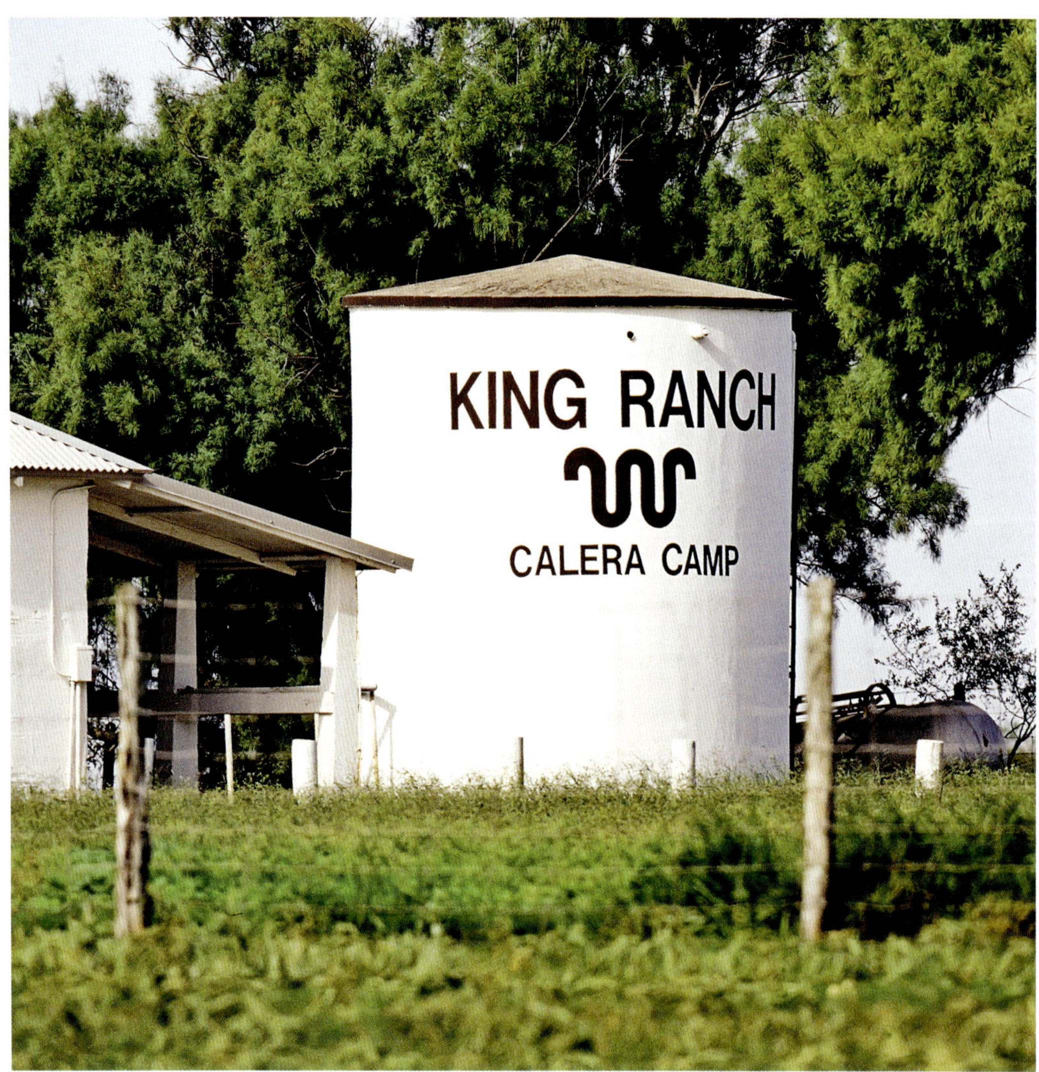

Storage Tank
King Ranch, Kingsville, Texas

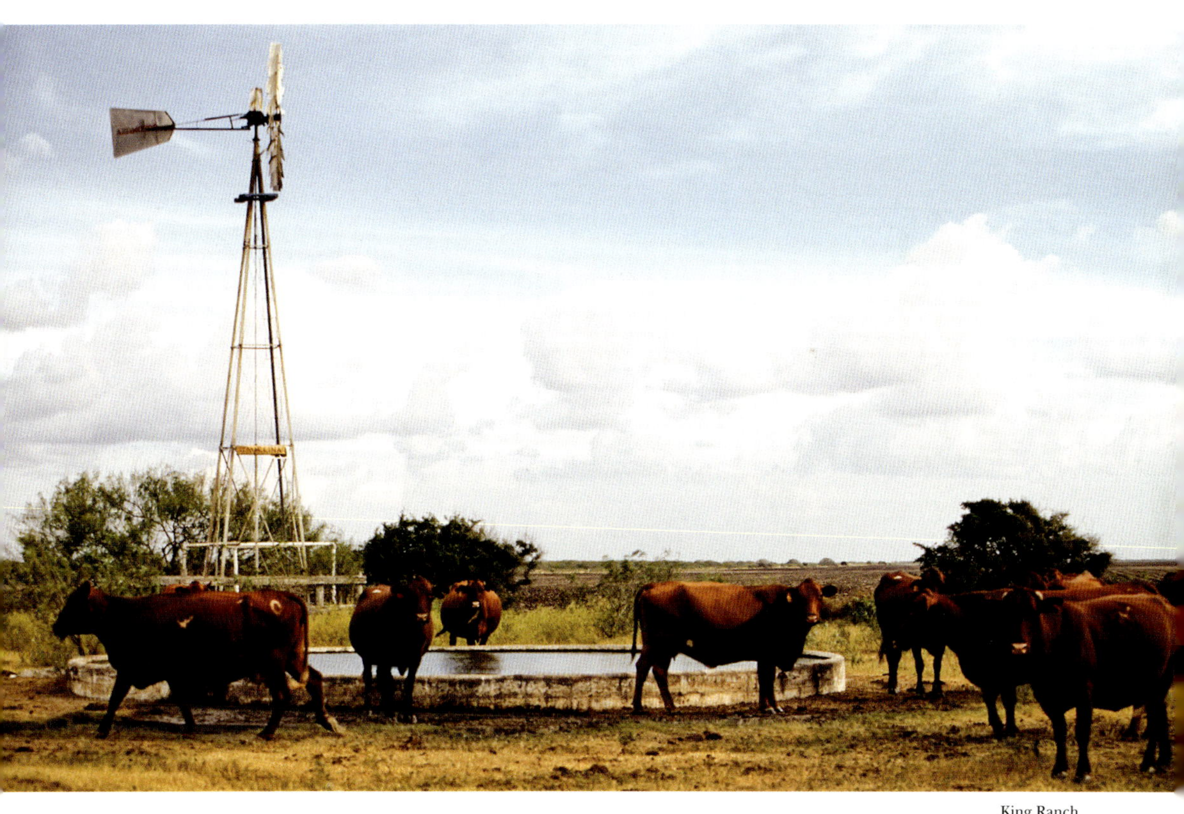

King Ranch
Kingsville, Texas

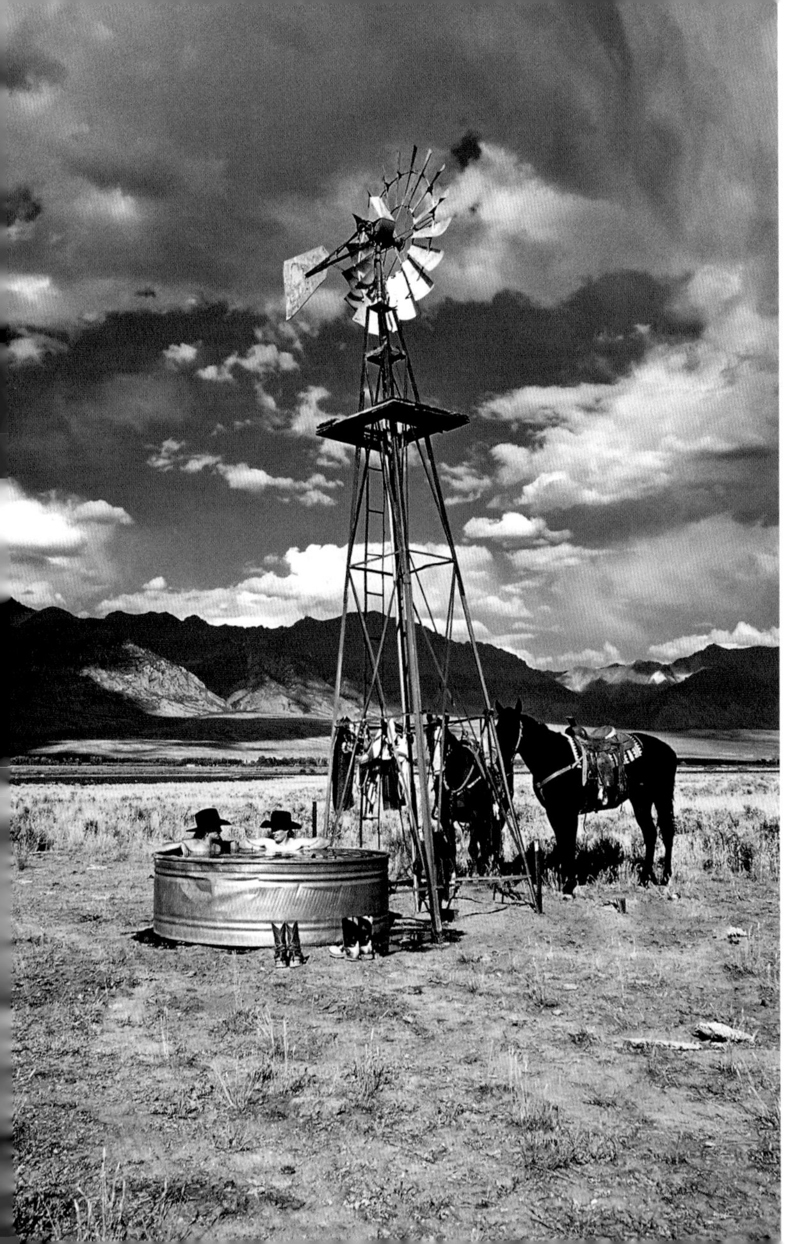

Waiting for the Boys
Kendra Kinghorn and Monique Hack
Mackay, Idaho

Takin' a Break

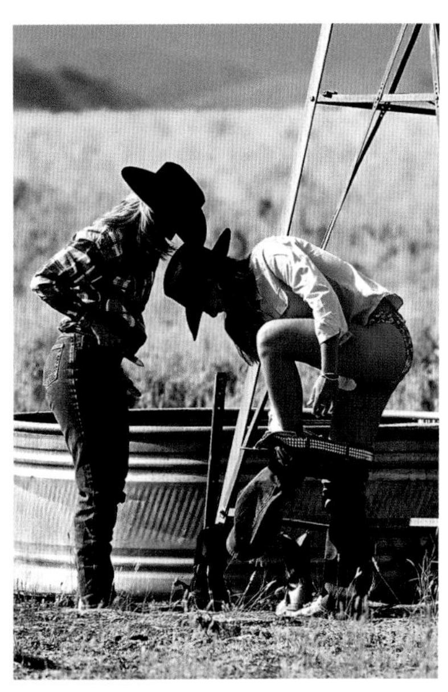

My sisters and I grew up on a lonesome starve-to-death ranch in New Mexico during the late '30s. We were the best "hired men" my dad could afford. The ranch had a series of windmills to water the cattle scattered over the countryside. Late one hot summer afternoon, we were riding for some stragglers that had dropped out of the last gather a week or so earlier. The heat and wind had just about dried us out like raisins. On passing one of the windmills, we noticed the cool, clear water sitting in the tank—it was too inviting to pass up. There weren't ever any men around and travelers in that part of the country were a rarity, so we stripped off our sticky-necked shirts and dusty britches and dove in. As we were reclining against the cool steel rim of the tank, wouldn't you know it, we noticed a rider traveling along the wagon road that passed pretty close to the tank. Low and behold, it was the preacher approaching! We'd forgotten it was his week to travel this part of his circuit. The windmill and tank were on a small rise above the trail and a person had to ride right up to it to see the water in the tank. The preacher must have watered his horse at the windmill back up the road, because he didn't come up to the trough. Our horses and clothes were off over the hill and couldn't be seen from where he pulled up. He did, however, get off his horse to rest and tied him under the only scraggly tree near the tank. He sat down cross-legged in the shade, then took a small Bible out of his vest pocket and started to read for what seemed like an eternity. We were hunkered down as quiet as church mice, praying he wouldn't come over to the tank and discover us. Finally, he mounted up and went on his way. We were getting kind of cold by the time he left because the sun was starting to go down. The next day in church we looked at each other and couldn't help but giggle when that preacher walked in.

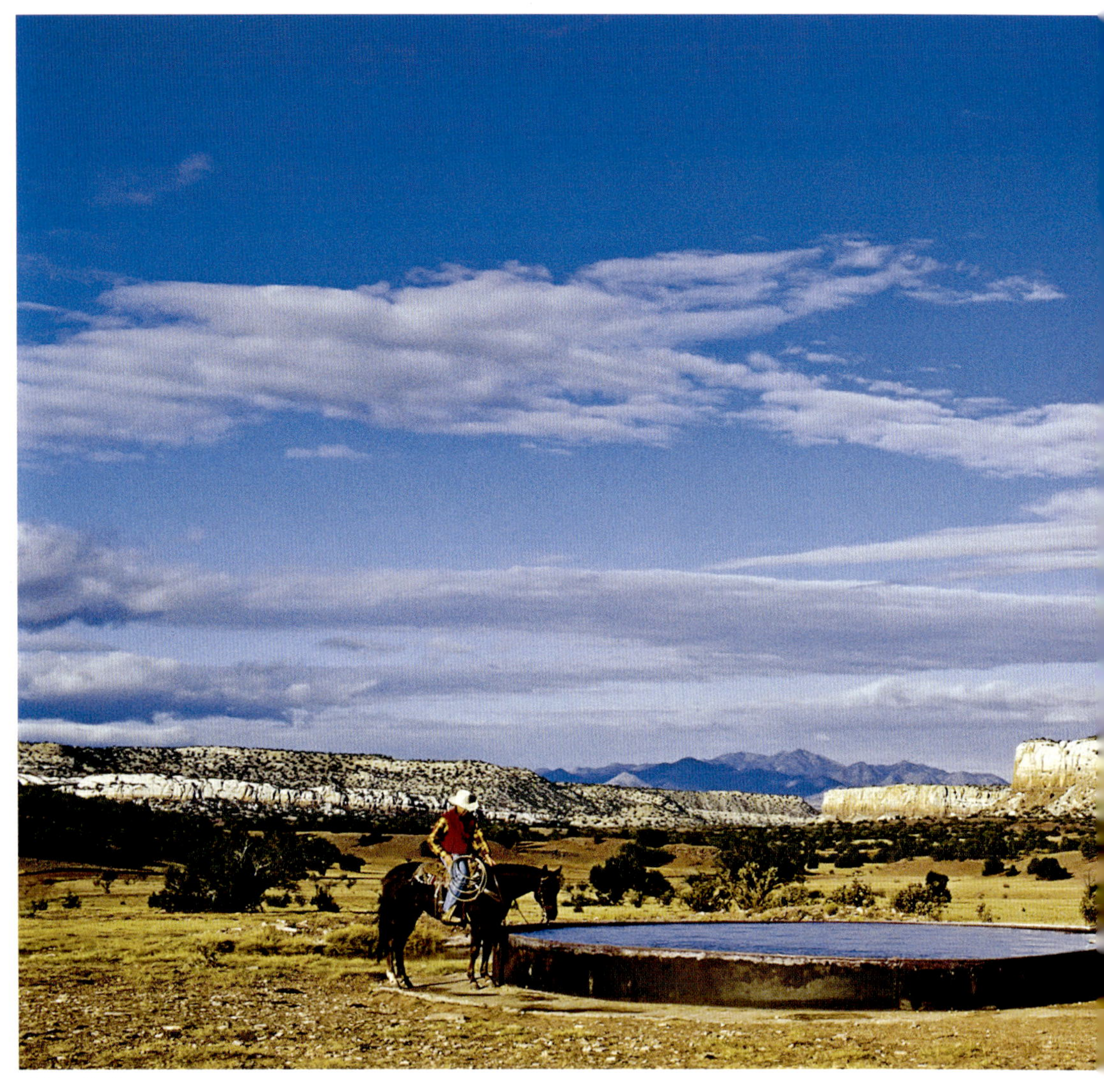

Taking His Time
Bob Patterson
Singleton Ranch, Lamy, New Mexico

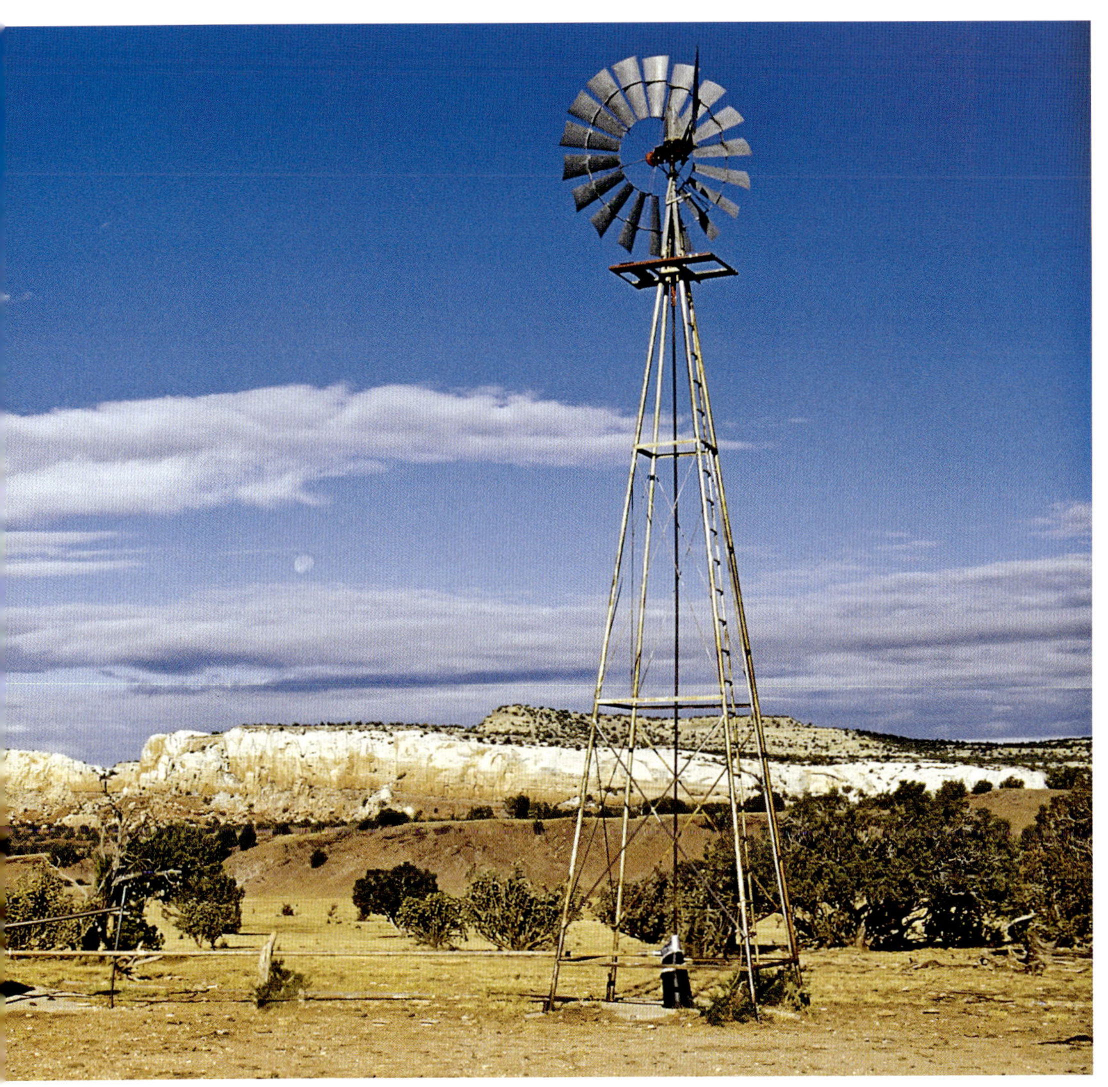

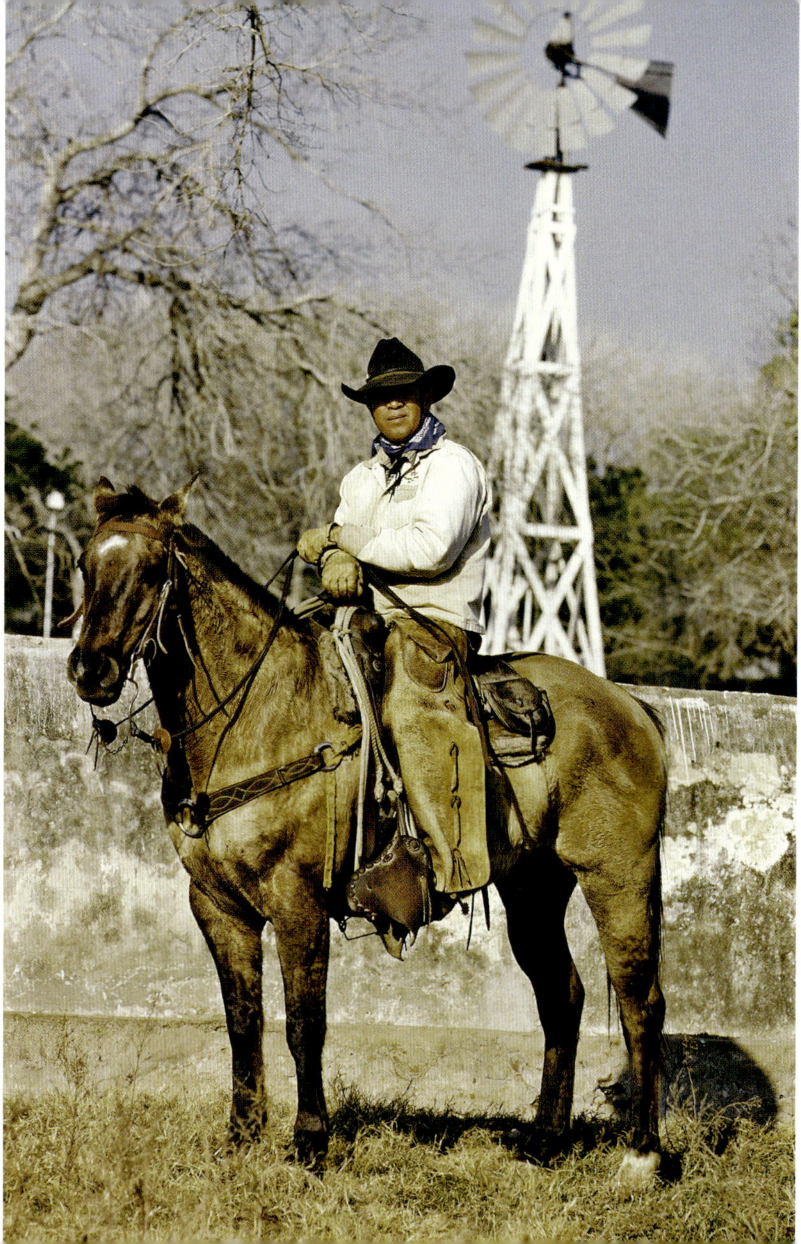

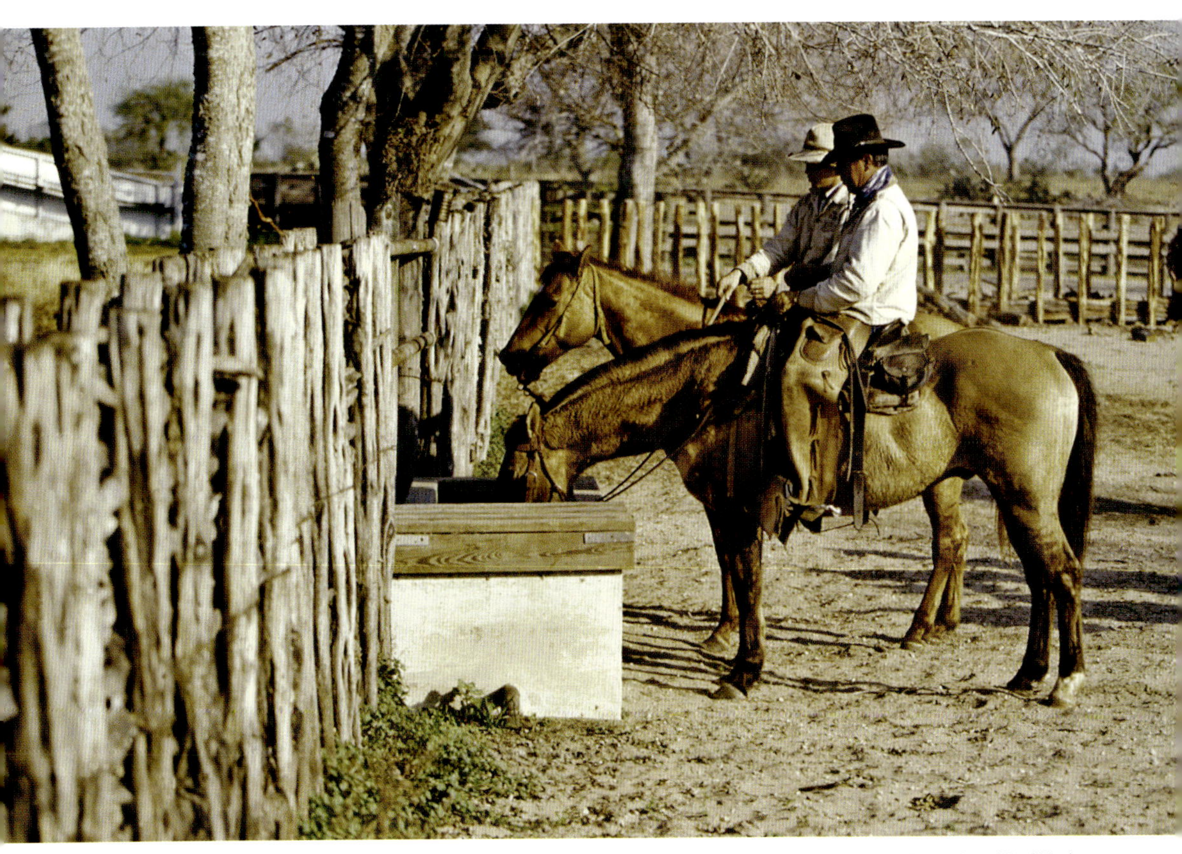

Pride
Juan Luis Longoria
McAllen Ranch, Linn, Texas

Juan Luis Longoria and Raul Trevino
McAllen Ranch, Linn, Texas

The radiant colors of sunset on the prairie transform windmills into delicate dancing ladies of the evening. They twist and spin, humming a faint song into the fading blue light. Darkness turns the graceful dancers back into artistic towers of steel and twirling blades.

Sunset at the Mill
06 Ranch
Fort Davis, Texas

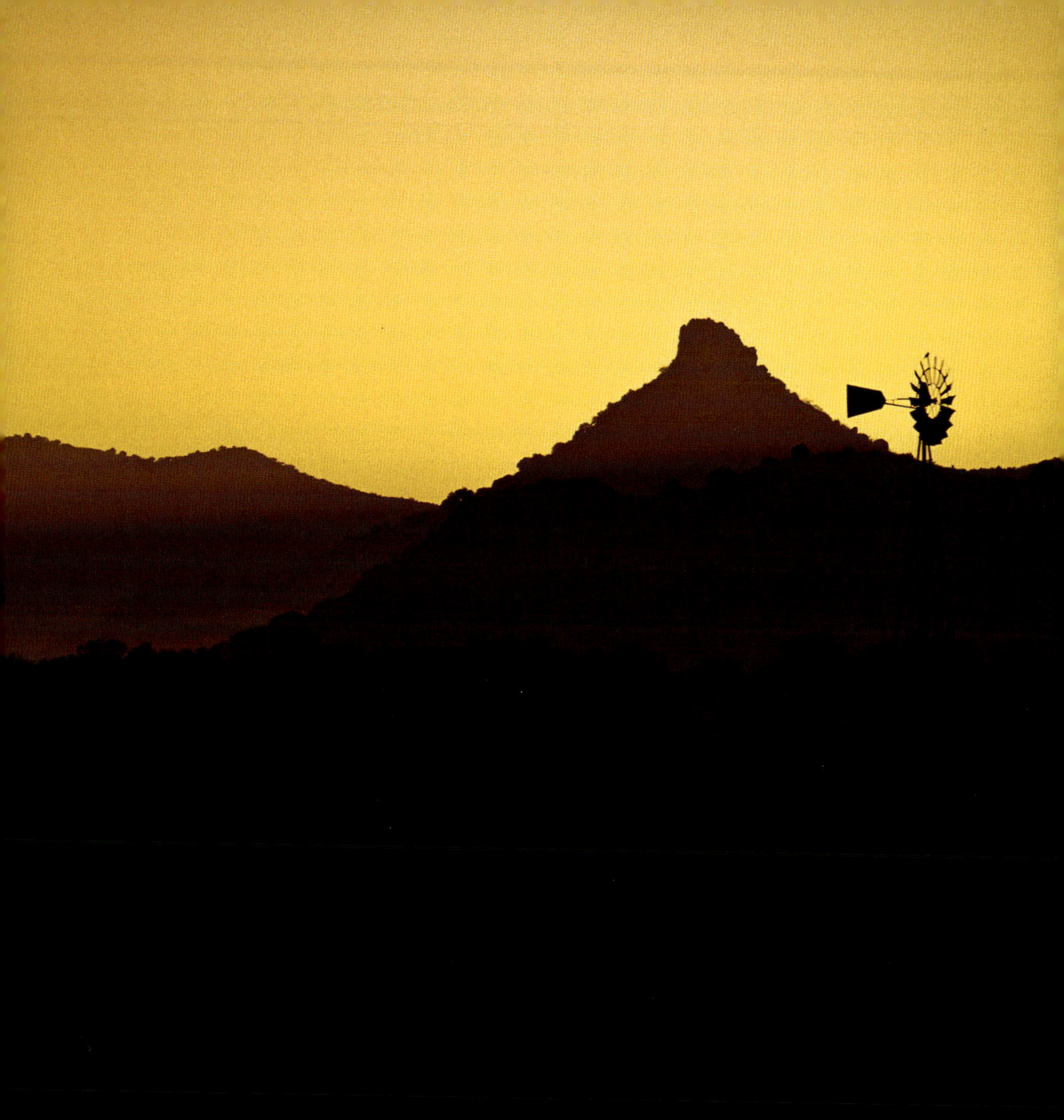

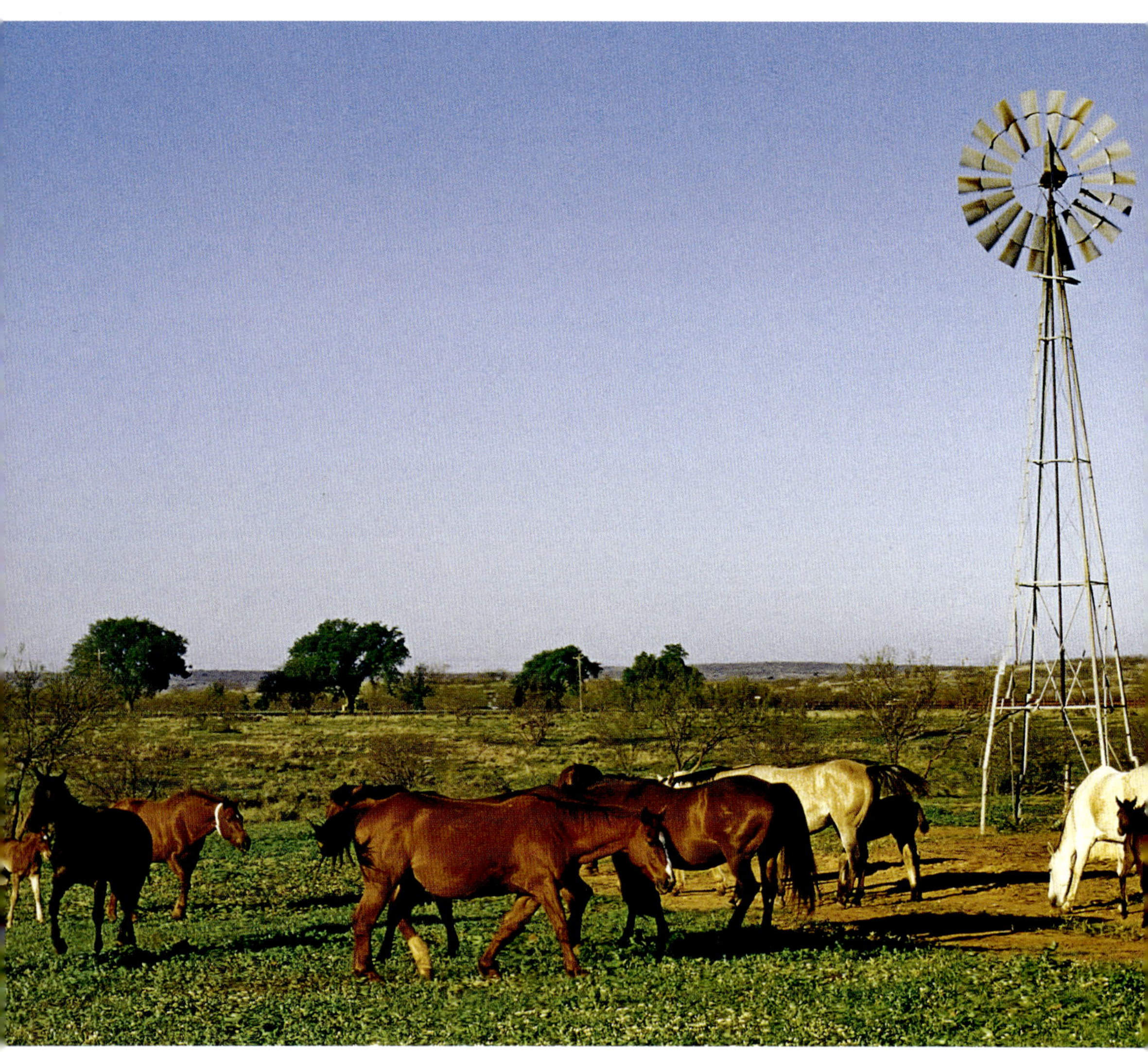

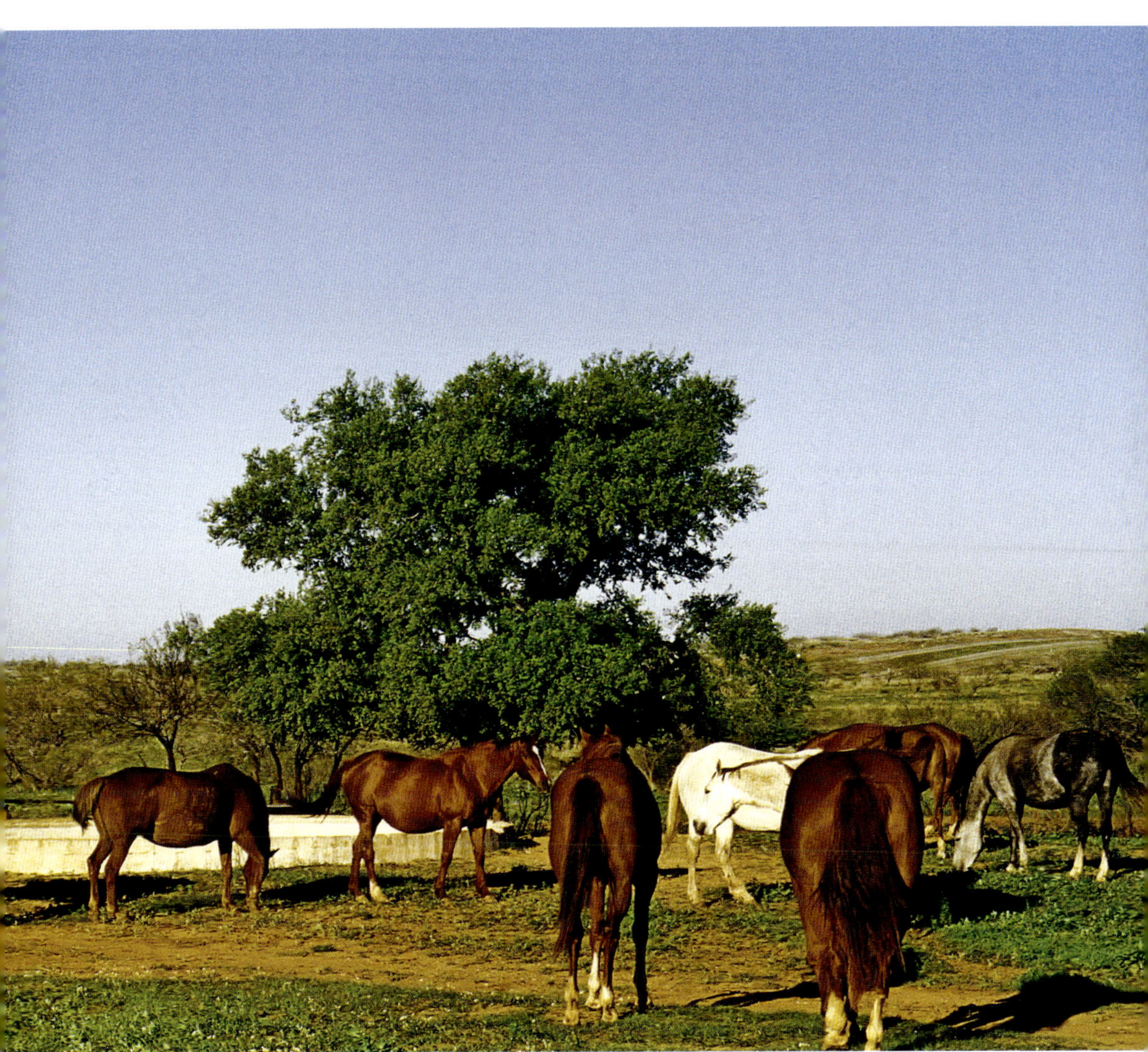

Mare Pasture
Pitchfork Ranch, Guthrie, Texas

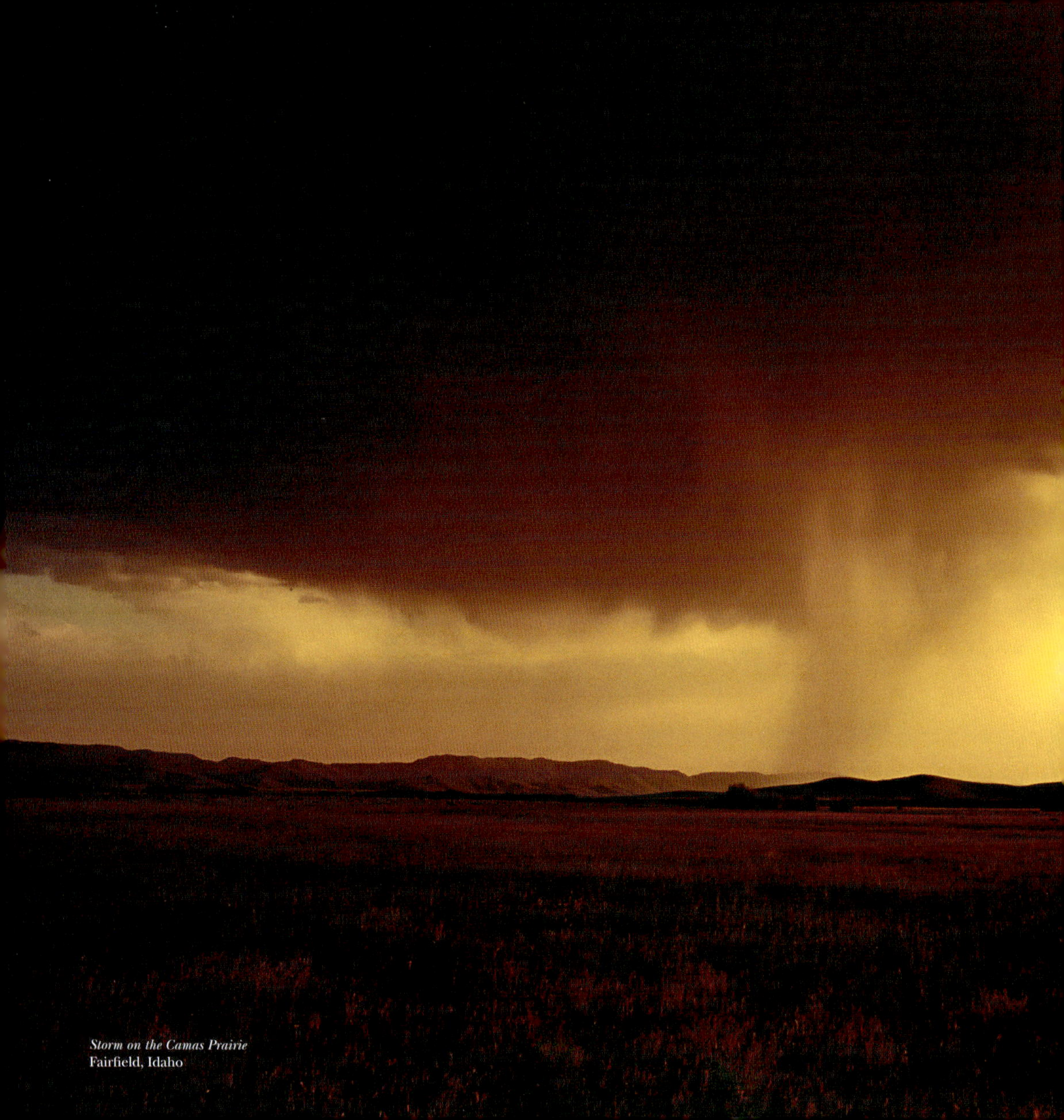

Storm on the Camas Prairie
Fairfield, Idaho

"The wind blows where it wants, and you hear the sound thereof, but can not tell from where it comes, and where it goes: so is every one that is born of the Spirit."

—John 3:8

Blow ye 'ole wind against my sails,
Blow ye hard and blow ye true,
Blow me round and round,
'Cause I need to water 'ole Blue.

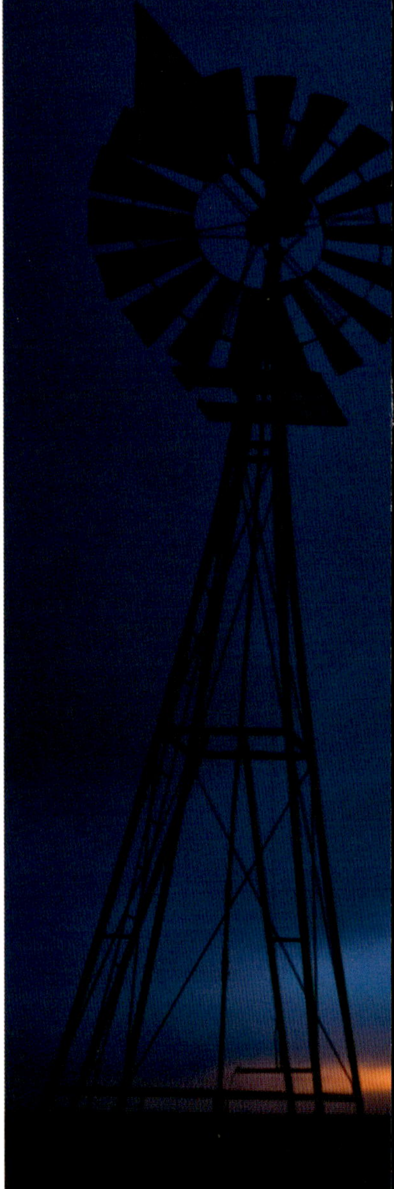

Clearing Storm
Adolfo Lozano and Richard Woodrome
Cluck Ranches, Gruver, Texas

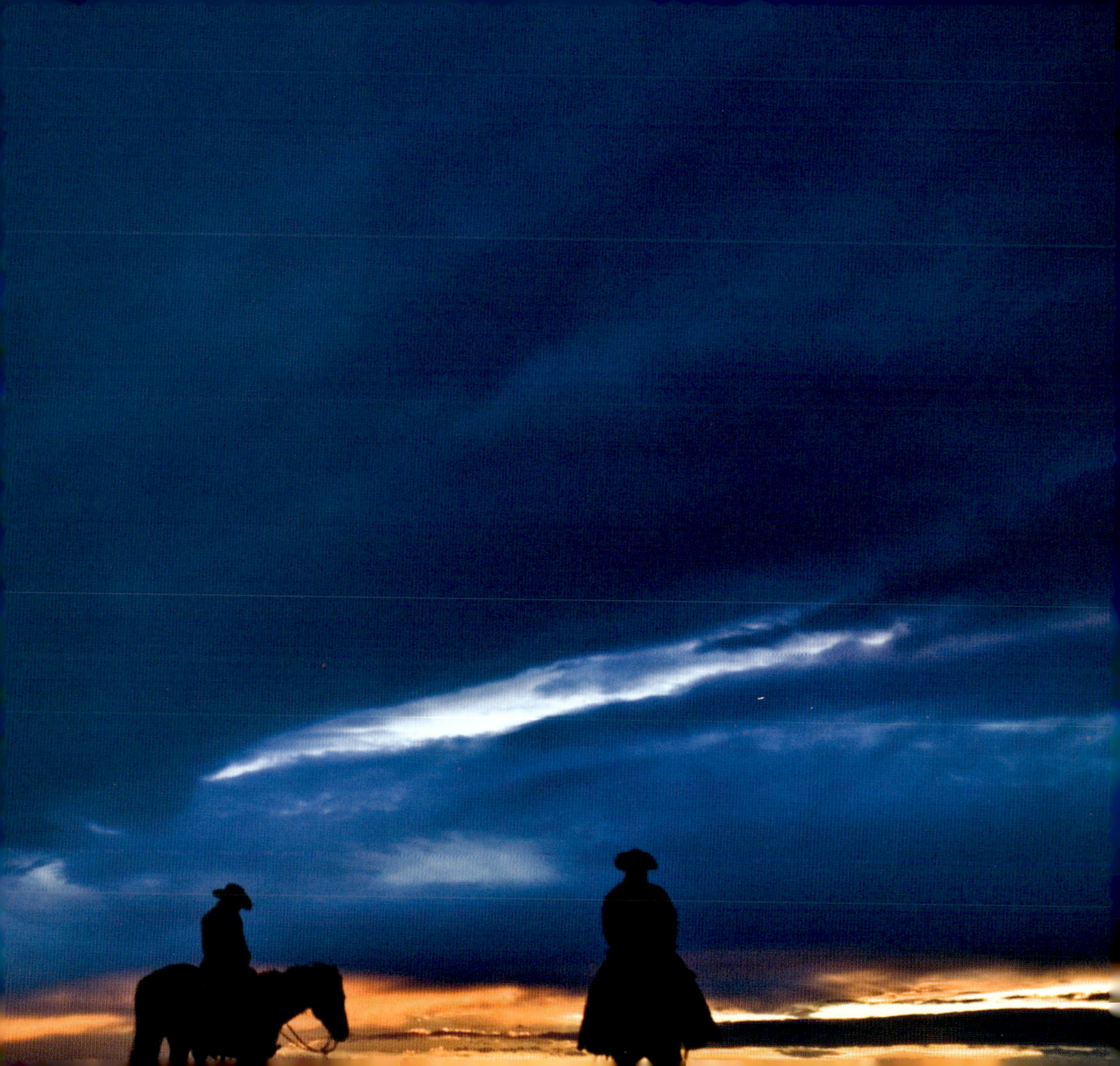

A Christmas Miracle

Daddy was a pretty good hand with young horses. He rode a lot of colts to make ends meet. We had a little place on the Platte River in western Nebraska. My father had bought the ranch with a down payment using his "mustering out pay" after the war in '45. He milked a few cows, broke horses, worked around during harvest, and tried to make a go of the ranch any way he could. One fall he was breaking a big half-draft colt for John Berry, the auctioneer who ran the sale yard. That horse bucked him off and broke his pelvis. He was immobile for many, many months. Mother fixed him a cot in the living room so she could tend to him a little easier. There he stayed, flat on his back, his dignity in shambles, just looking out the window and falling deeper and deeper into despair as each day slowly passed. We helped Mother out as best we could for as young as we were. If it weren't for the welfare of our church and the neighbors, our little cornfield would never have been harvested. We had no money, so we lived off the garden vegetables stored in the root cellar, some fruit Mother had canned, and our milk cows. Christmas was approaching and our desperate situation just drove Daddy further into depression. The night before Christmas we heard some sounds from out in the barnyard. When we looked out the window we couldn't believe our eyes. My little sister and I screamed and jumped up and down. Daddy had been sleeping and was startled awake by our shrieks. There, out the window, the windmill had been decorated with Christmas lights. When he saw those pretty colors on the big wheel he couldn't hold back any longer. I'd never seen my father cry before, nor did I ever again. On the porch were boxes and boxes of canned fruit, jerky, and coffee. Two beautiful cloth dolls had been left for my little sister, Sadie, and me. We never found out who touched our lives in such a wonderful way that night. Sadie thought it was the Wise Men. I knew better; it was too cold for camels, so it had to have been Santa himself.

Bar Horseshoe Ranch
Mackay, Idaho

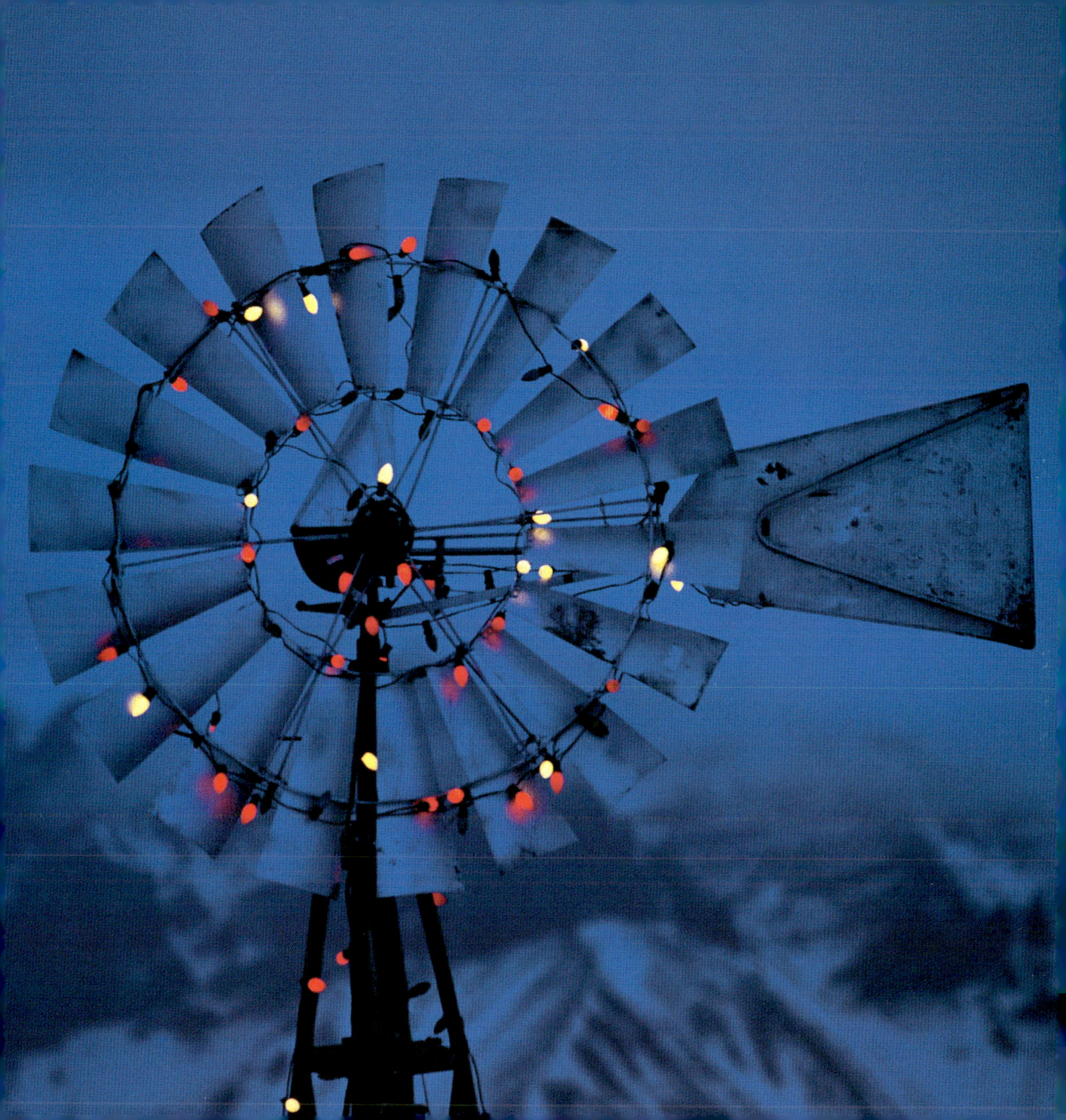

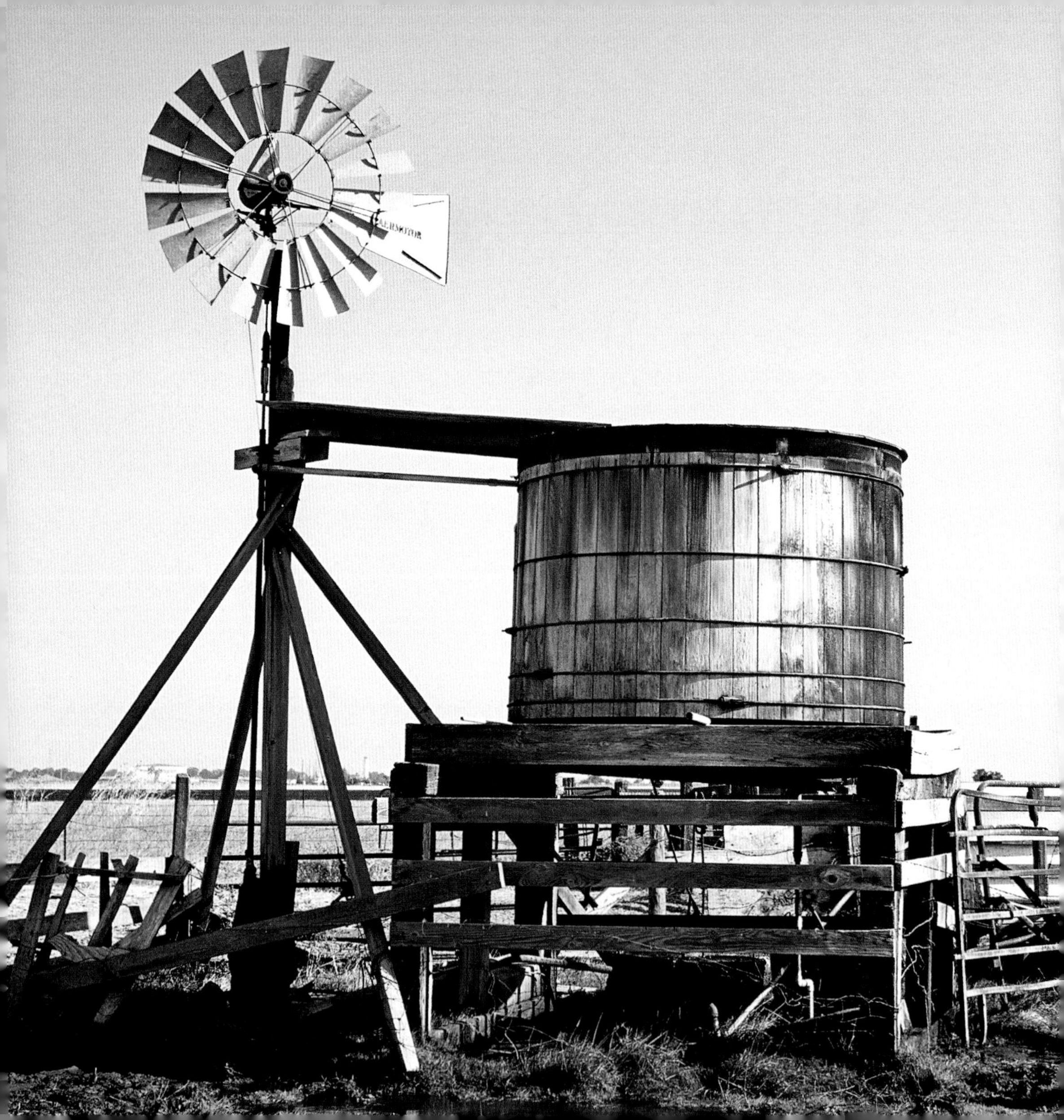
AERMOTOR

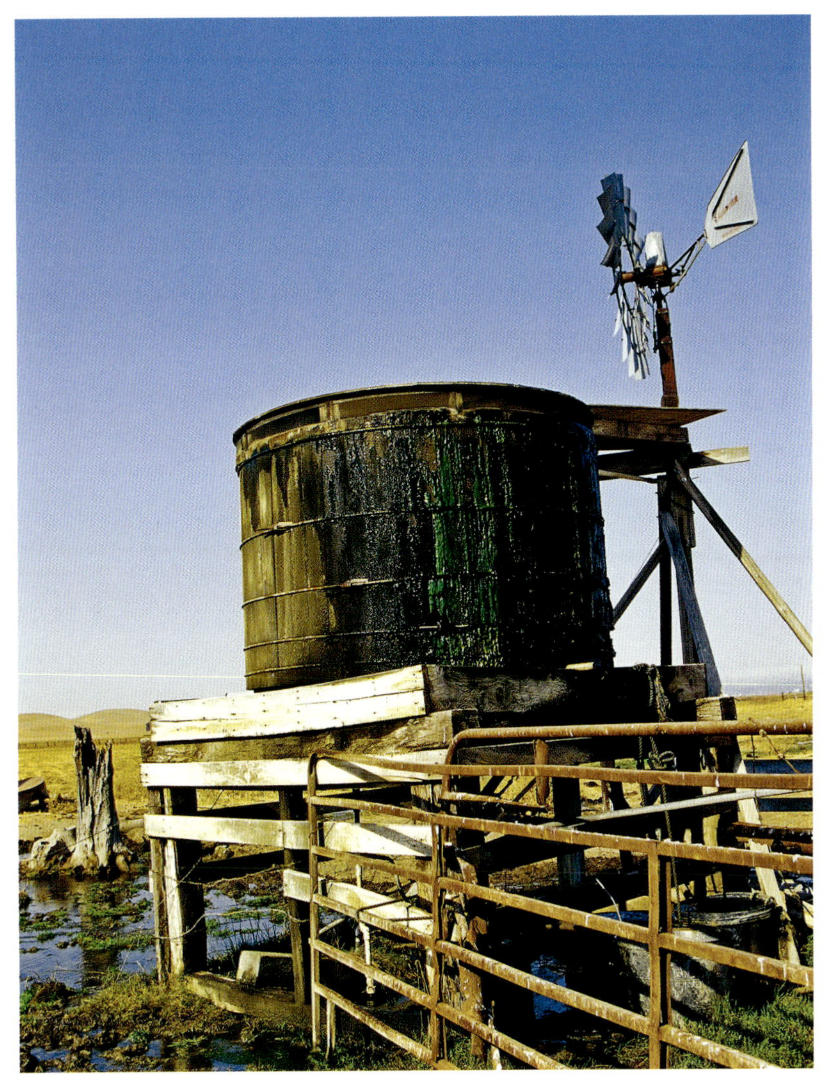

Needs a Little Work
Fairfield, California

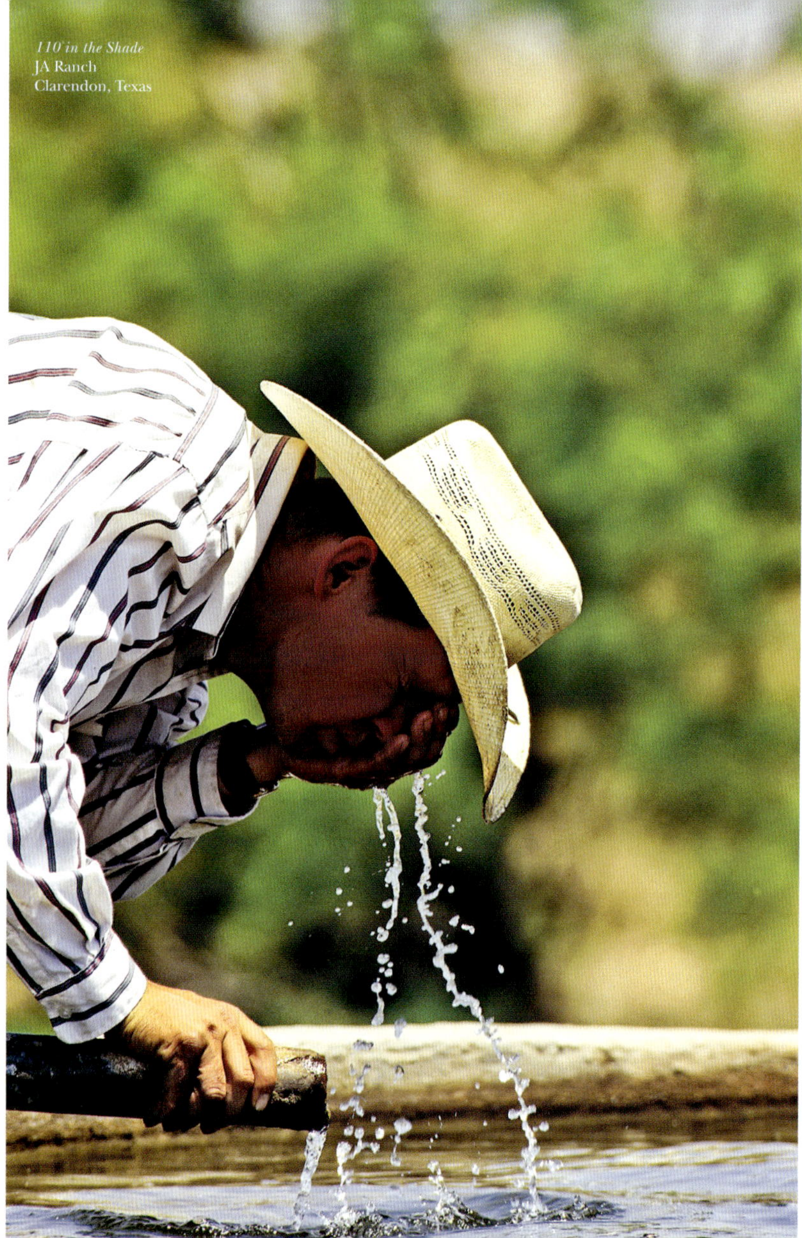

110° in the Shade
JA Ranch
Clarendon, Texas

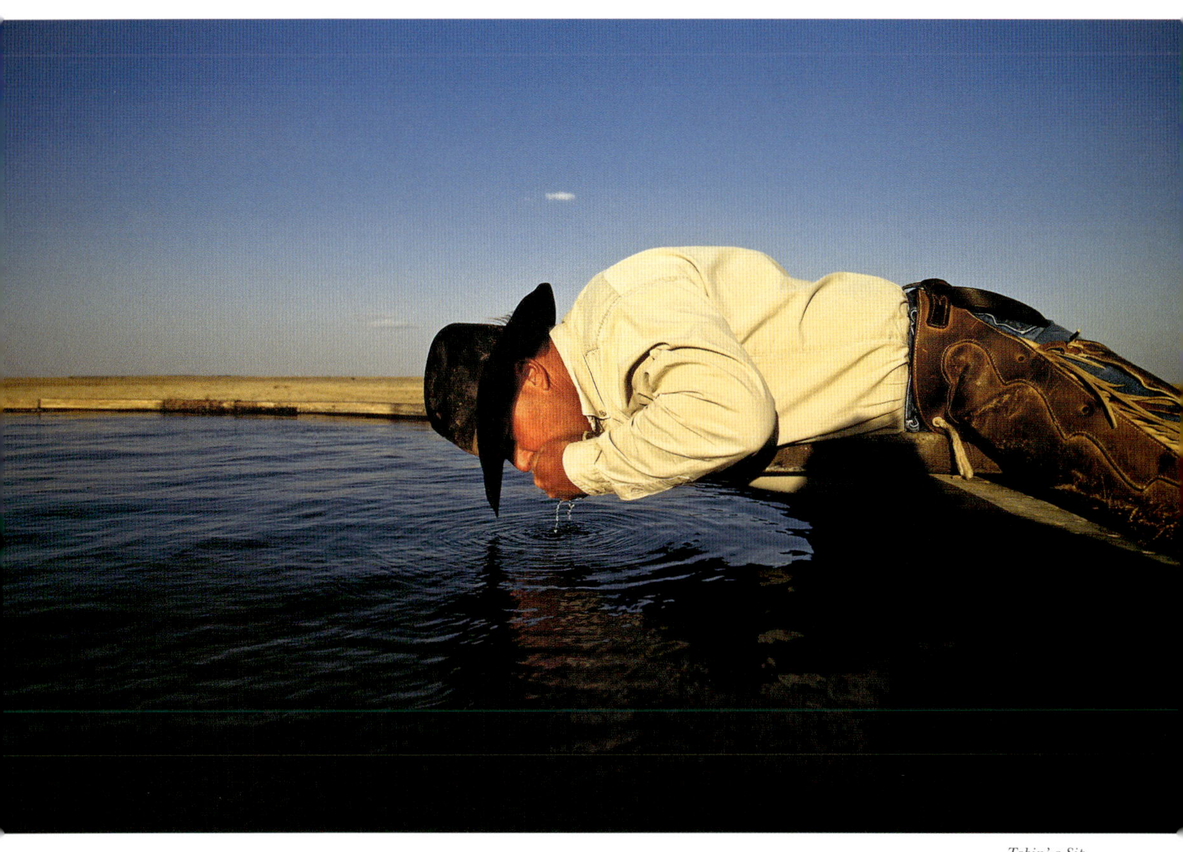

Takin' a Sip
Harrell Cattle Company
Claude, Texas

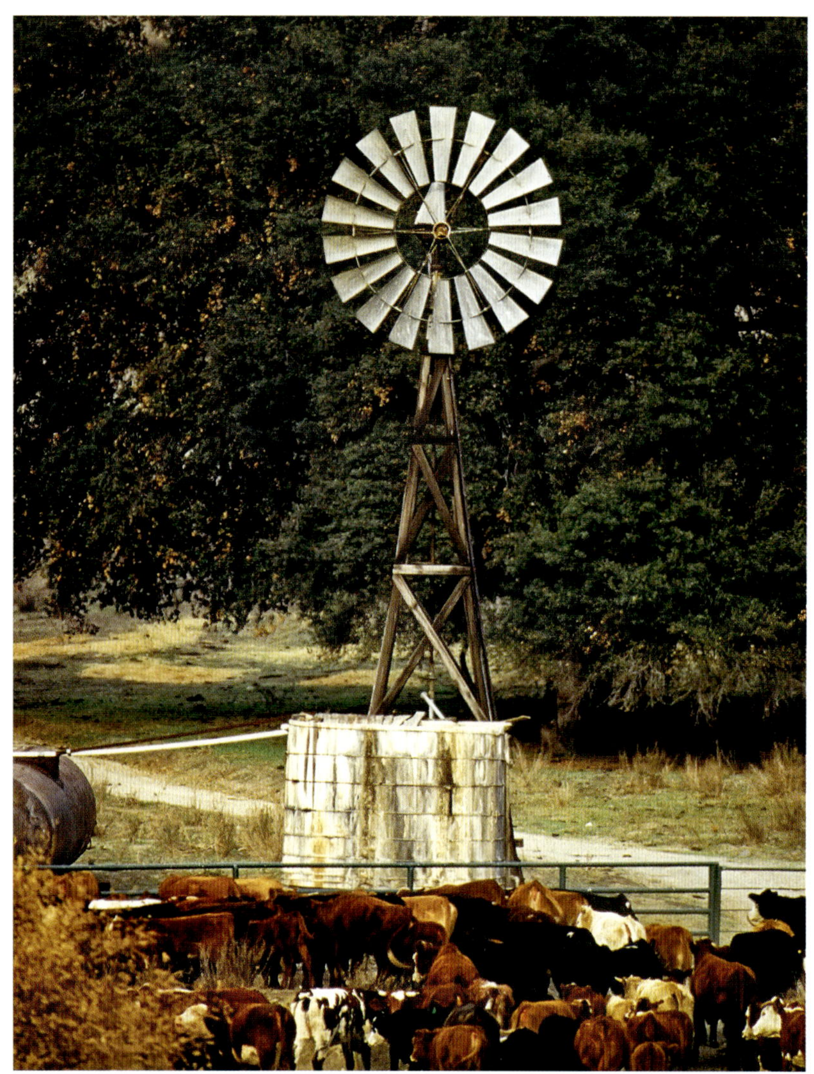

Baxter Black Memorial Windmill
Rancho Mission Viejo, San Juan Capistrano, California

Good Old California Tank
Fairfield, California

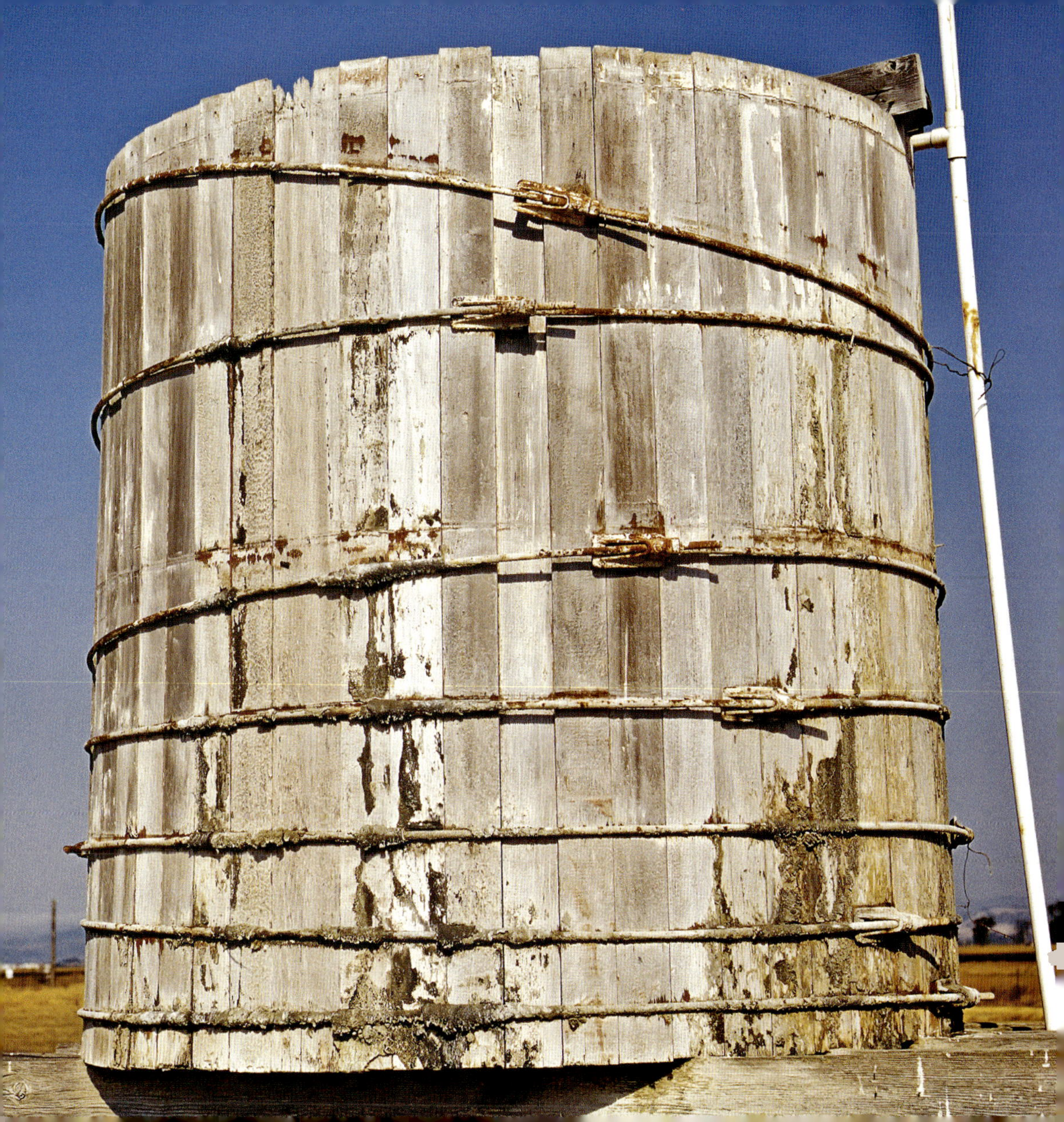

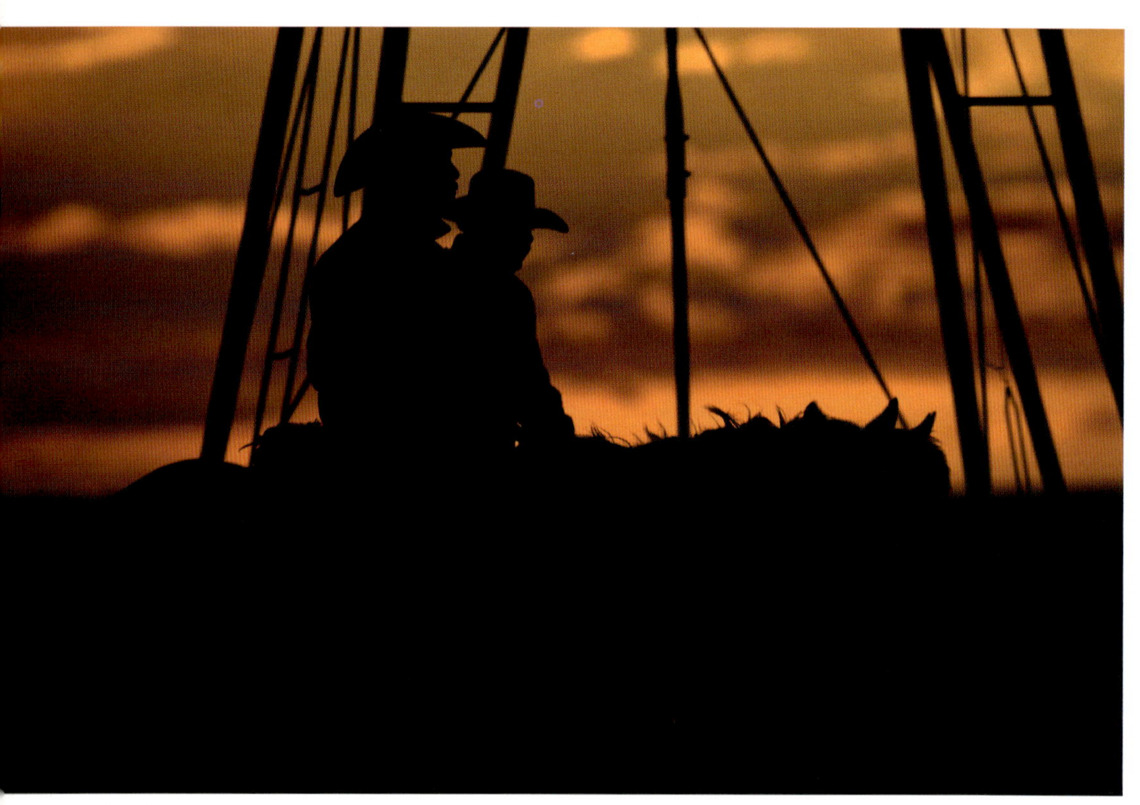

Going Home
Adolfo Lozano and Richard Woodrome
Cluck Ranches, Gruver, Texas

Sittin' in the Shade on the Cool Mill Tank
Thomas Saunders and Johnny Stewart
West Texas

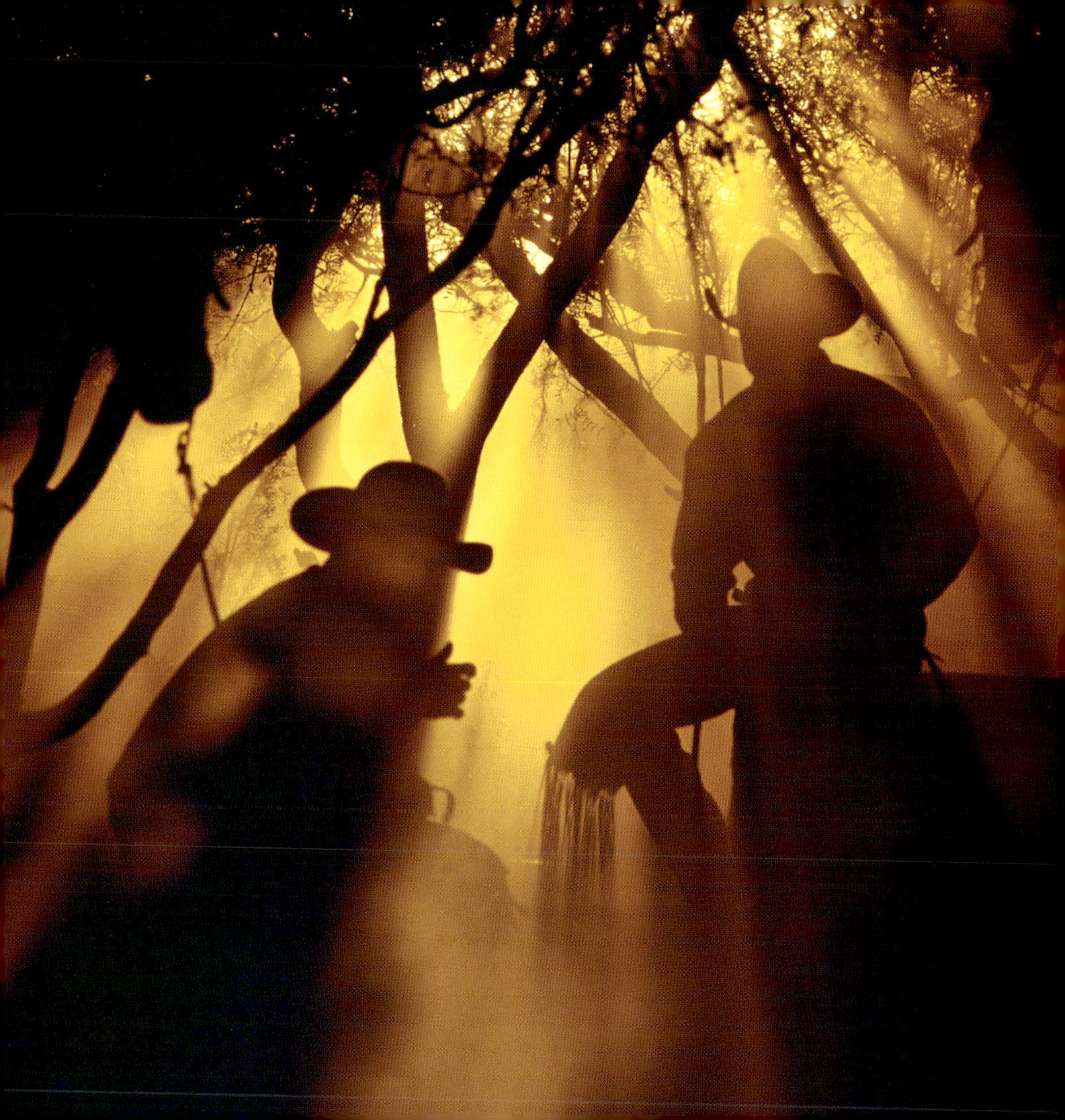

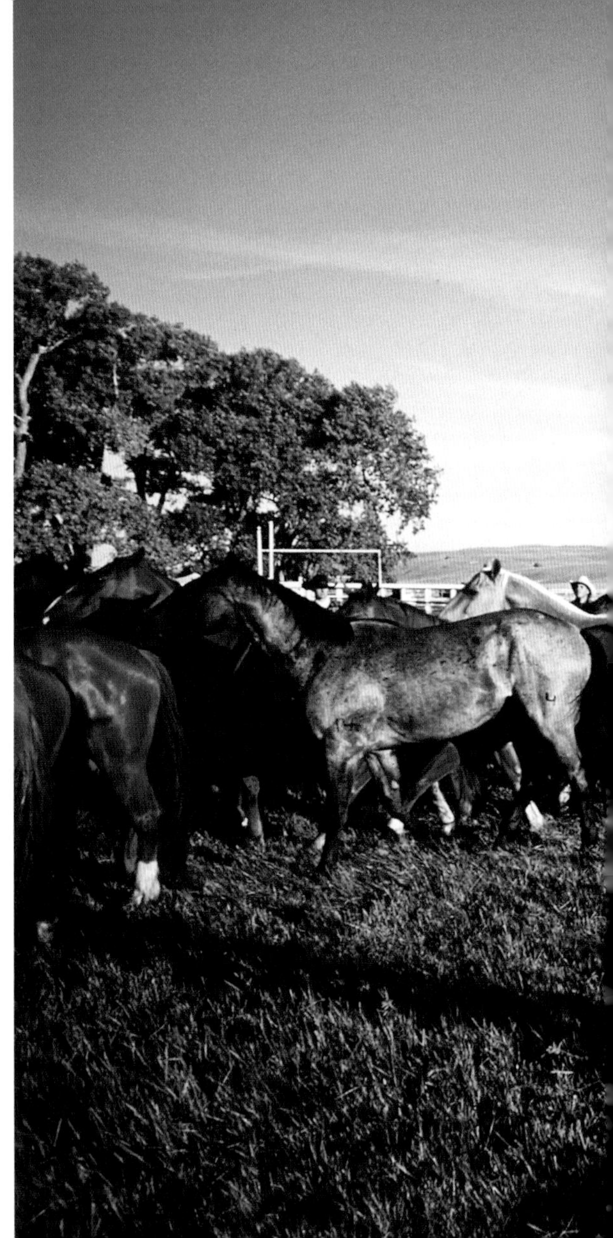

Lookin' for Old Gray
Craig Haythorn
Arthur, Nebraska

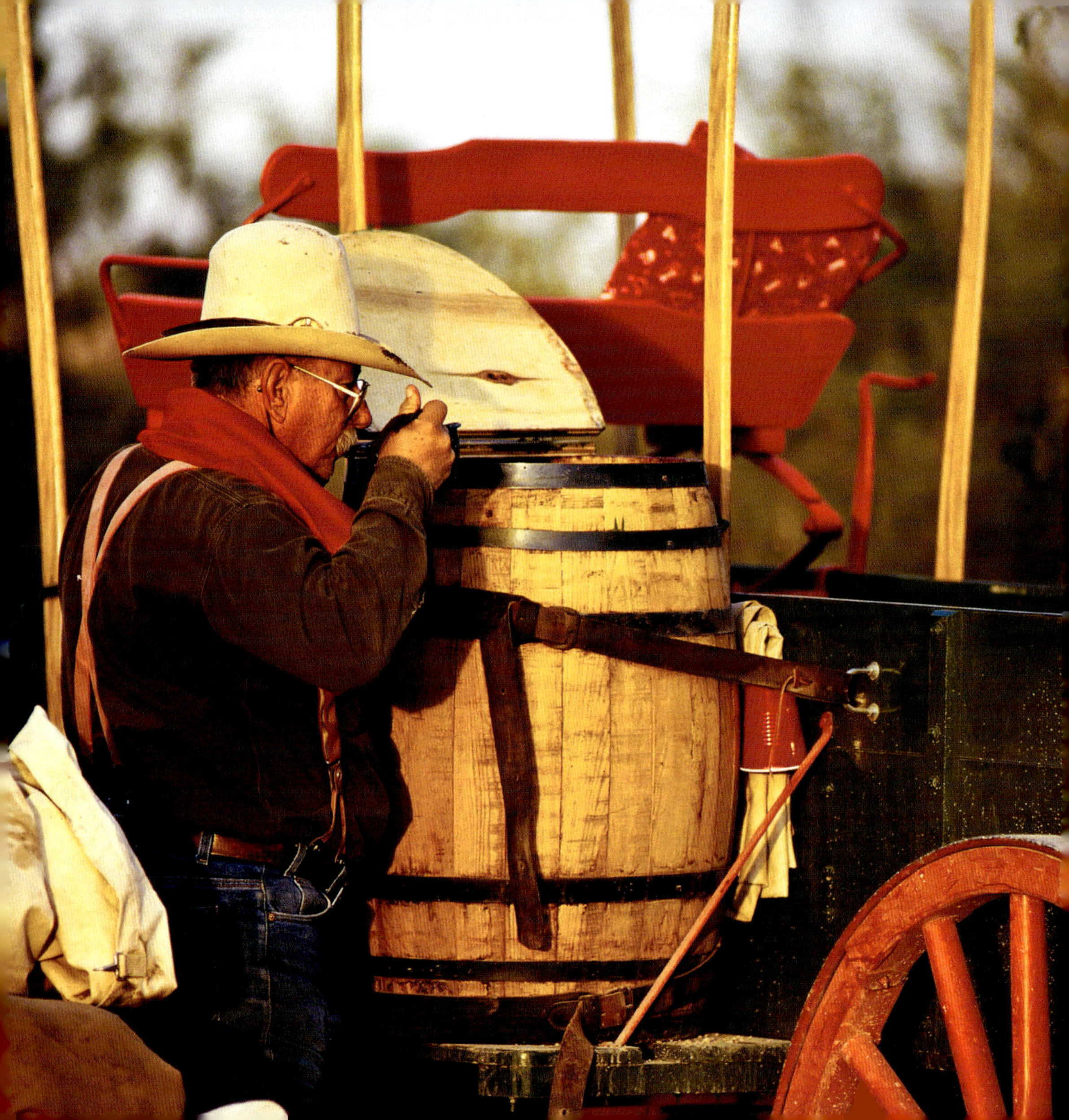

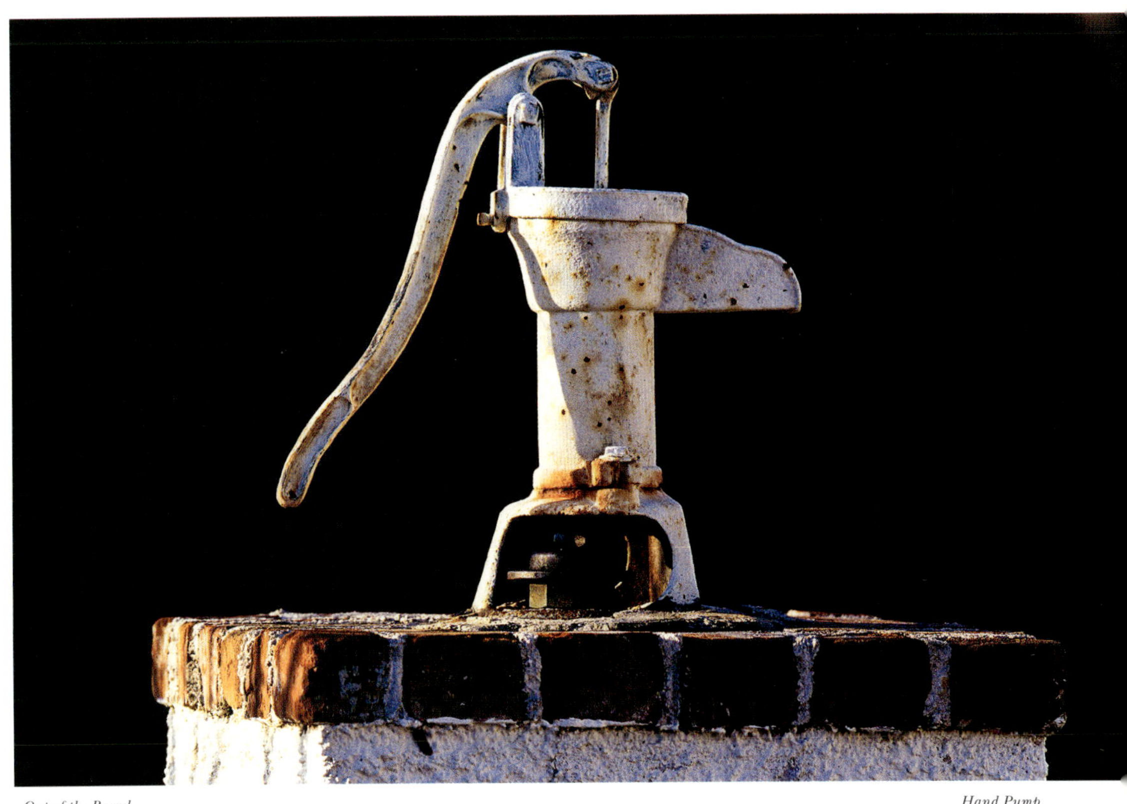

Out of the Barrel
Tom B. Saunders
Weatherford, Texas

Hand Pump
Bellota Ranch
Tucson, Arizona

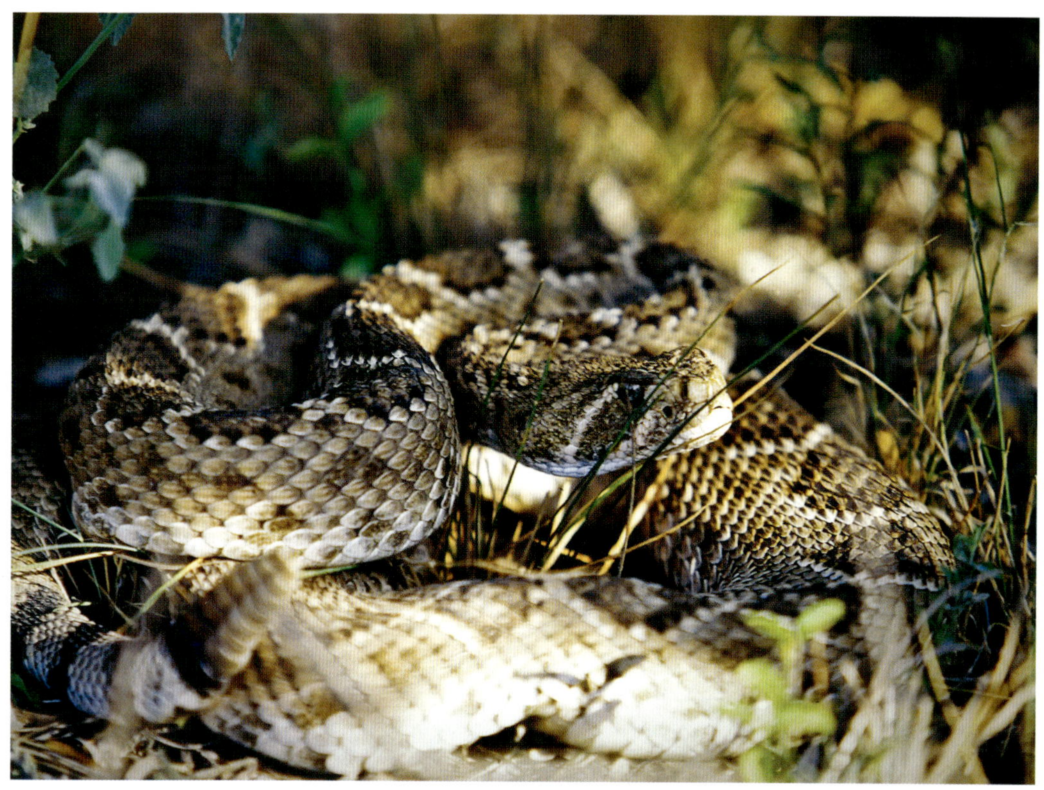

Rattlesnakes Hunt for Critters Near the Water
South Texas

Quarter Mile to the Mill
Eppenauer Ranch
Toyah, Texas

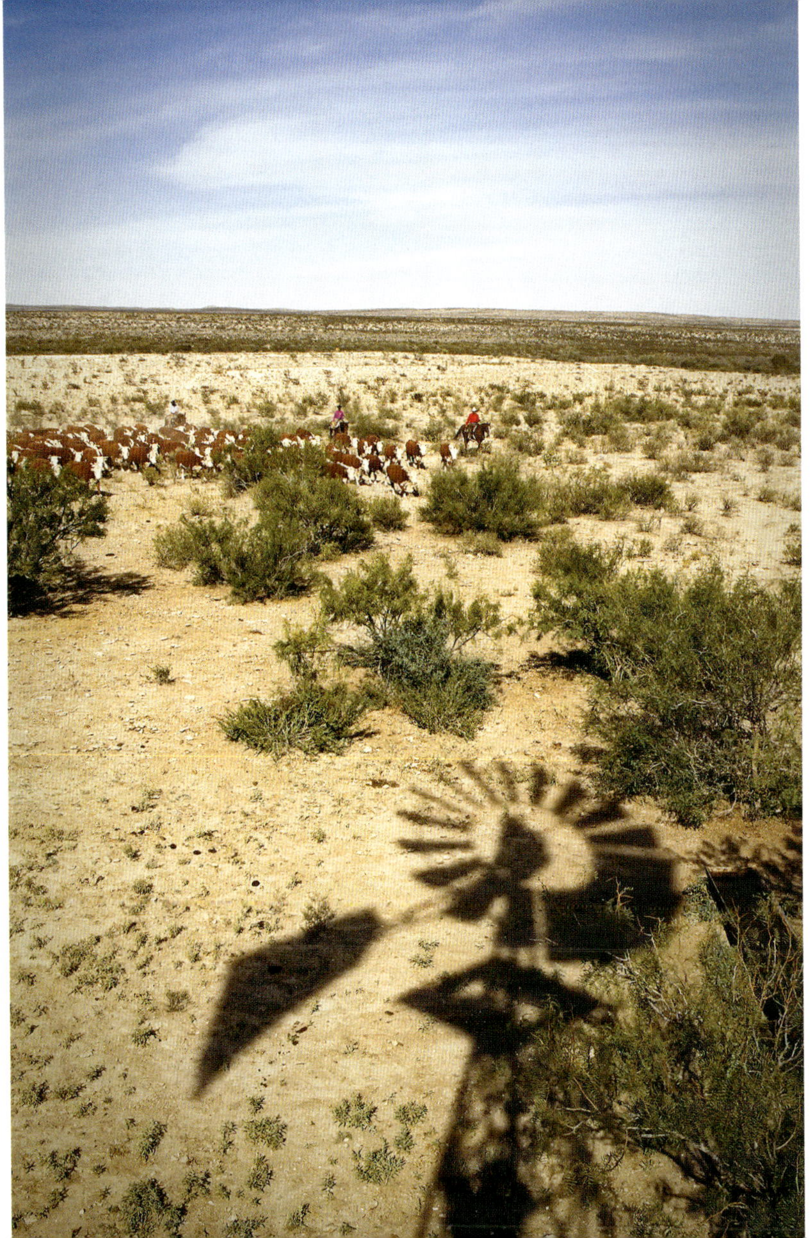

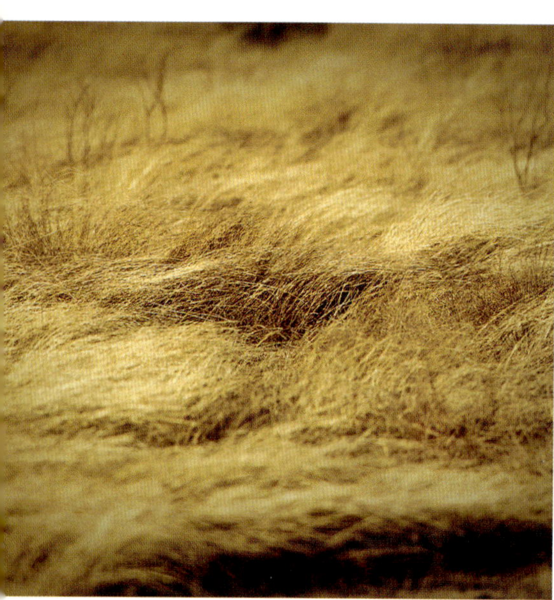

Waiting for Rain
Pitchfork Ranch
Guthrie, Texas

Sunset
Southern Utah

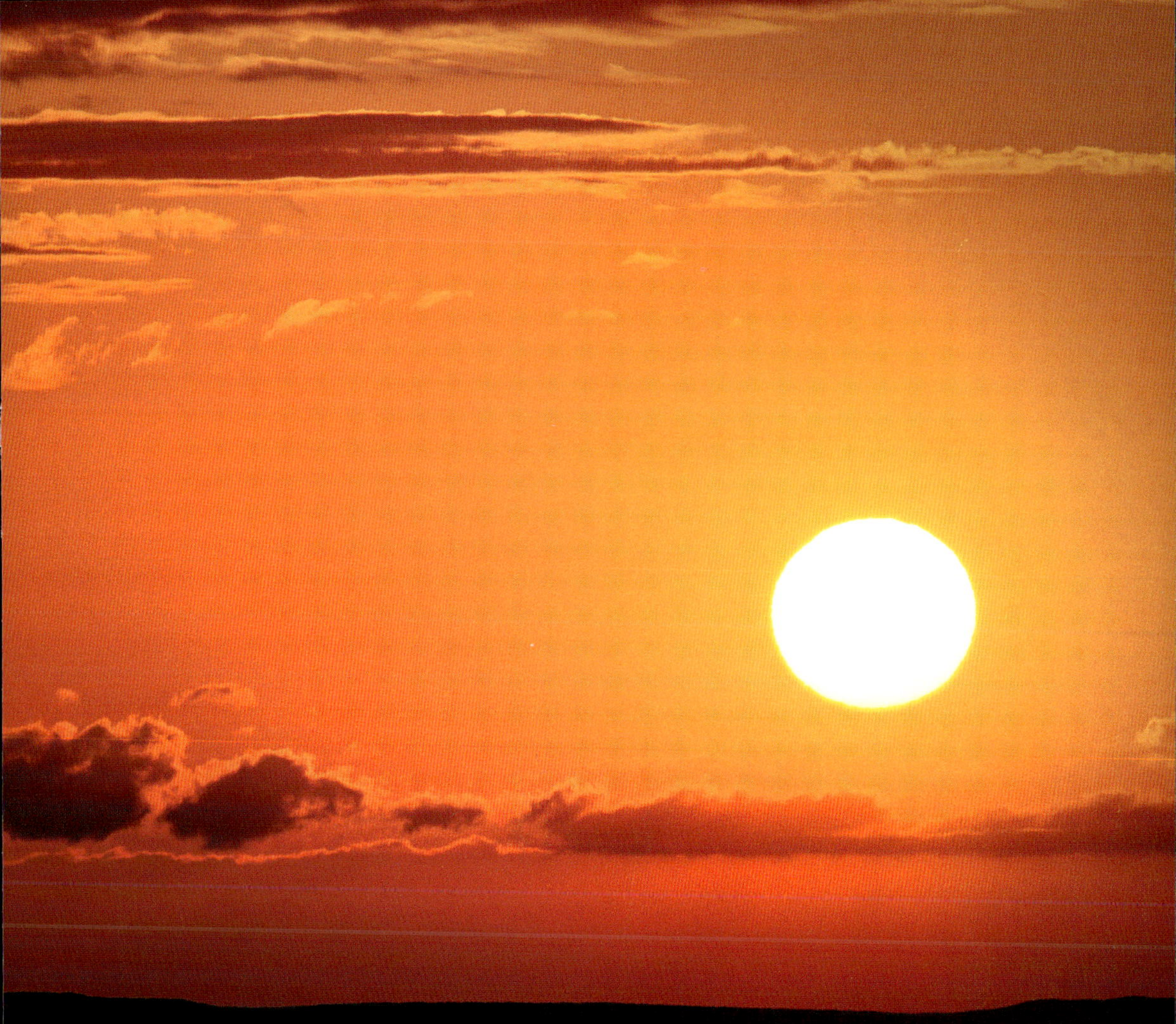

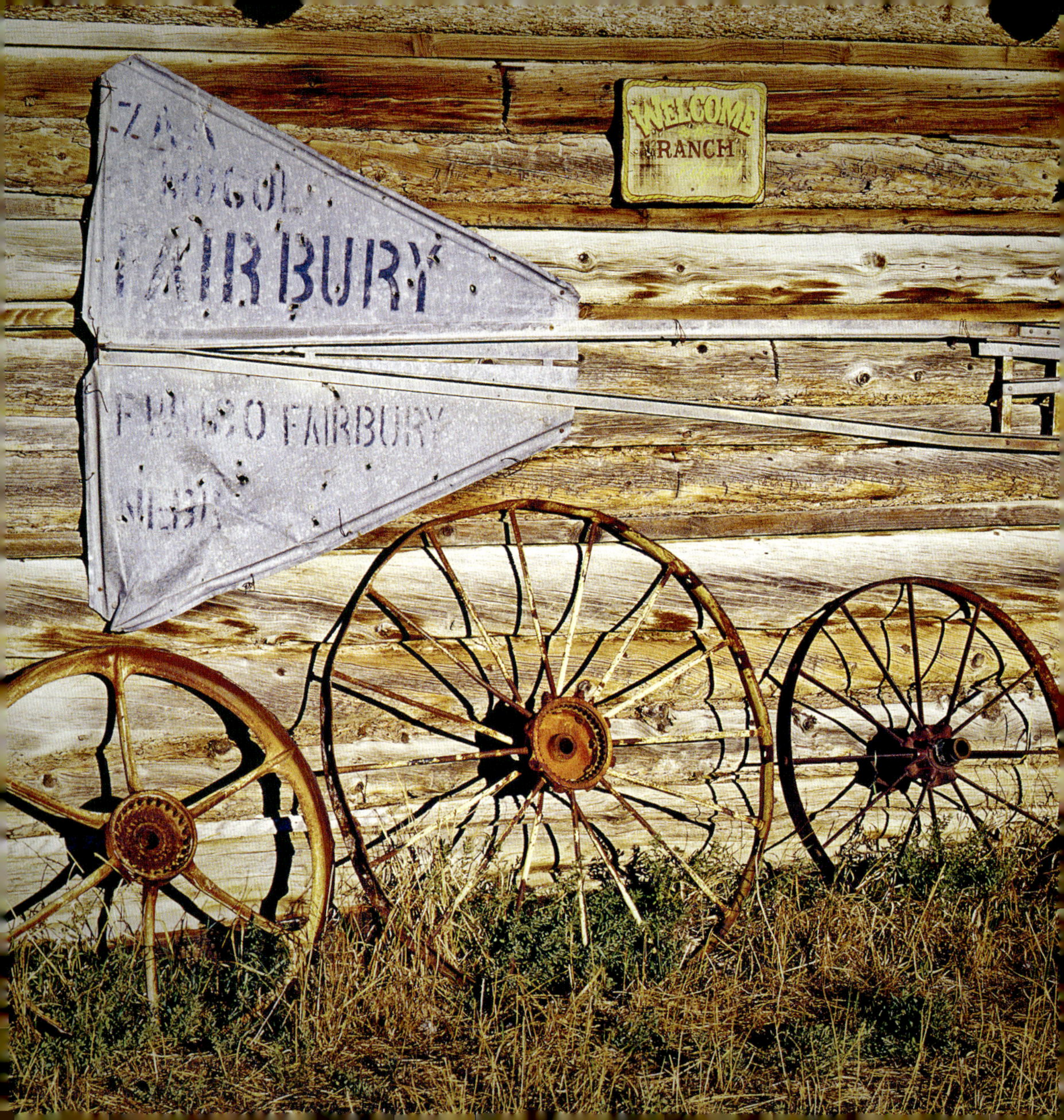

WELCOME
RANCH
FAIRBURY
FAIRBURY

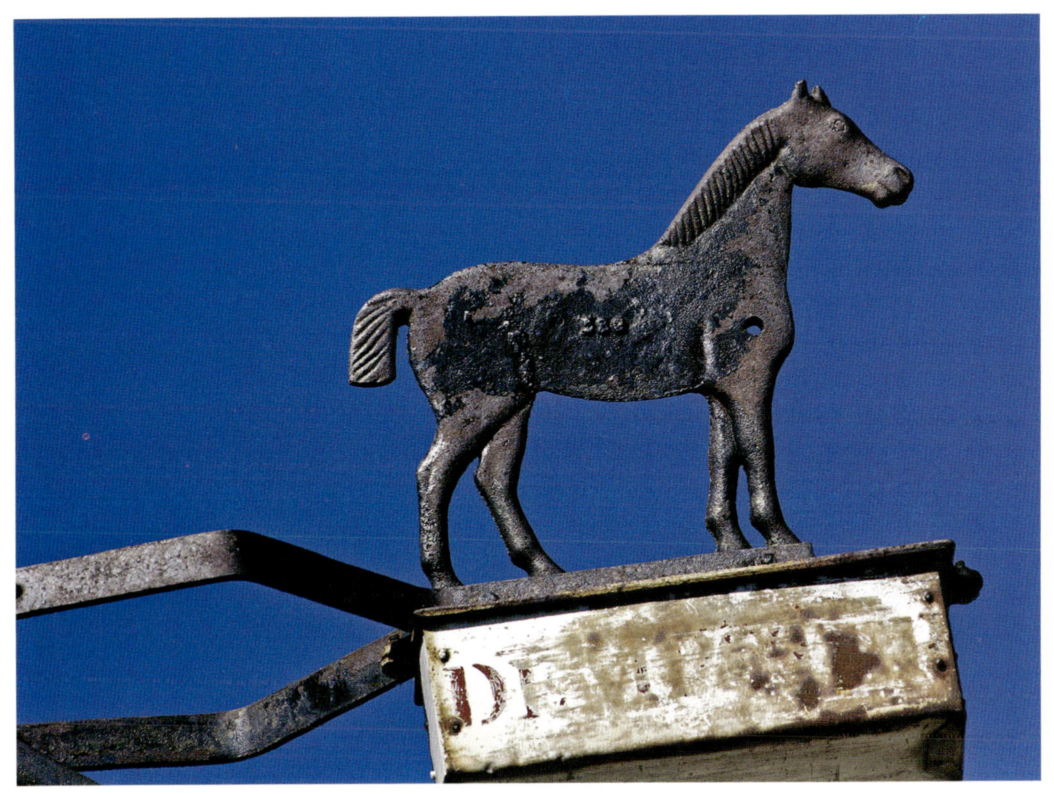

Old Windmill Weight

Bar Horseshoe Ranch
Mackay, Idaho

How to Stop a Runaway

While taking this photo of Jim Bob Walton I asked him, "If the fan breaks loose, how do you keep it from spinning?" His response was that you have to climb up the tower, get on the platform, and slowly back your rear end into the fan blades until it stops.

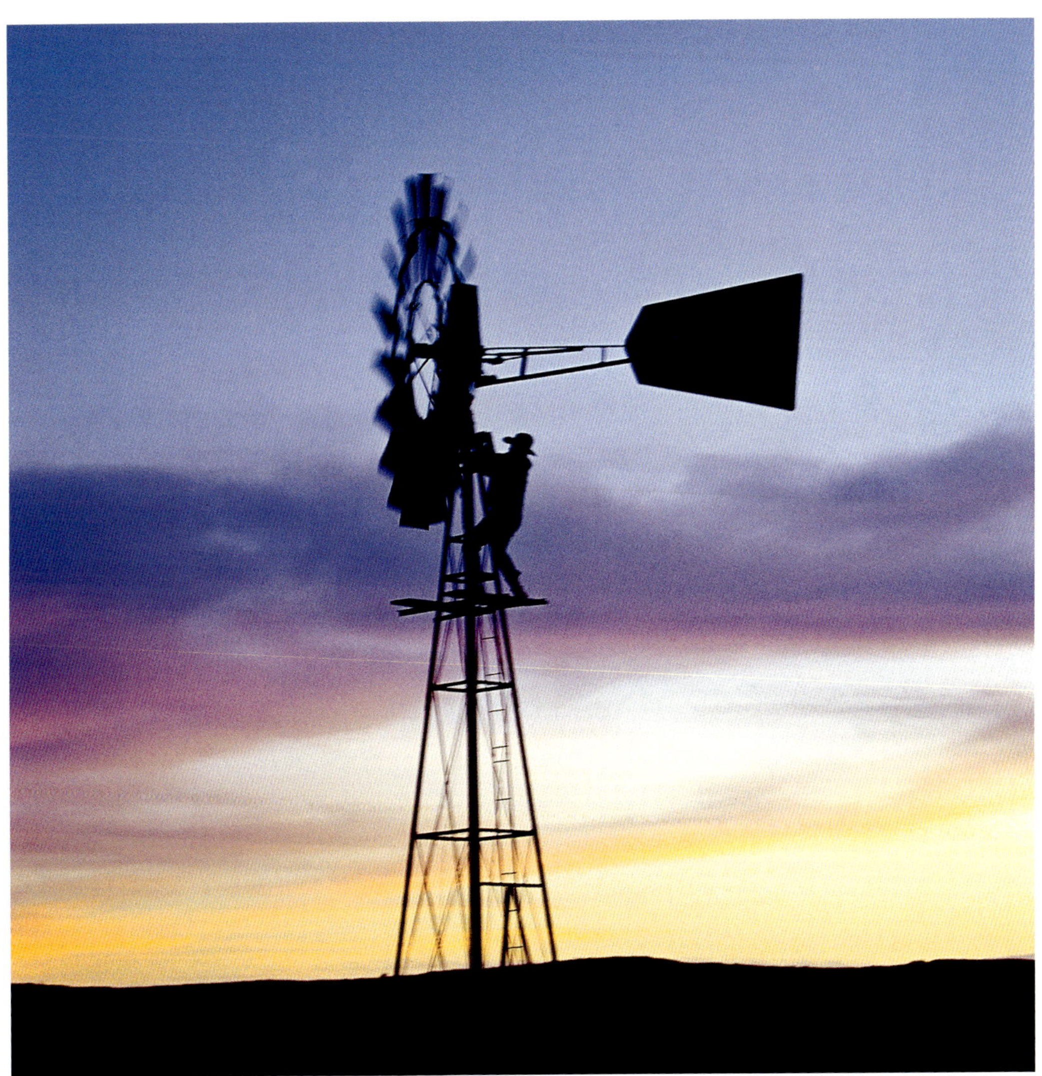

LX Ranch, Amarillo, Texas

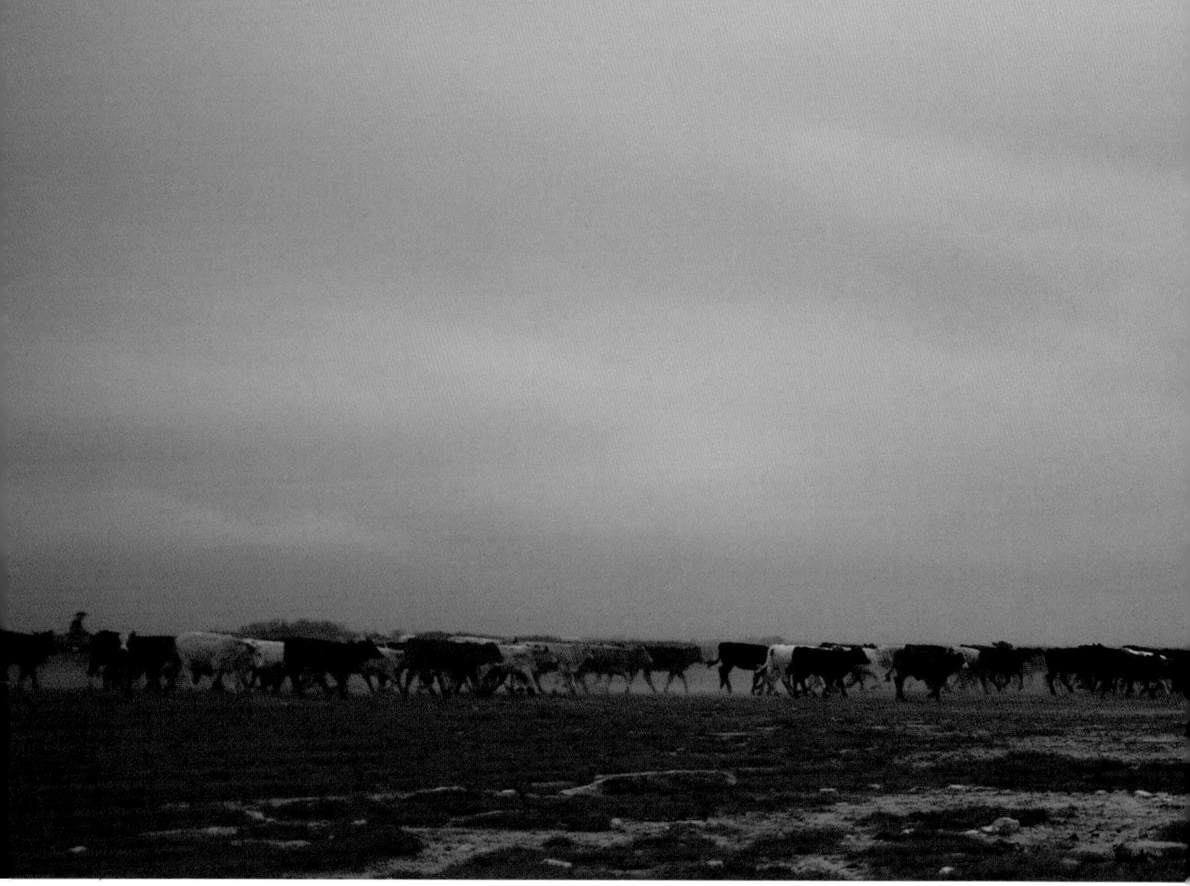

Got to Get There Before the Storm
Cluck Ranches
Gruver, Texas

"Does the wind blow this way all the time?" asked a visiting investor to the XIT Ranch. "No mister," answered the ranch

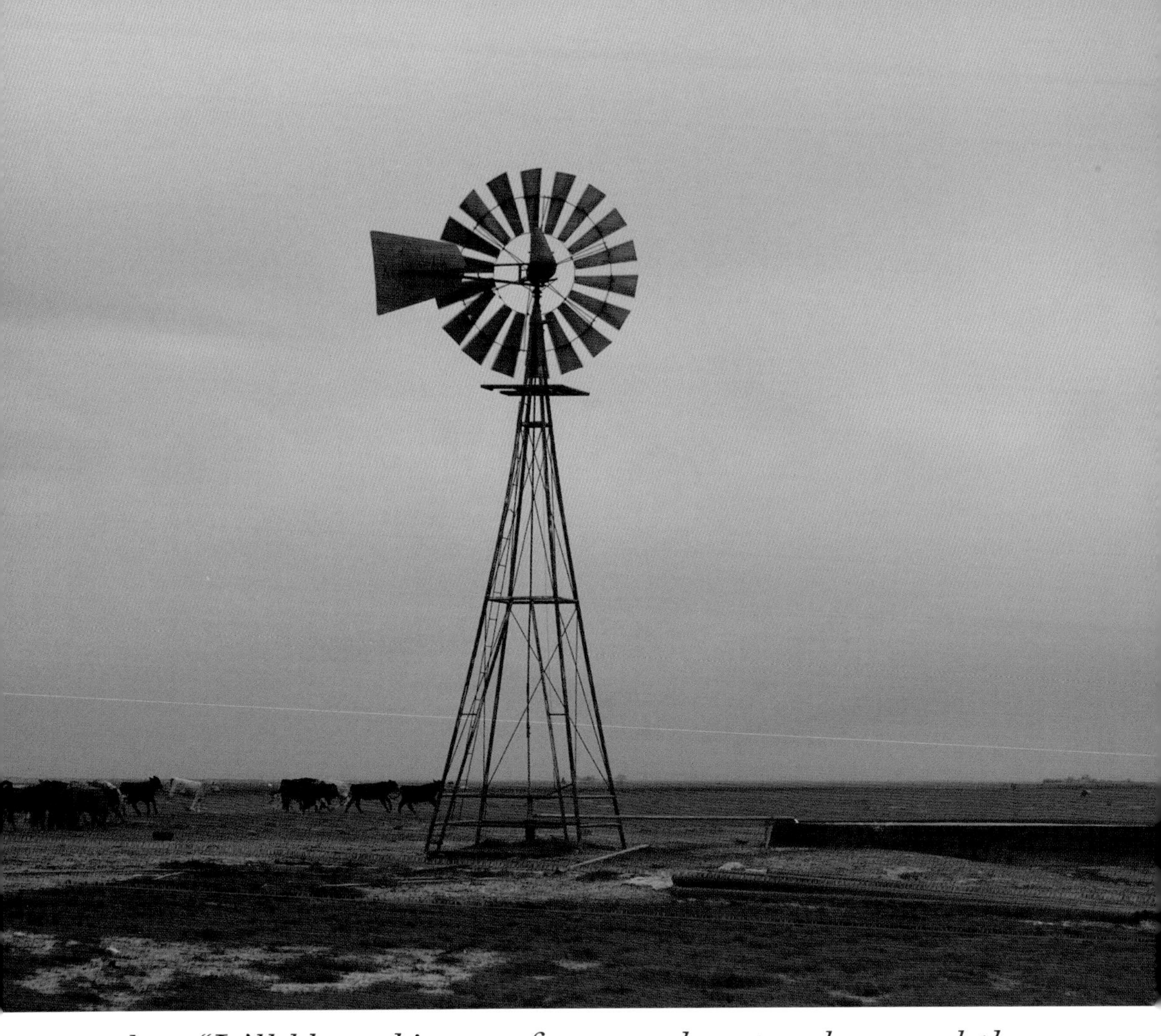

cowboy. "It'll blow this way for a week or ten days, and then it'll take a change and blow like hell for a while."

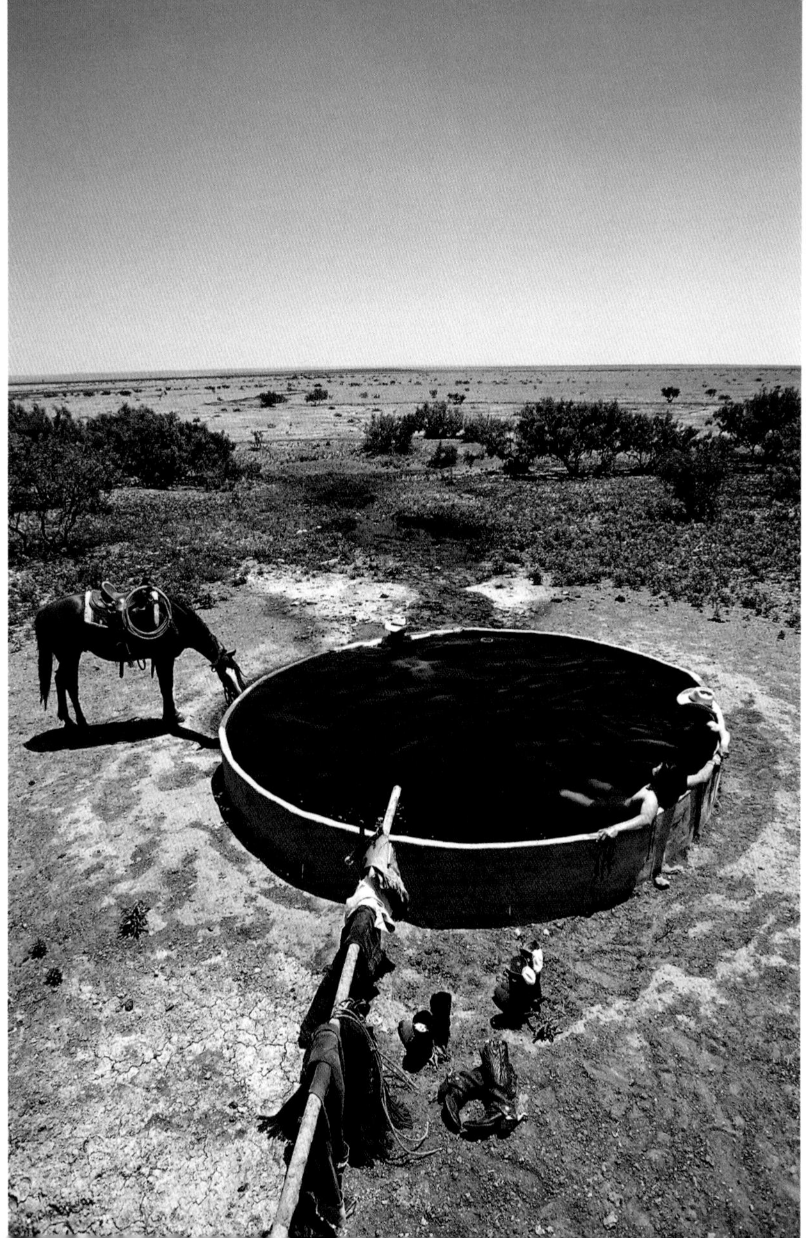

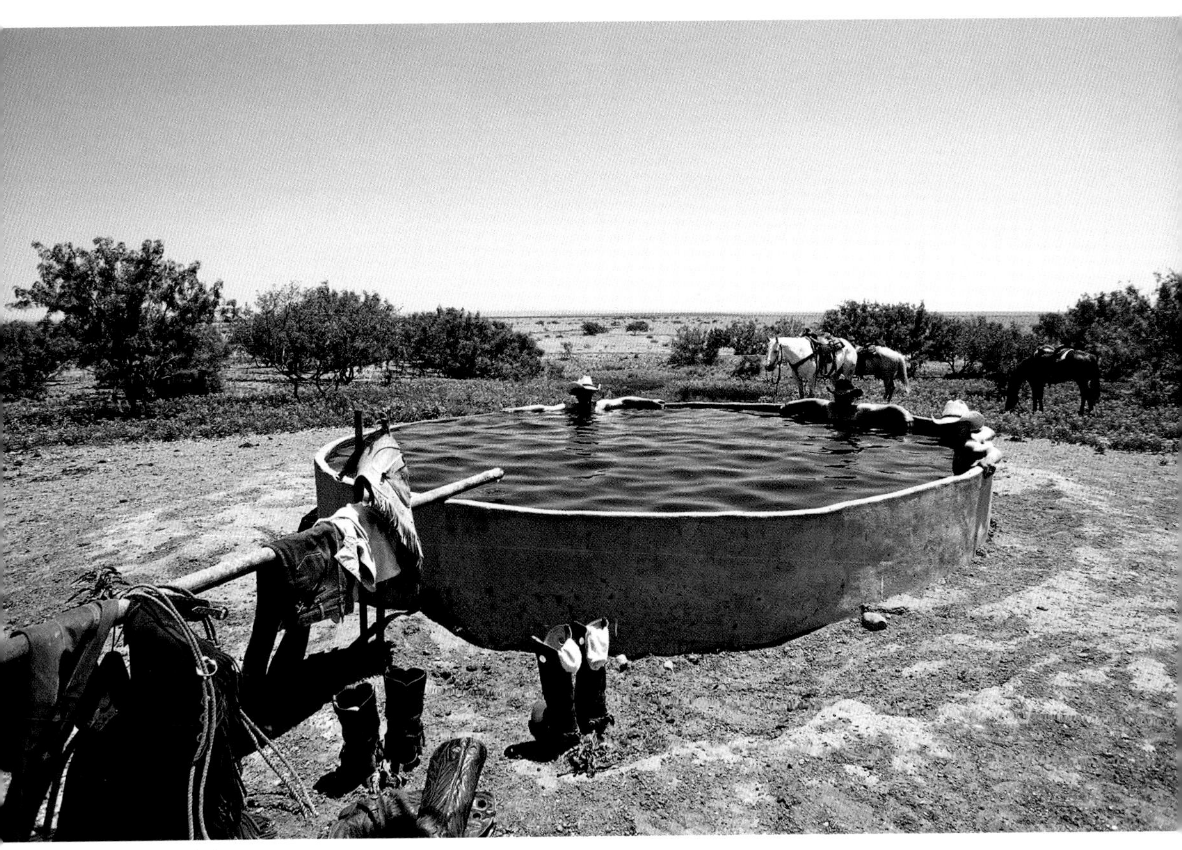

Cowboy Swimming Pool
JA Ranch
Clarendon, Texas

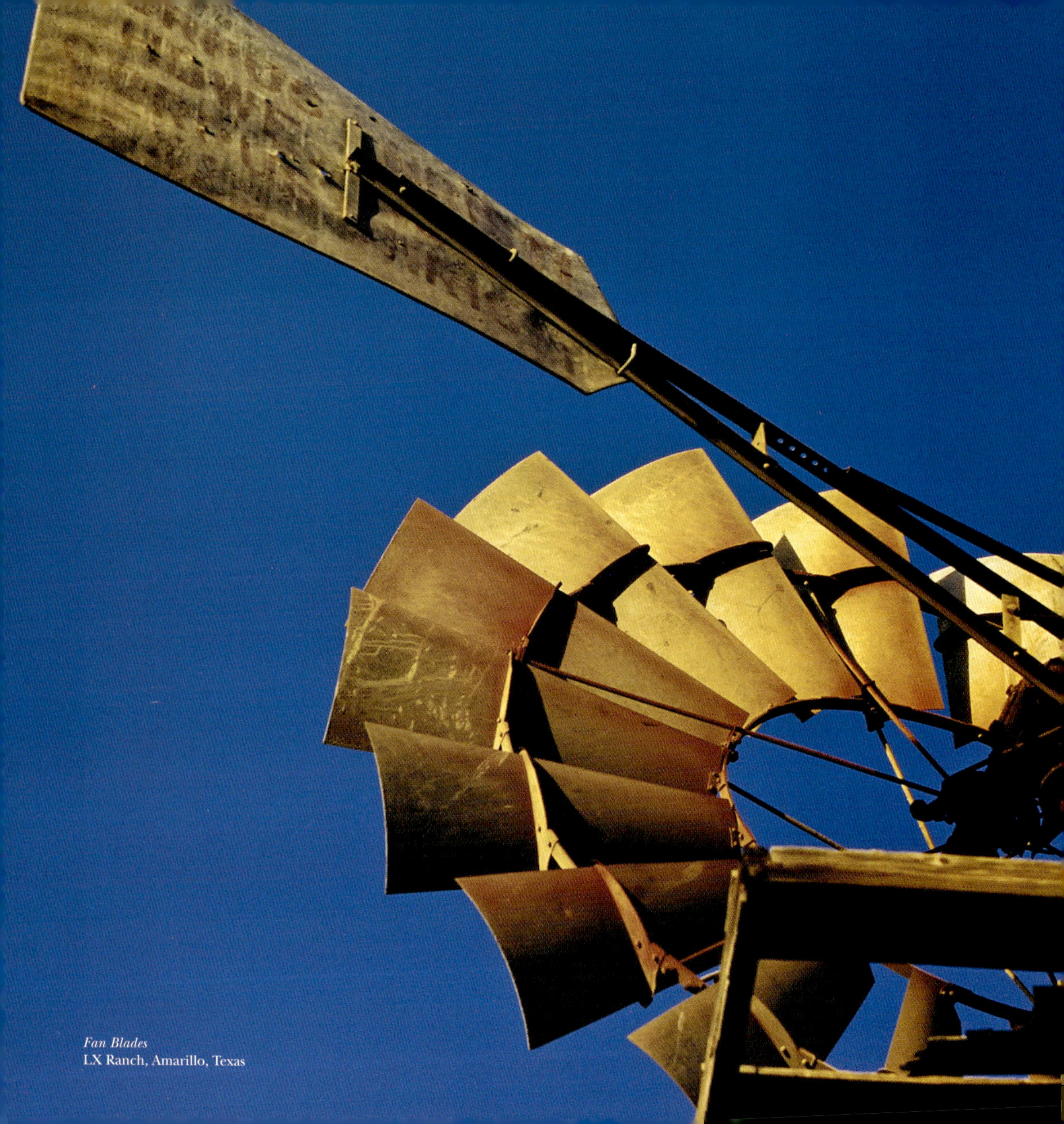

Fan Blades
LX Ranch, Amarillo, Texas

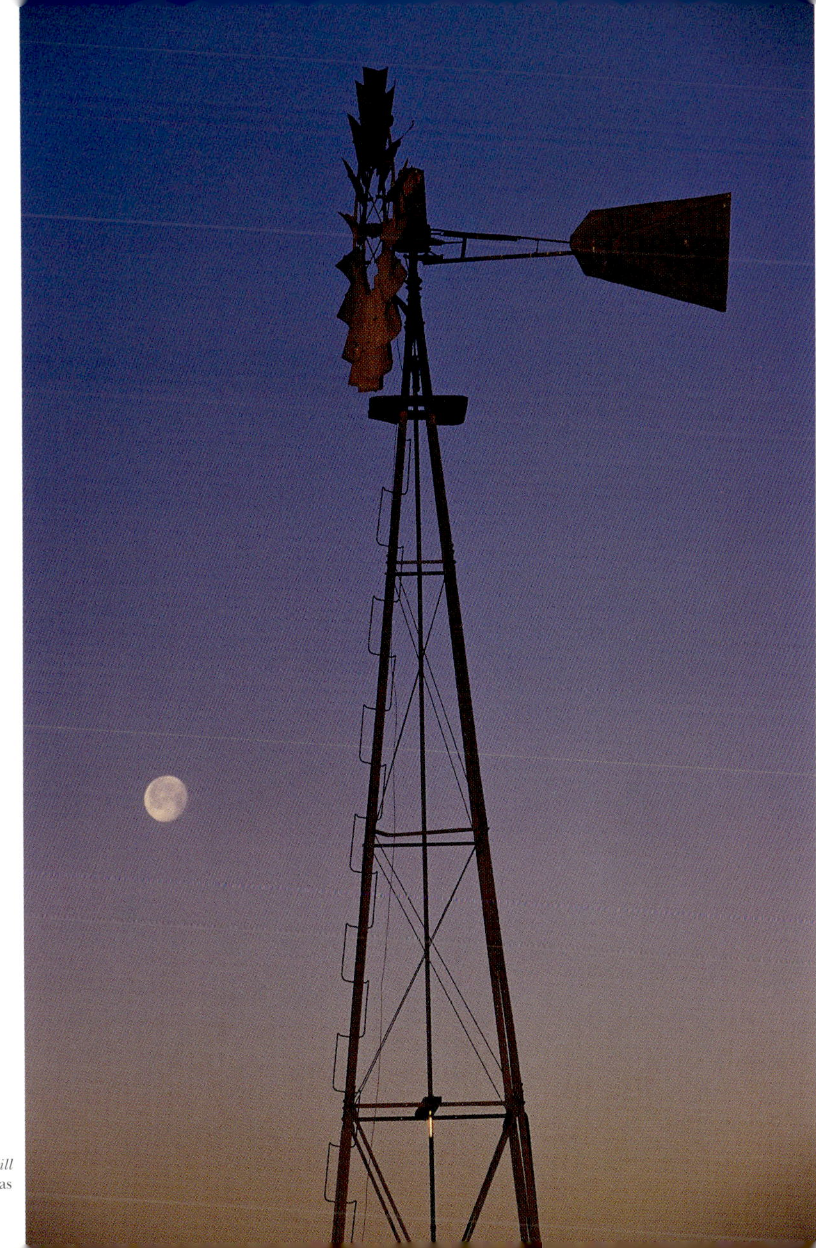

Moonrise and Mill
LX Ranch, Amarillo, Texas

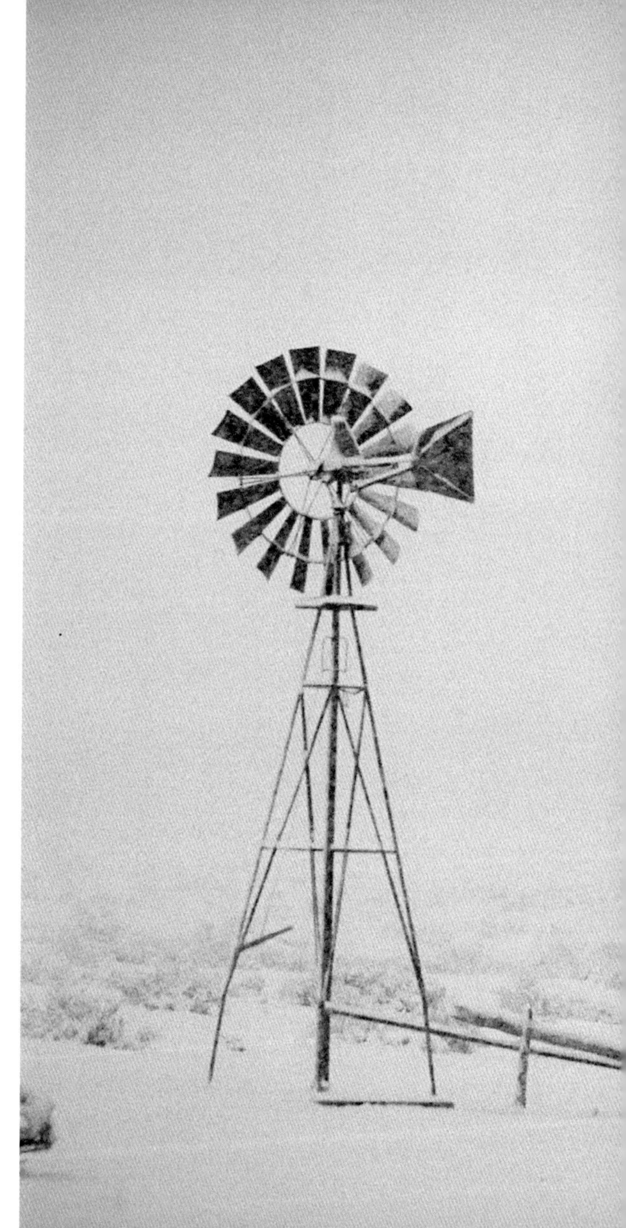

Spring Blizzard
Moab, Utah

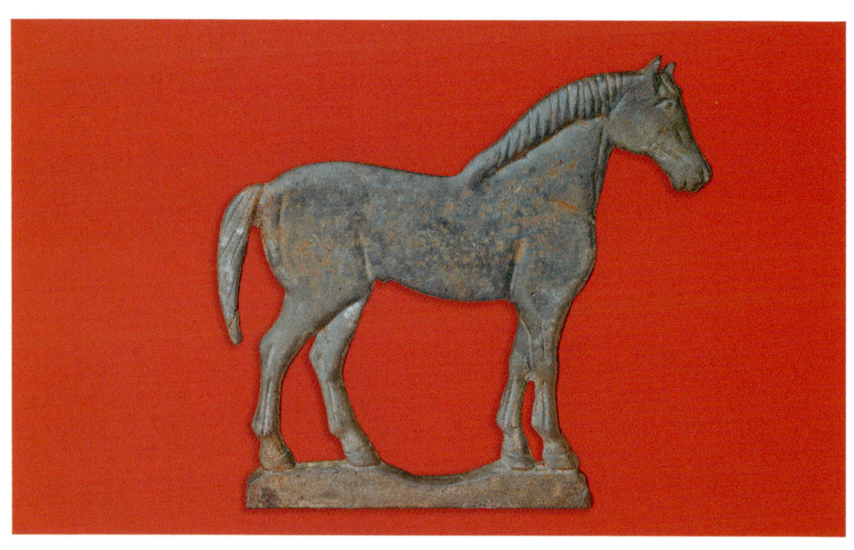

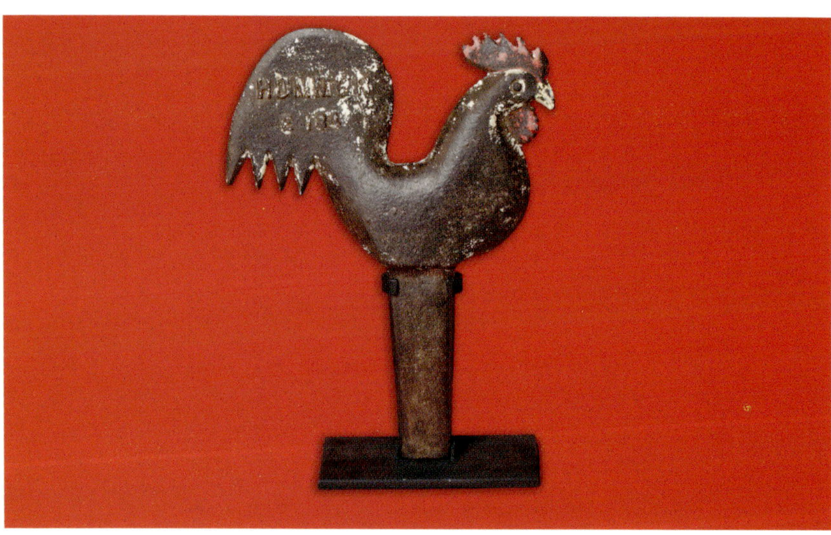

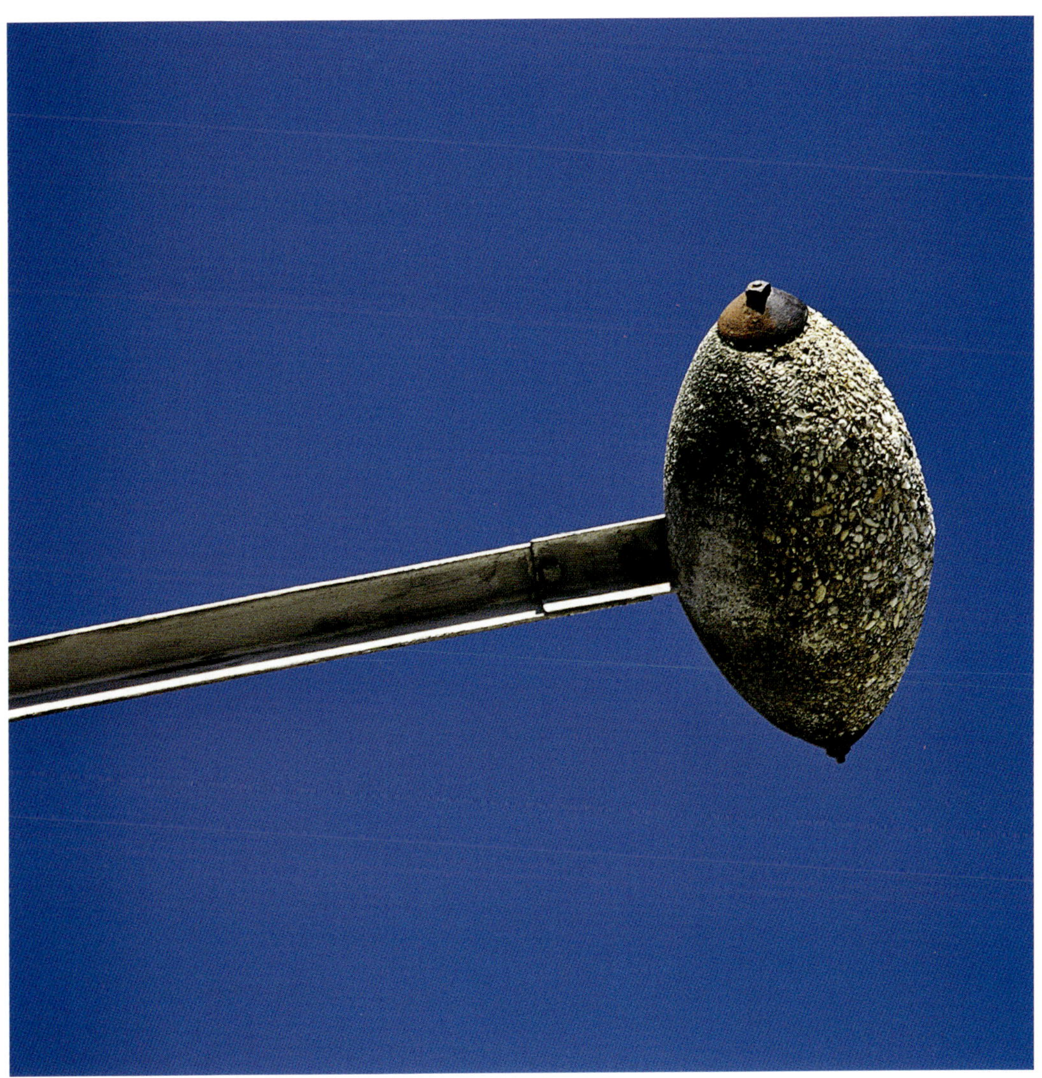

Antique Windmill Weights

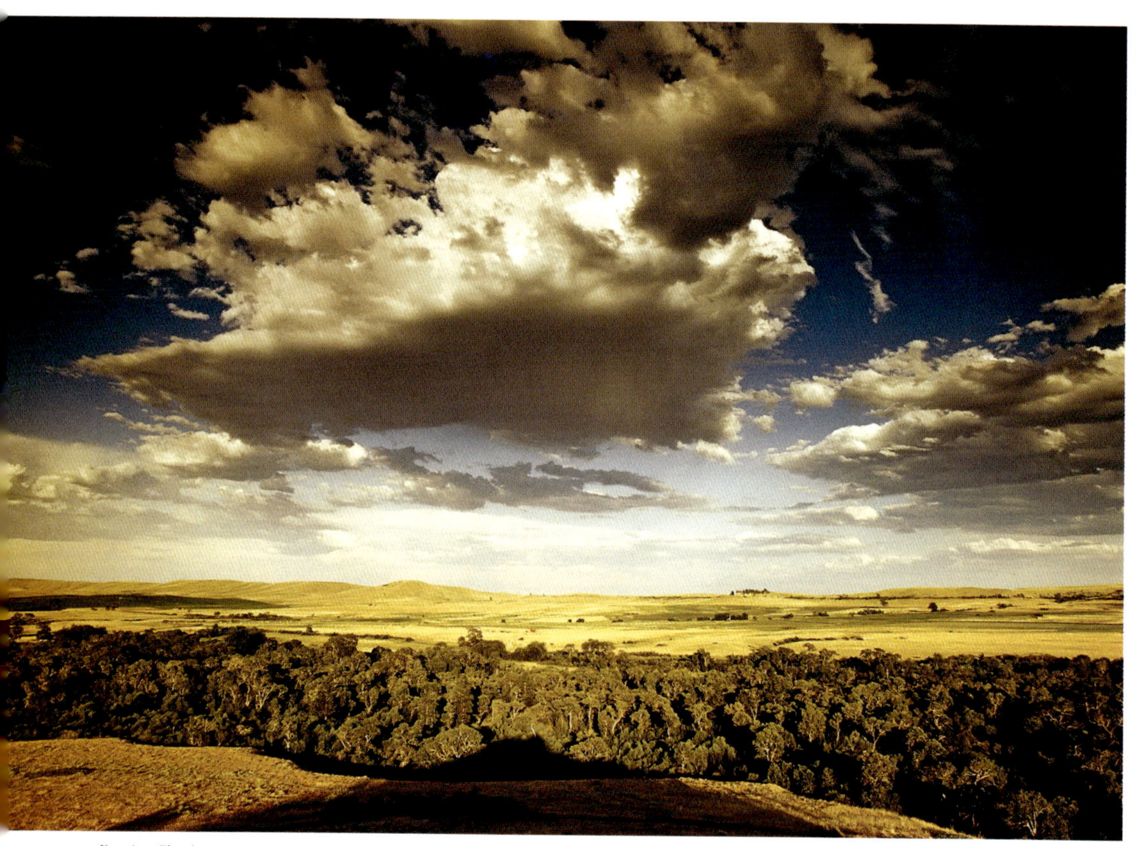

Evening Clouds
Sheridan, Wyoming

Storm Clouds
Padlock Ranch
Hardin, Montana

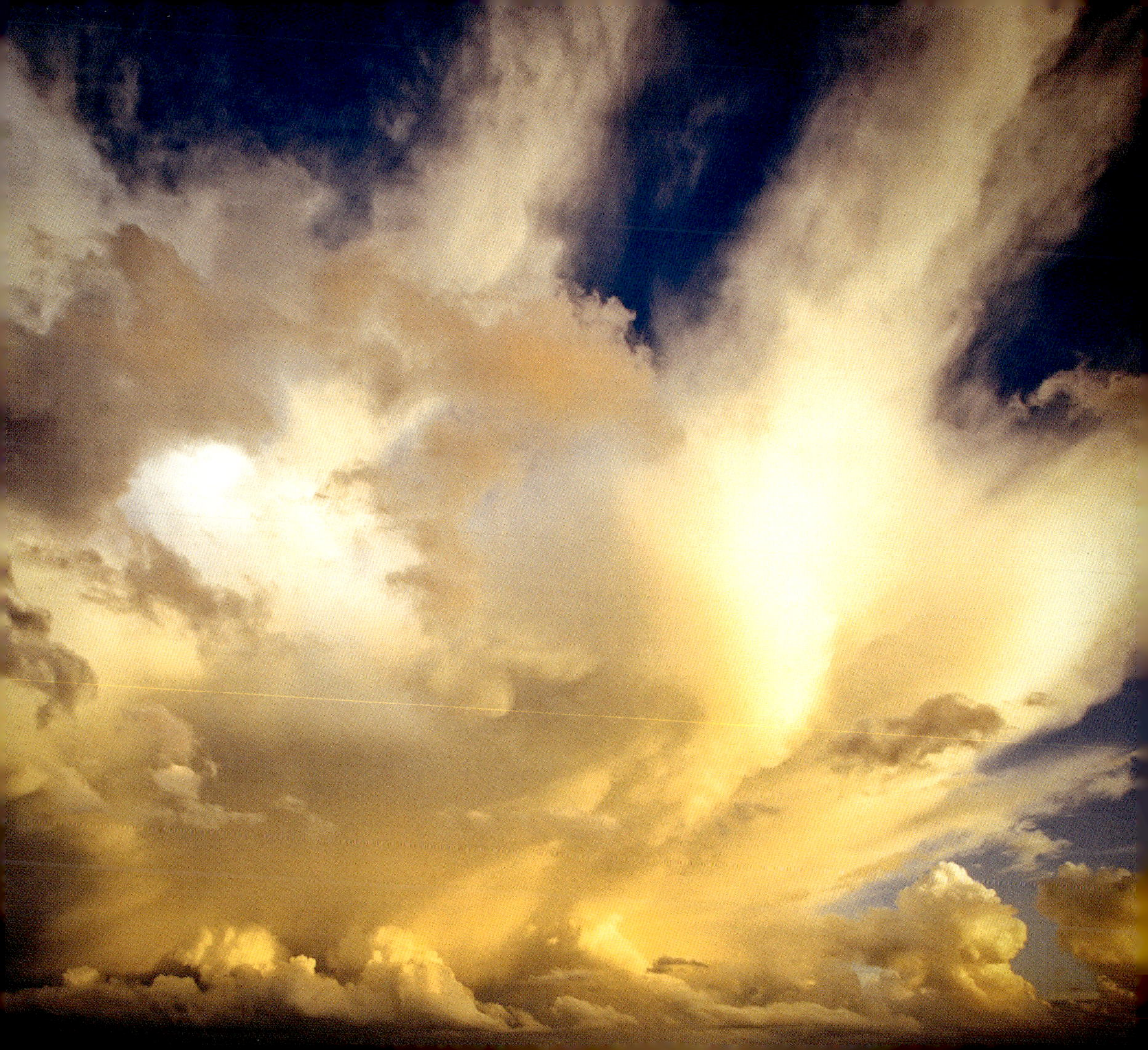

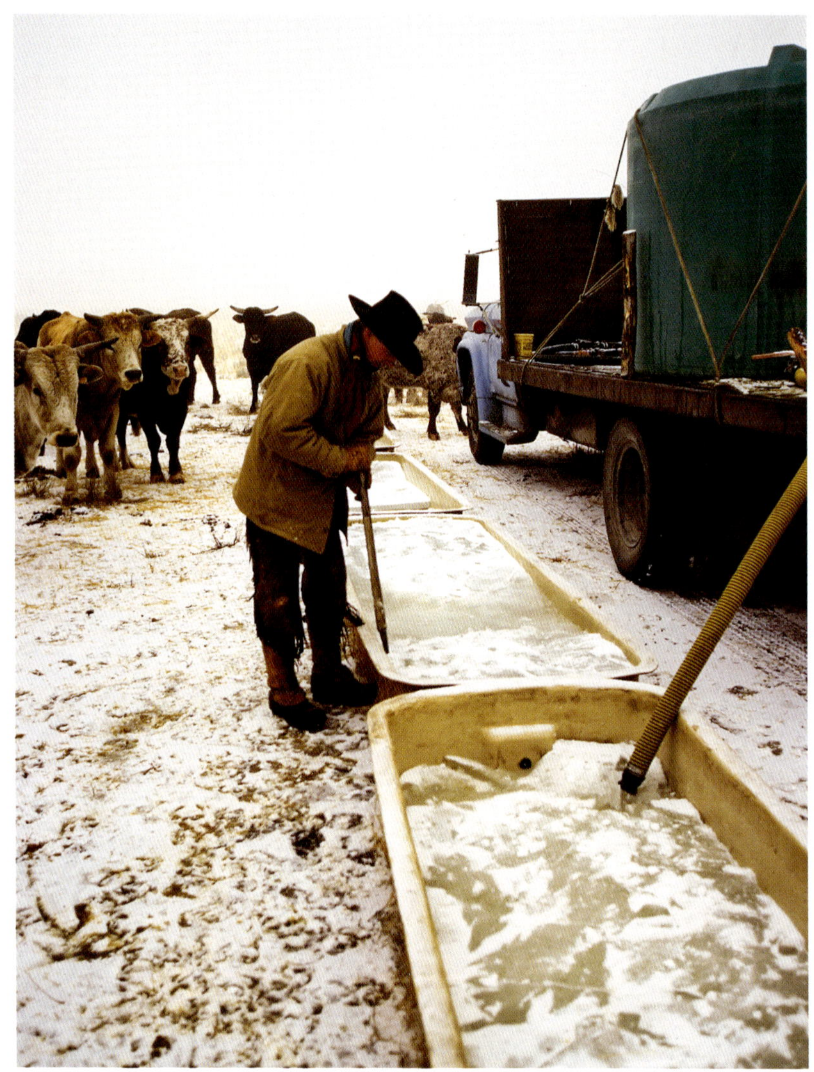

Mark Tilford Breaking Ice
Eastern Idaho

Fixin' the Mill in the Winter
Mackay, Idaho

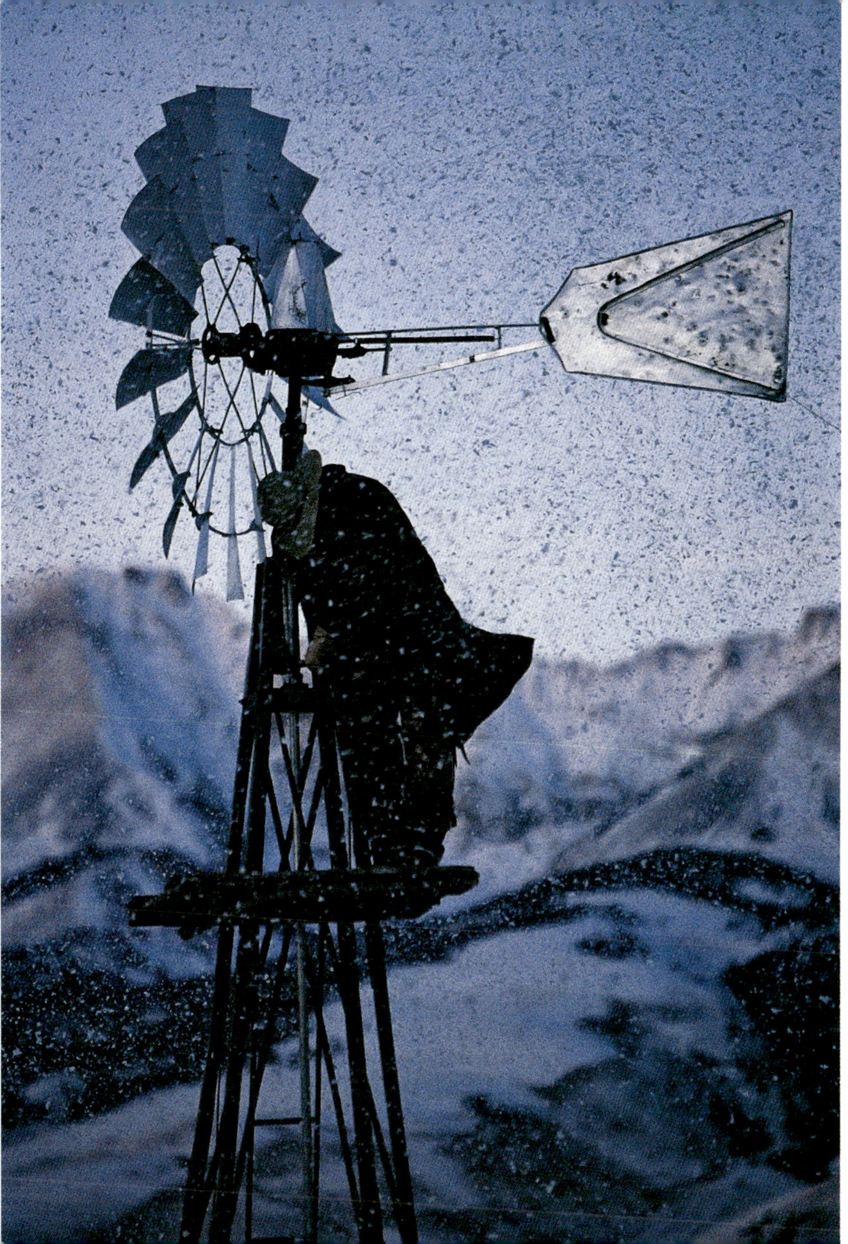

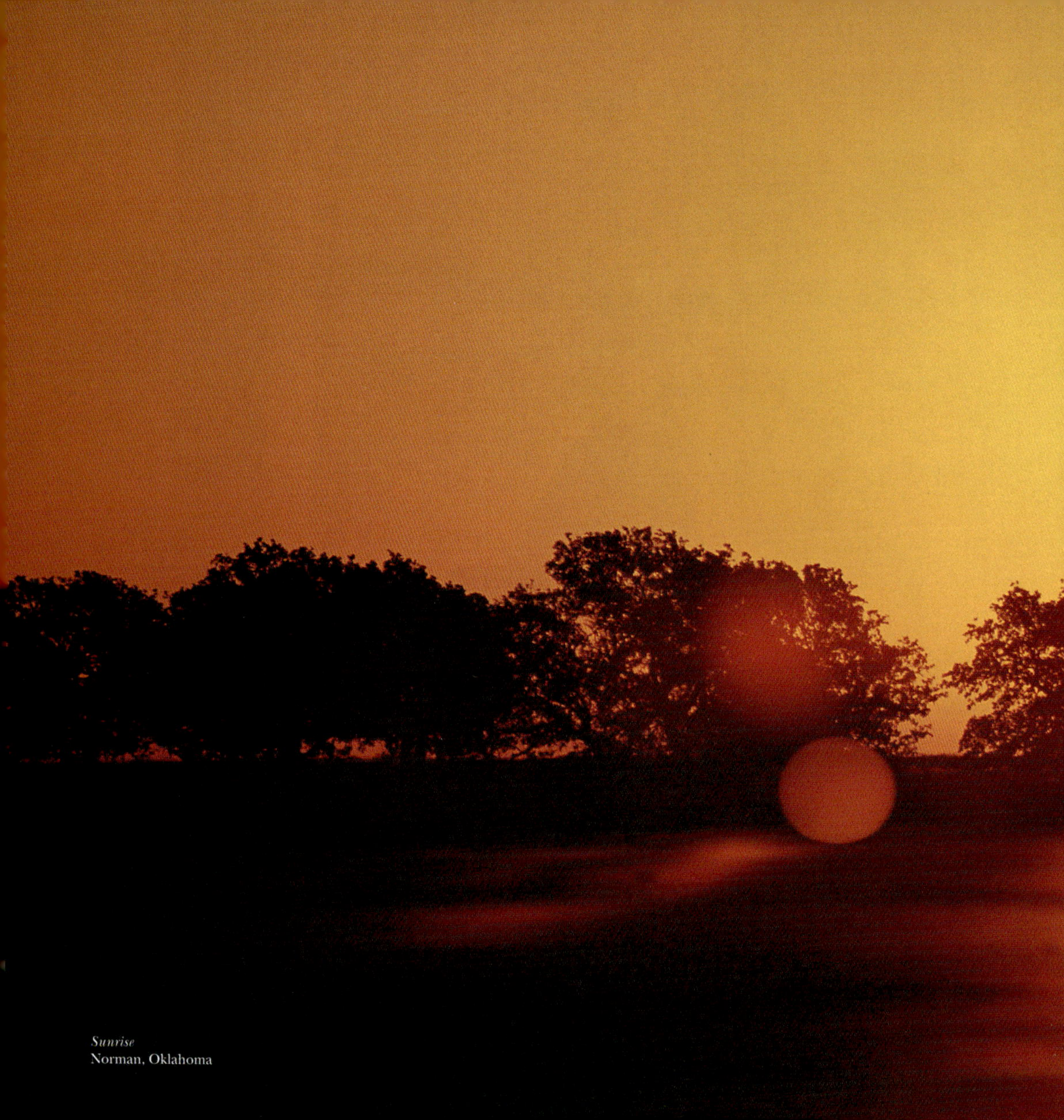

Sunrise
Norman, Oklahoma

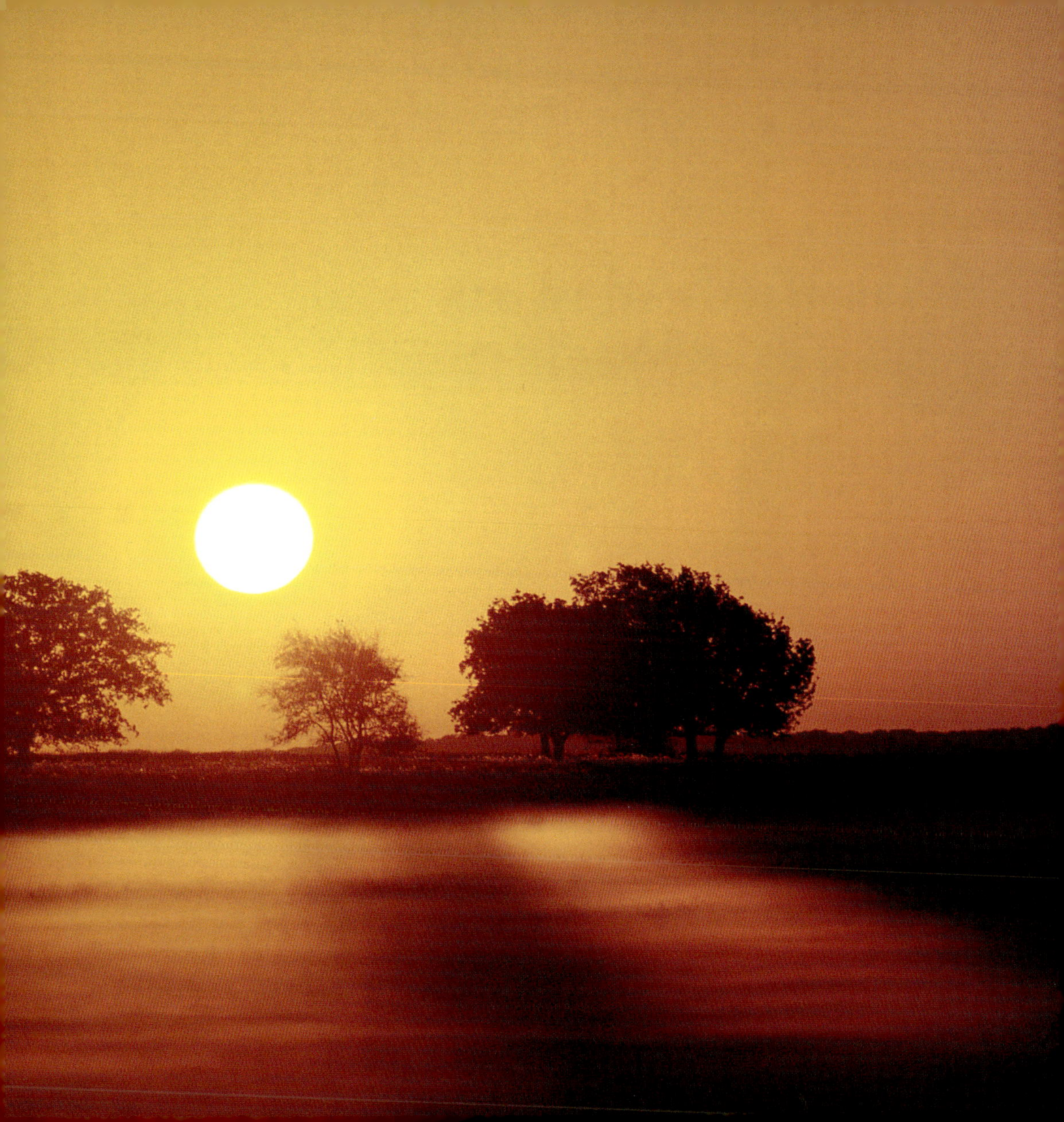

Classified Ad in an Old Texas Weekly:

Widower wanting wife
and mother for six kids.
Must be able to climb
windmill tower to keep
it oiled and greased. Will
send picture of windmill.

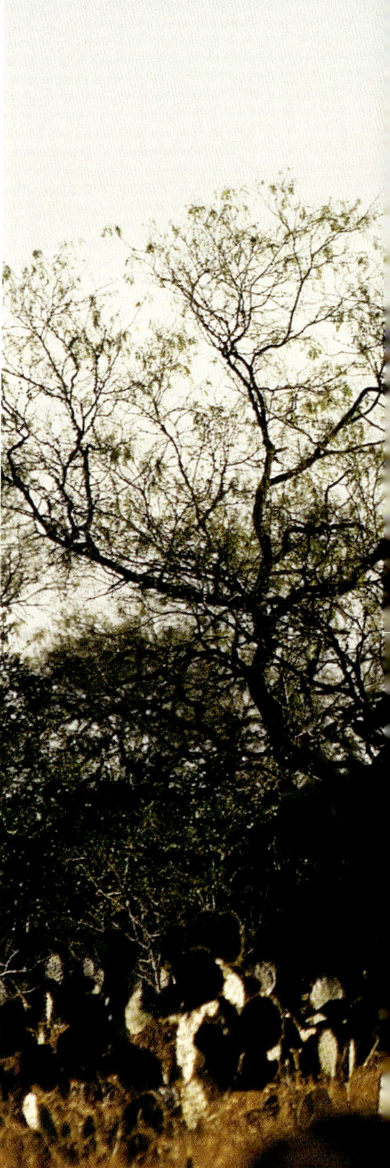

Roost
McAllen Ranch
Linn, Texas

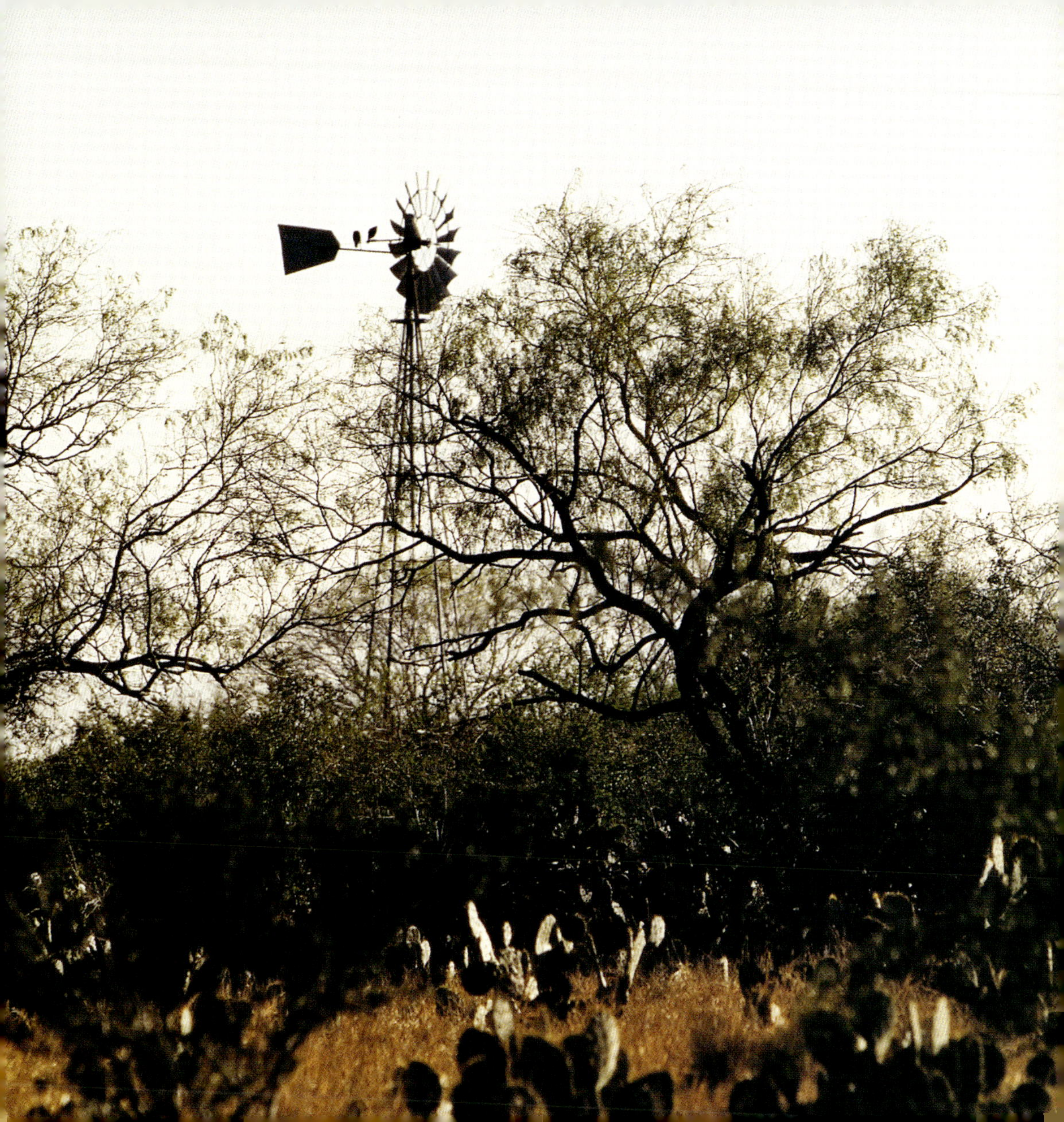

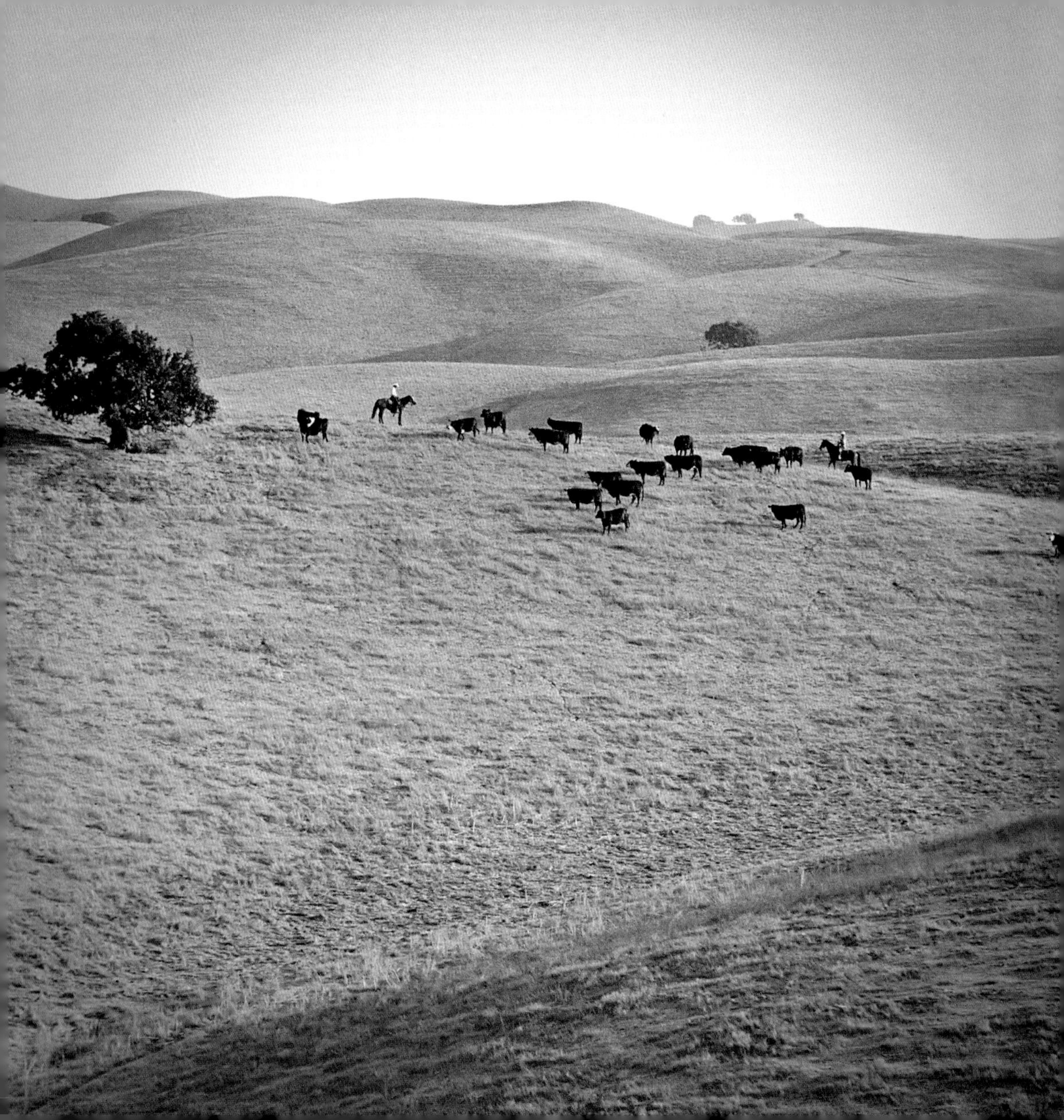

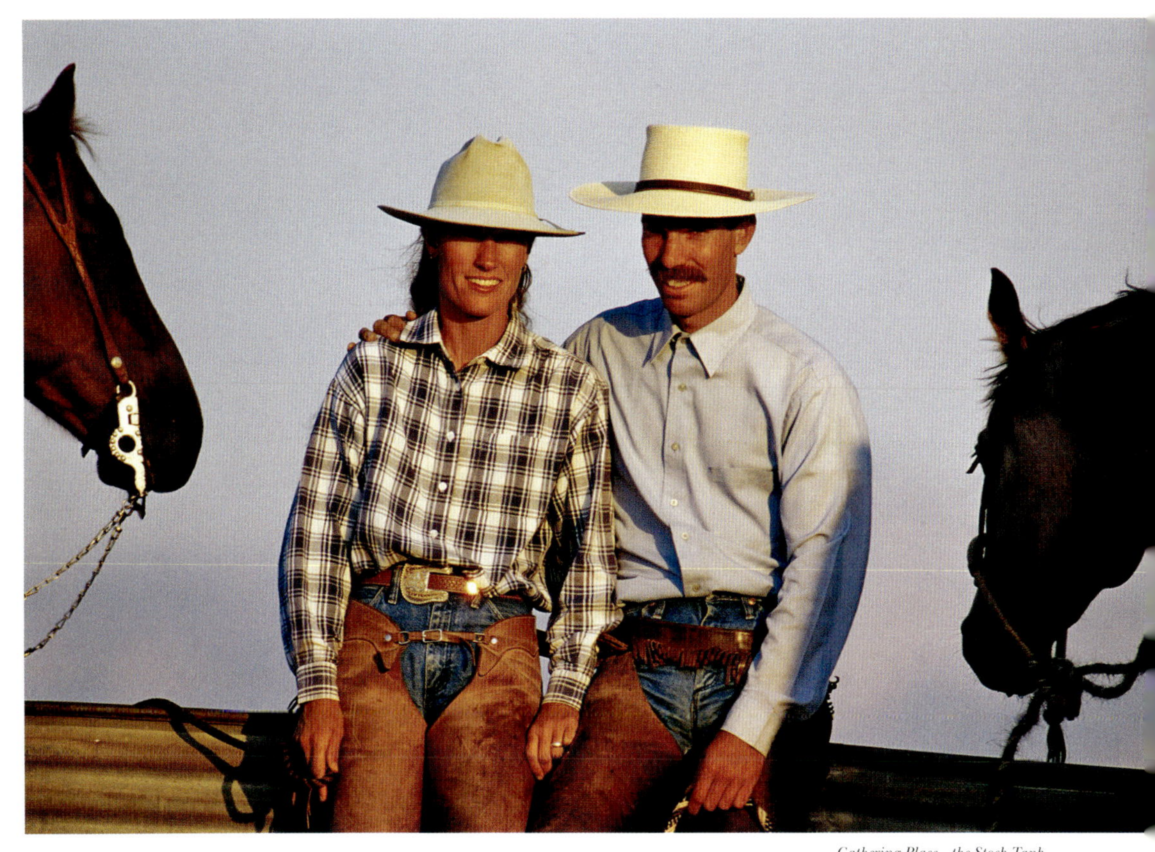

Gathering Place...the Stock Tank
Justin and Arleah Fields
Dunne Ranch, Hollister, California

Dunne Ranch
Hollister, California

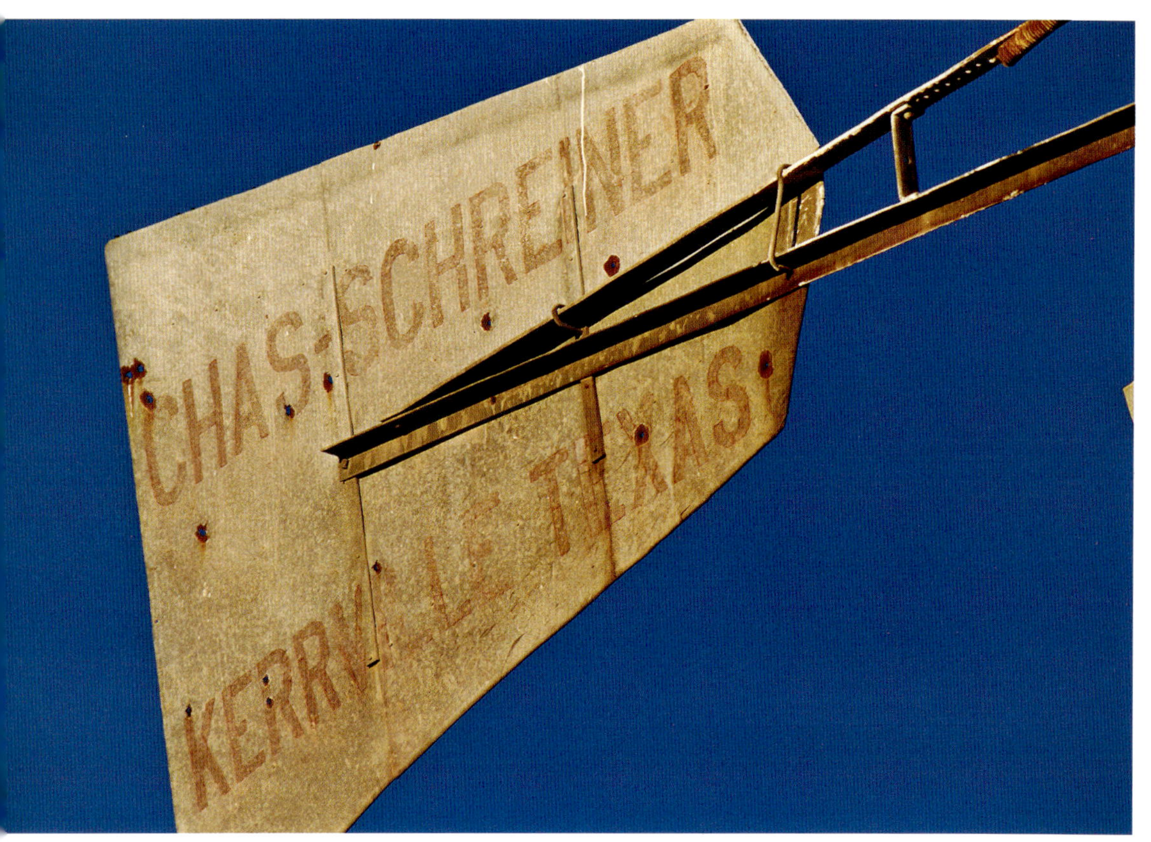

YO Ranch
Mountain Home, Texas

*Hotter Than *!#%*
Wayne Swain
Donnell Ranch, Fowlerton, Texas

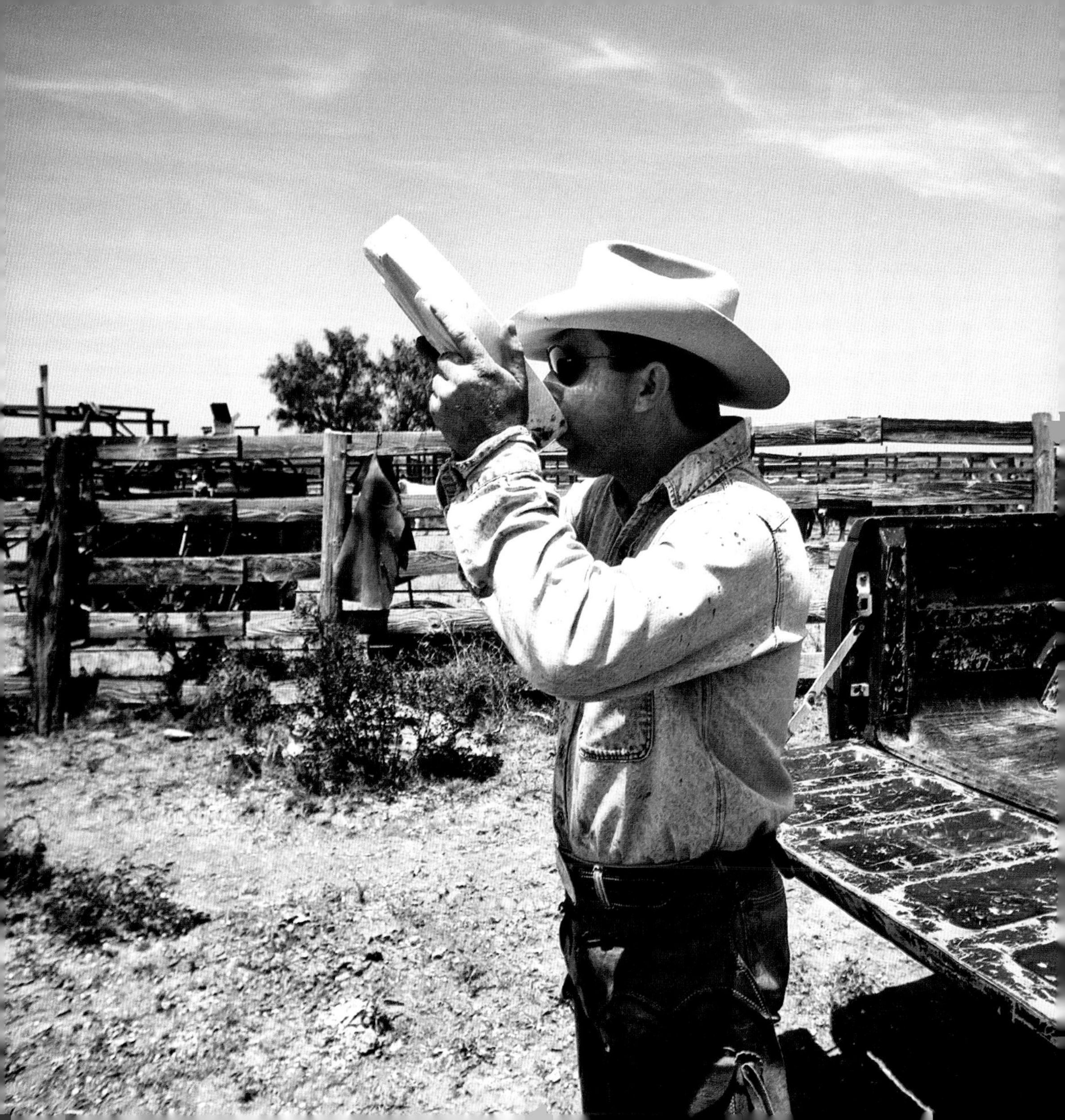

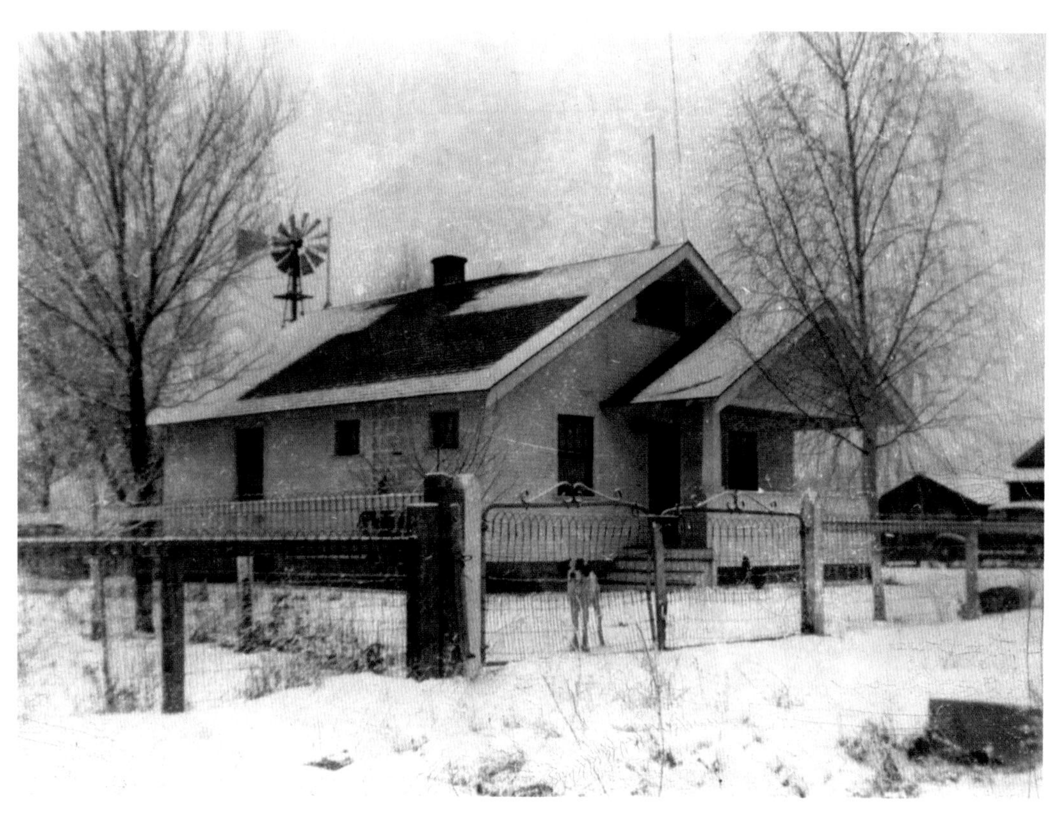

Original photos of Halverson House with the windmill in the backyard in Mackay, Idaho, 1940s

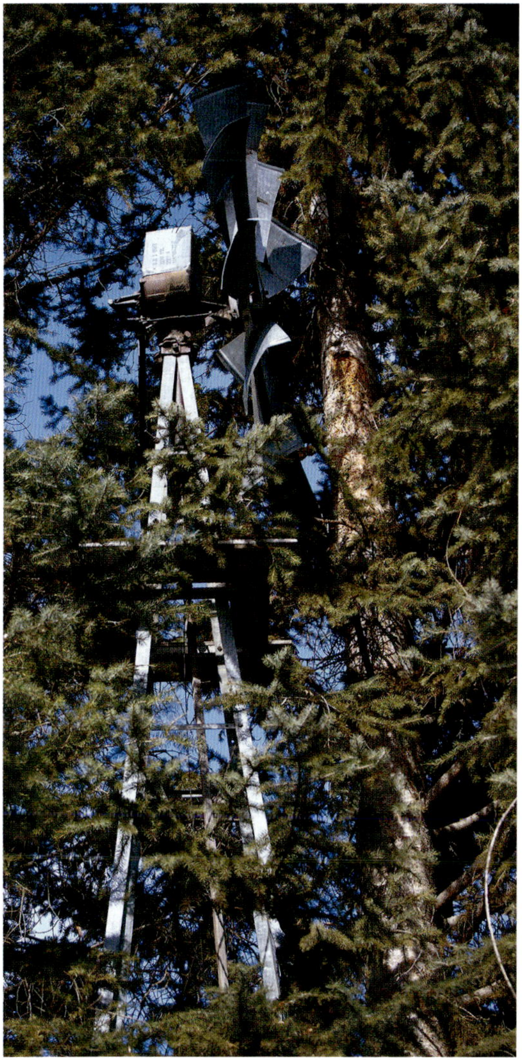

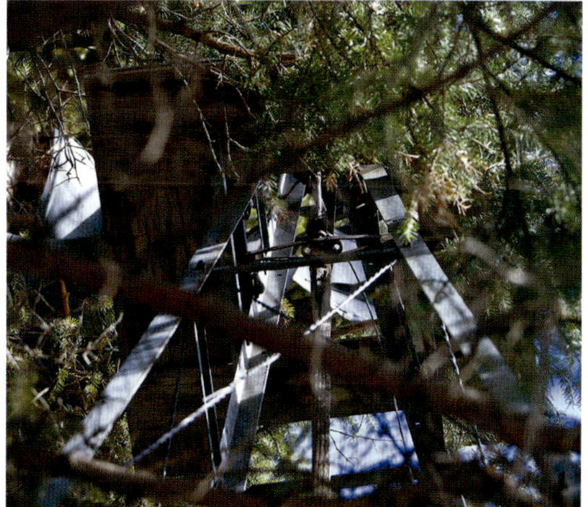

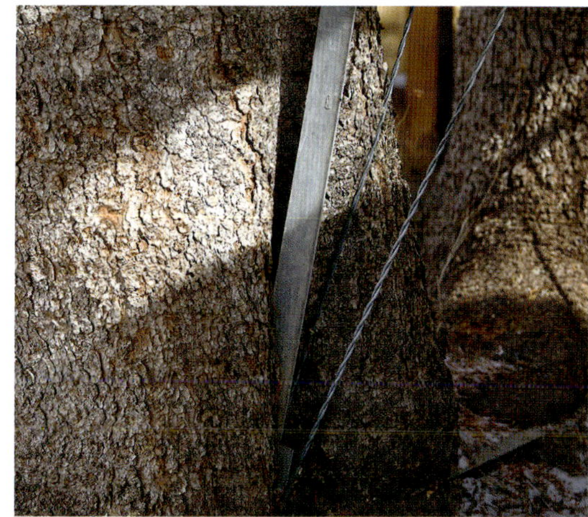

Photos today of the Halverson House windmill with trees growing around it. The mill still turns when the wind blows.

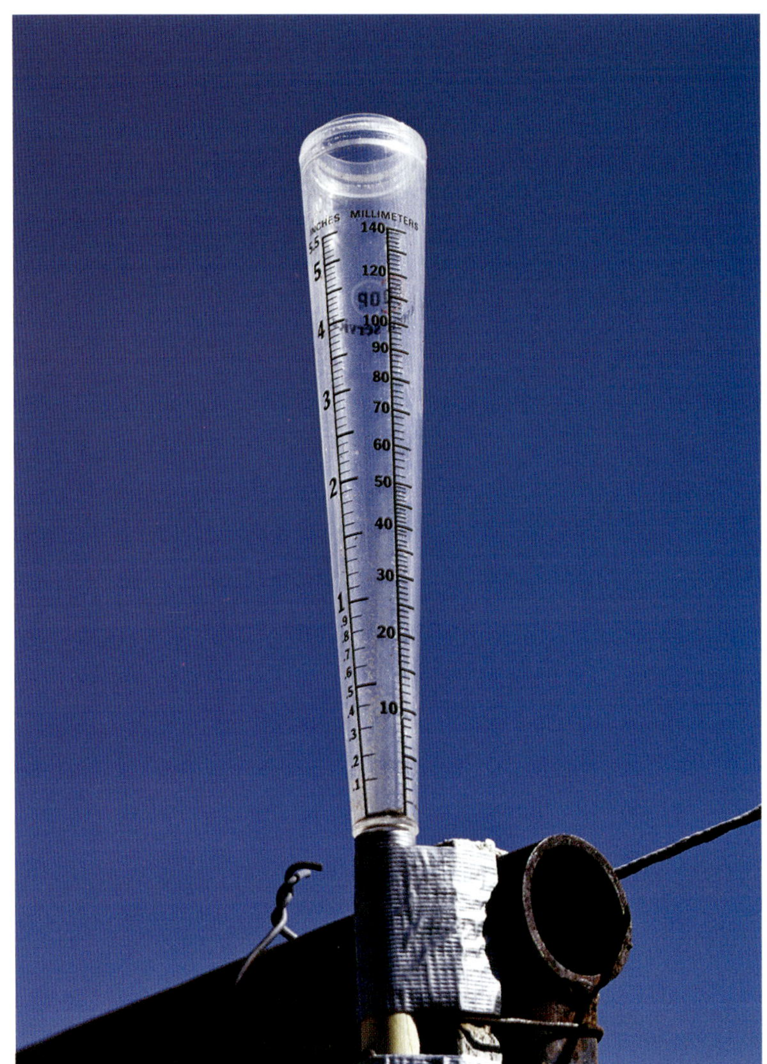

Rain Gauge
West Texas

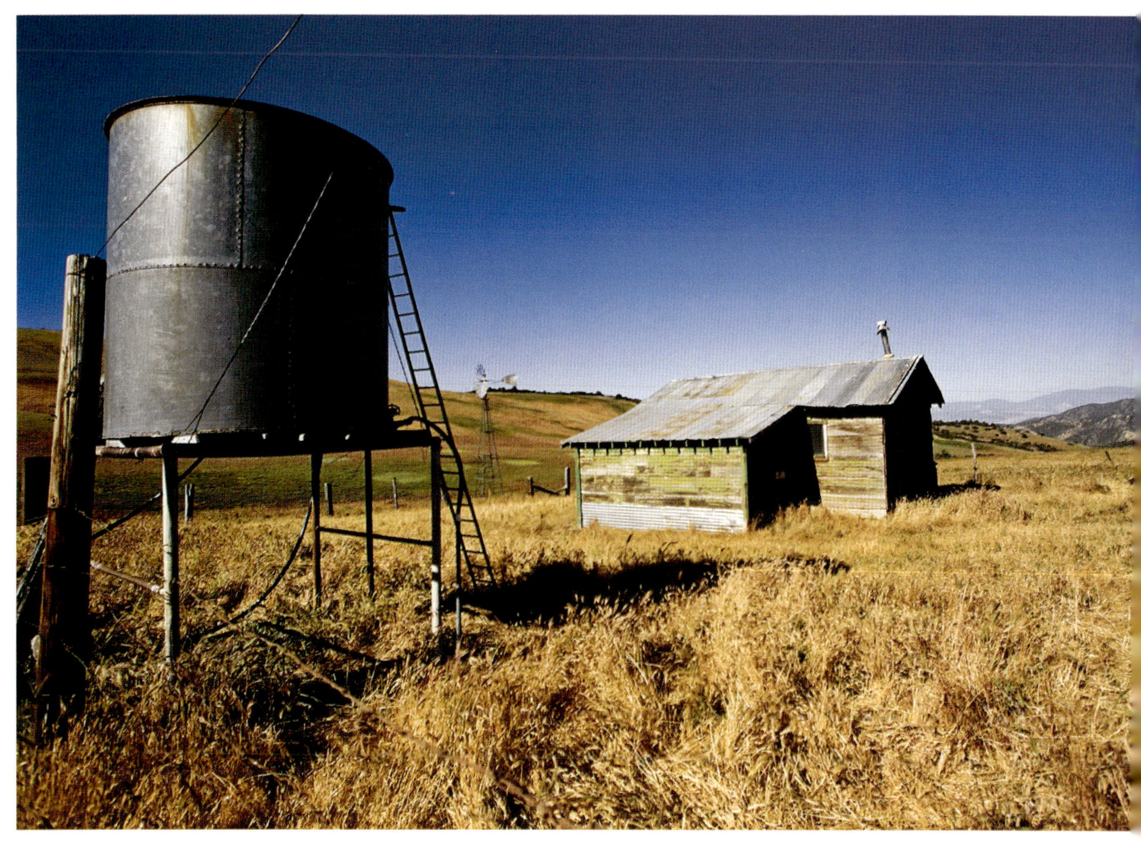

Cow Camp
Santa Barbara Canyon Ranch
Santa Barbara, California

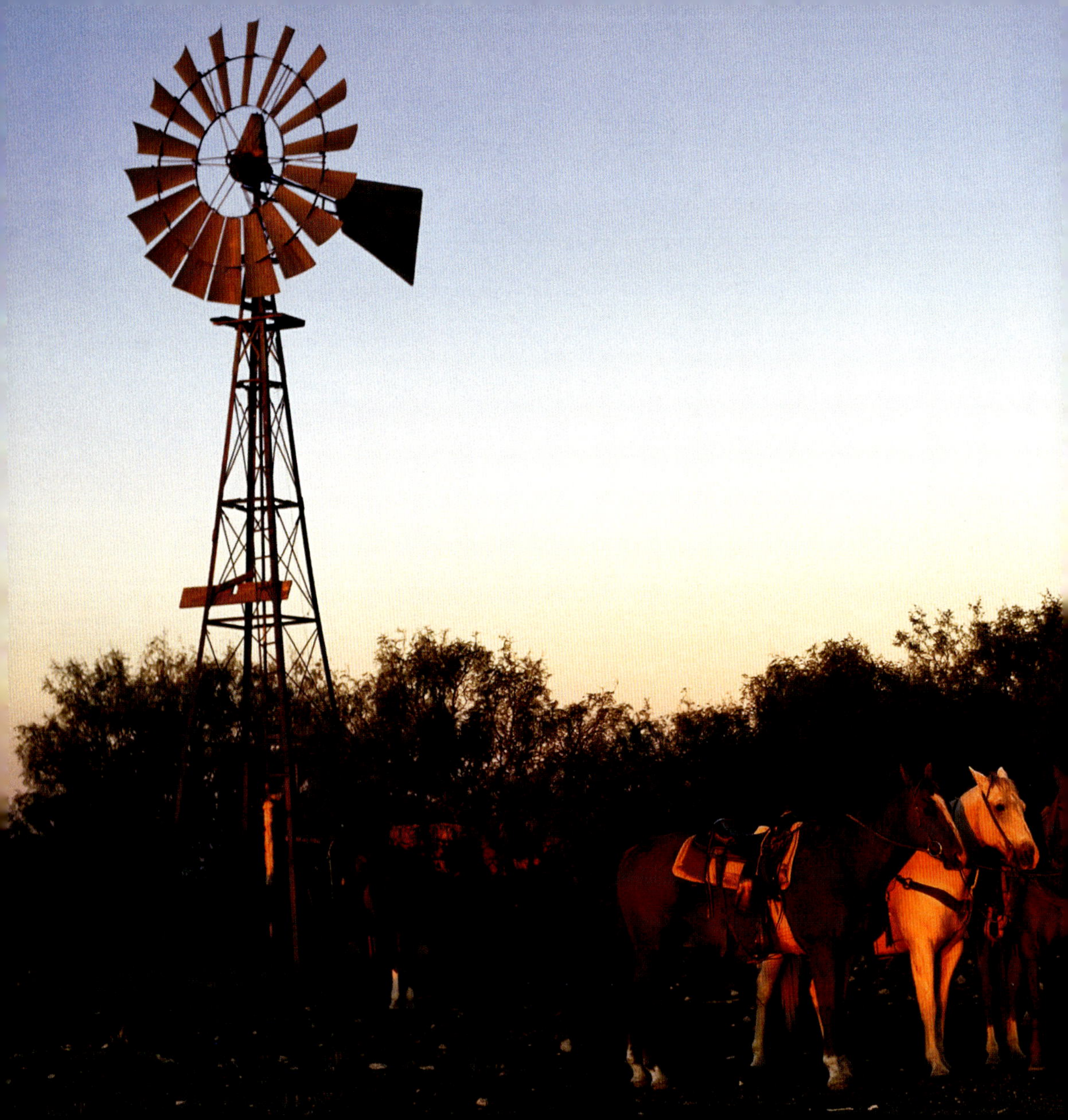

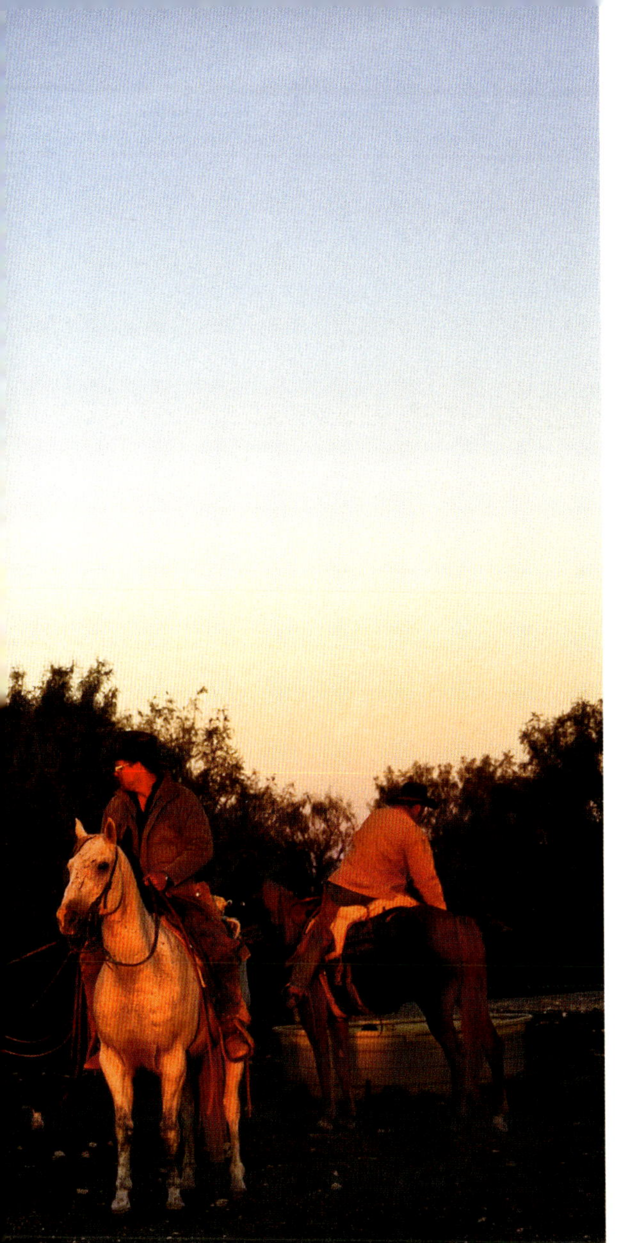

Taking the Horses to Water
West Texas

Evening Dancer

An old prairie tale told of a young woman who just wandered off into the emptiness one evening. They say the loneliness and the relentless wind drove her insane. She never came back nor did anyone ever find her. Her children would look for her every evening. Whenever they saw a windmill during those beautiful and peaceful hours, they would say, "Look! There's Momma dancing in the sunset. Look at her pretty bonnet, twisting and turning as she dances, her long dress spreading out and flowing from her neck down around her feet. Oh, how beautiful she is...someday she's comin' back for us."

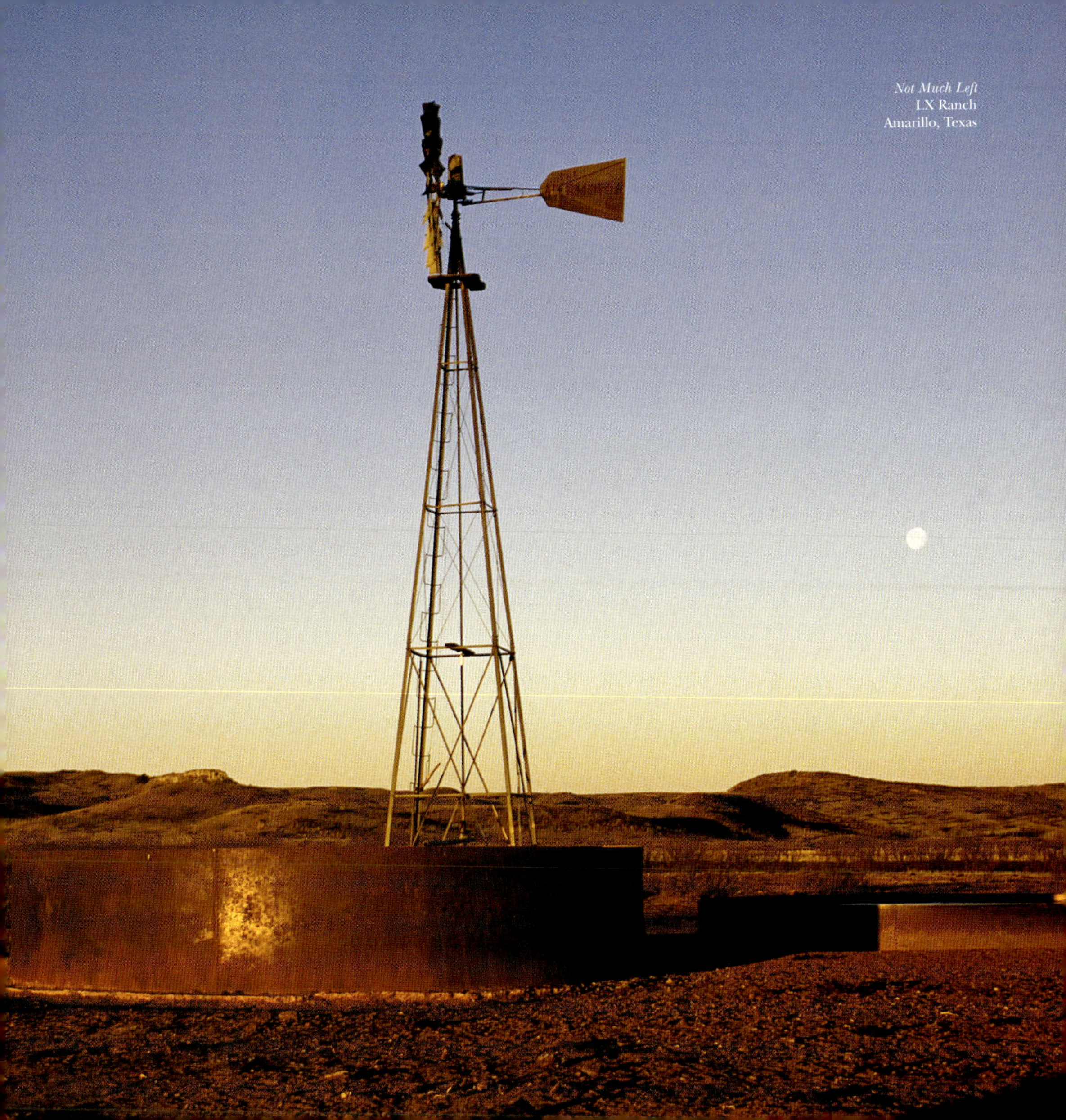

Not Much Left
LX Ranch
Amarillo, Texas

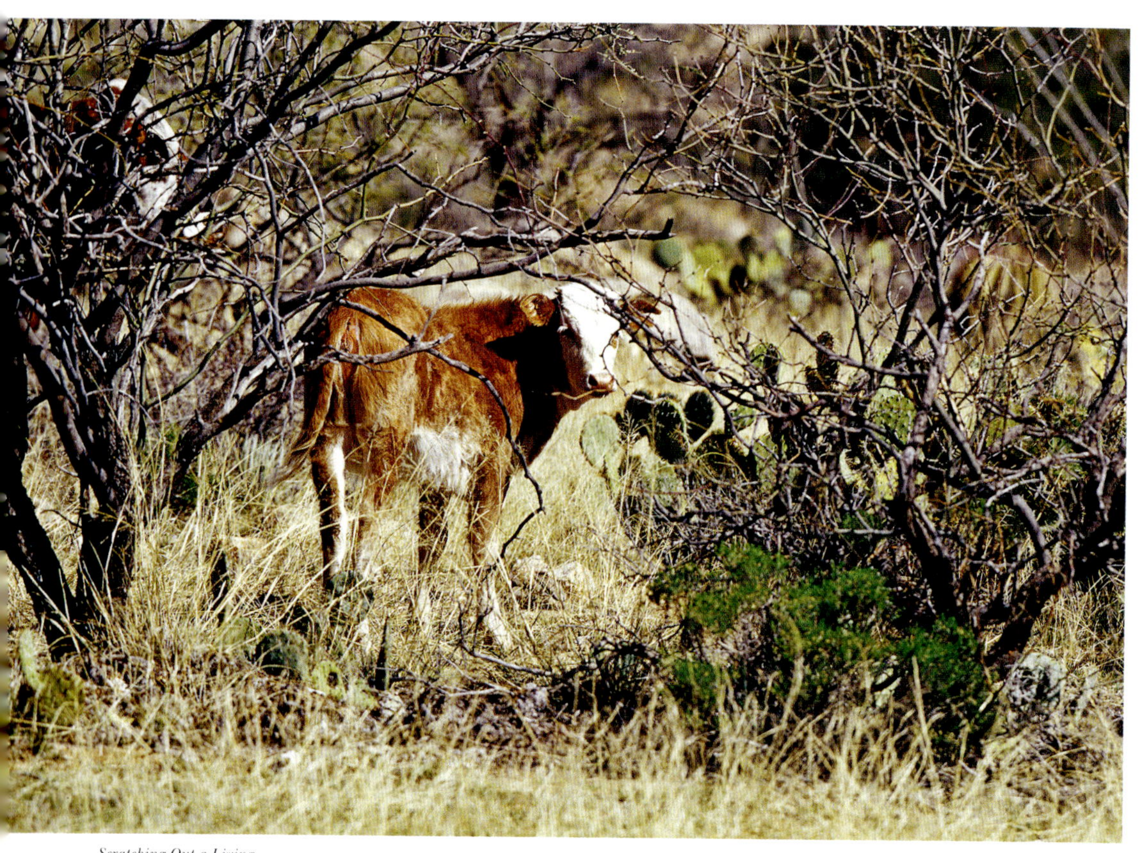

Scratching Out a Living
Bellota Ranch
Tucson, Arizona

Lookin' for Strays
Bellota Ranch
Tucson, Arizona

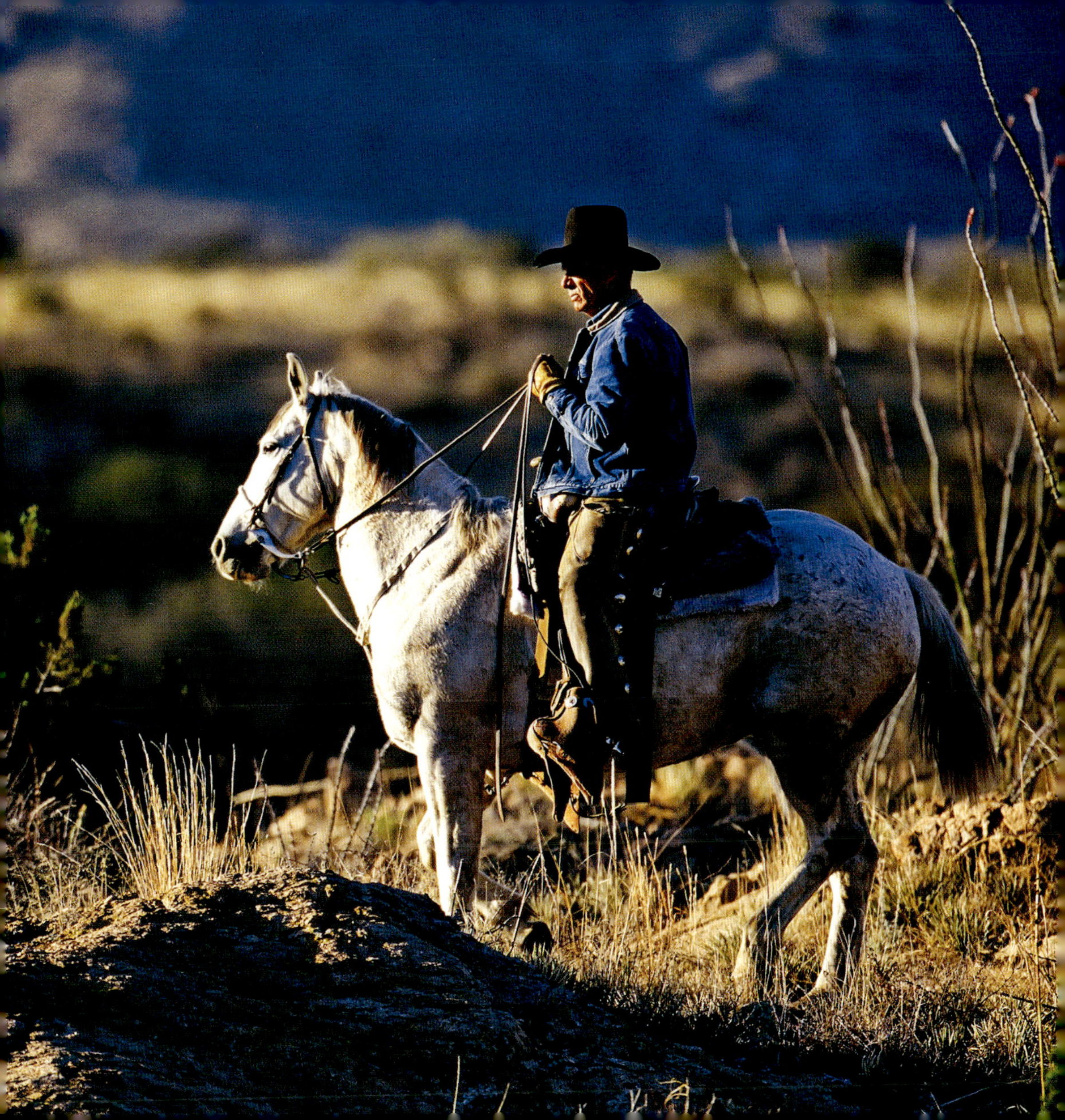

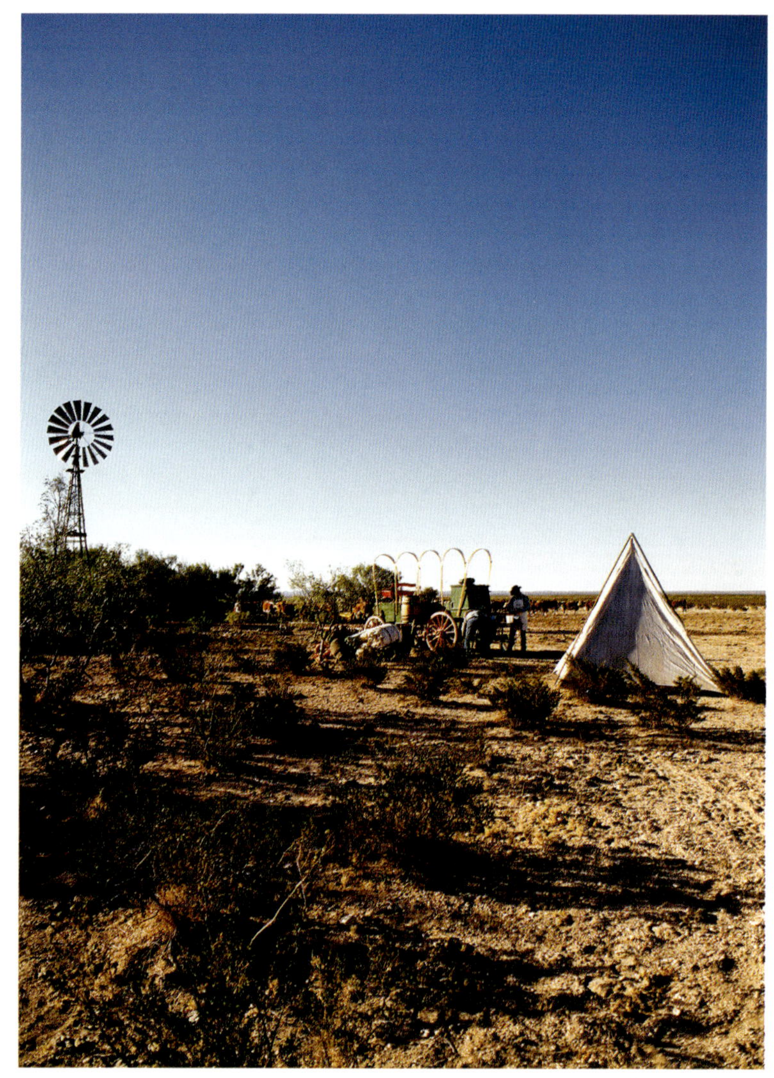

Camping at the Mill
West Texas

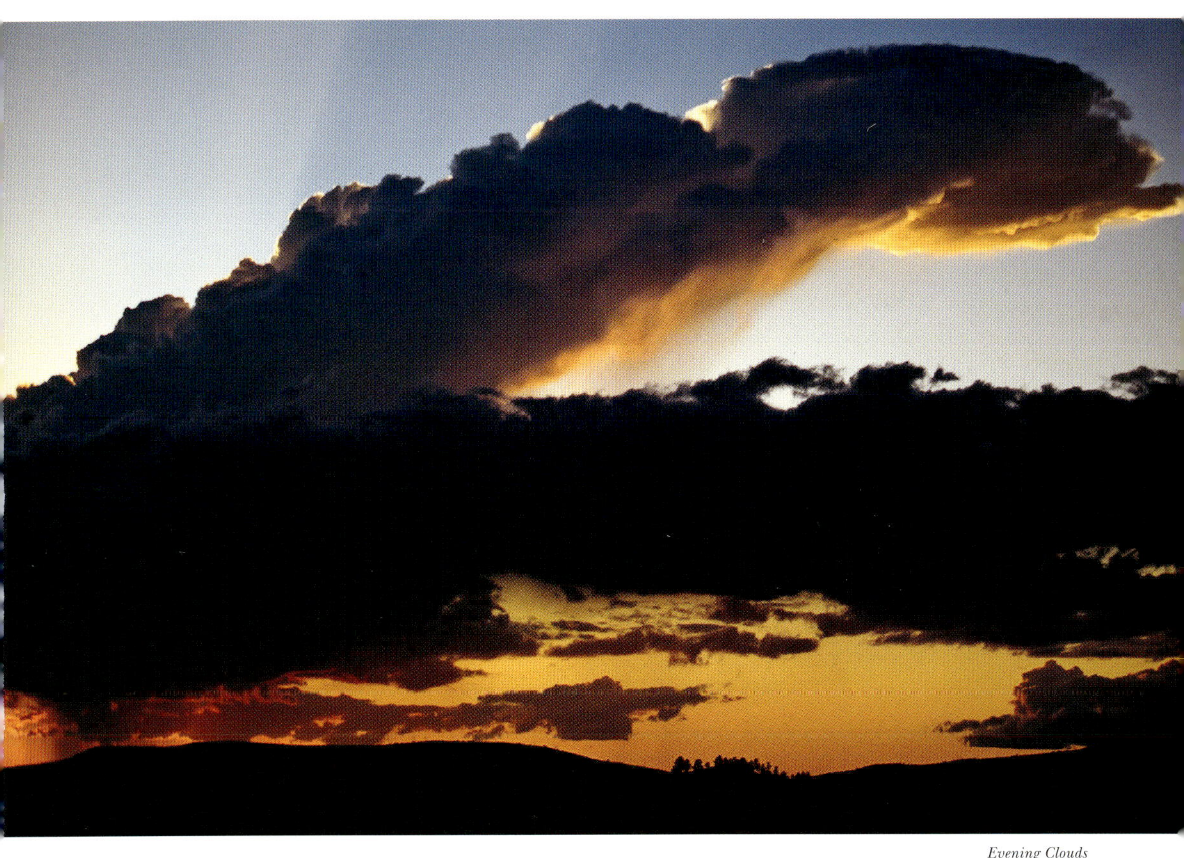

Evening Clouds
Eastern Montana

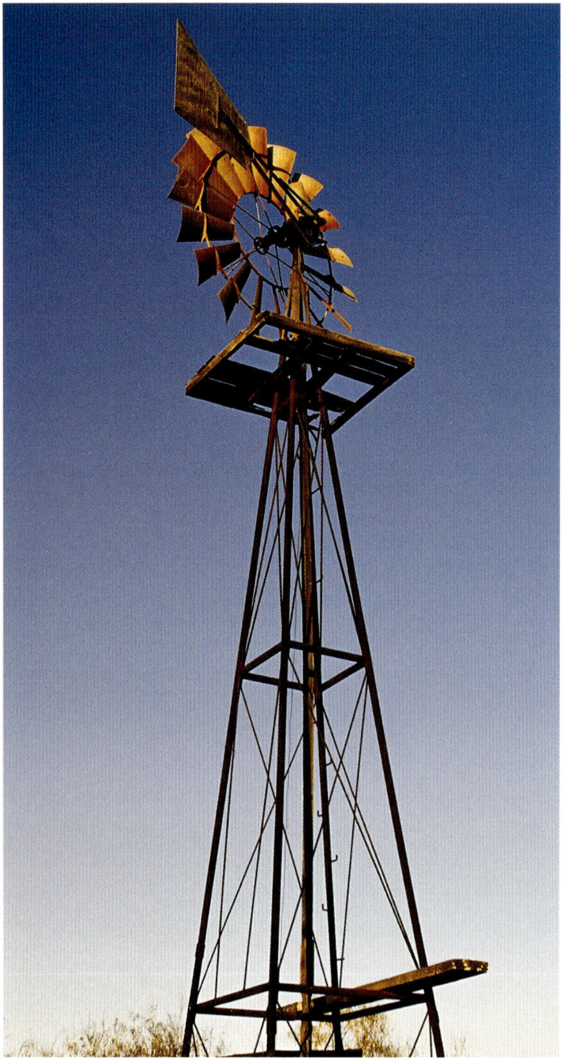

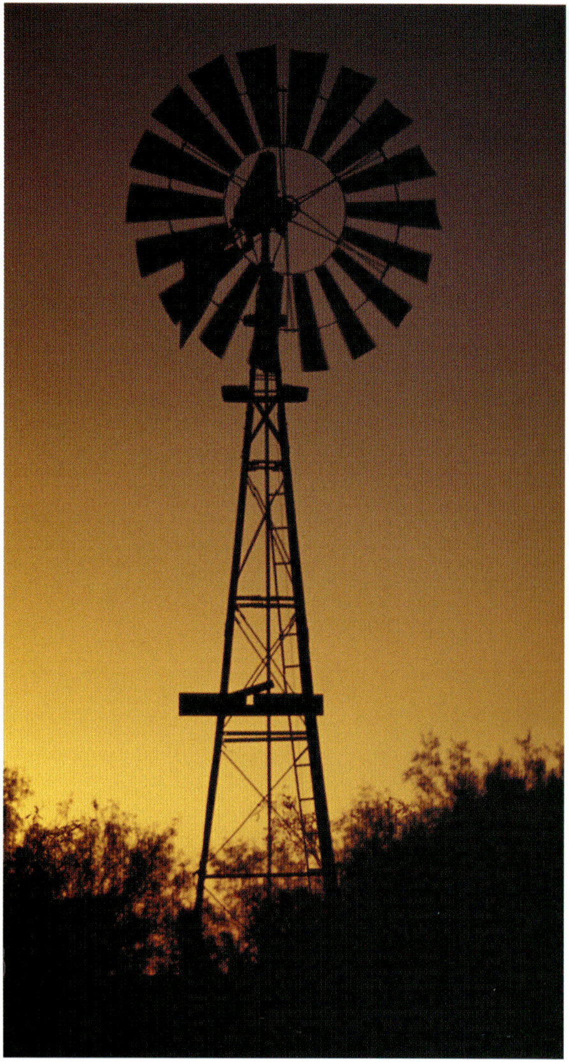

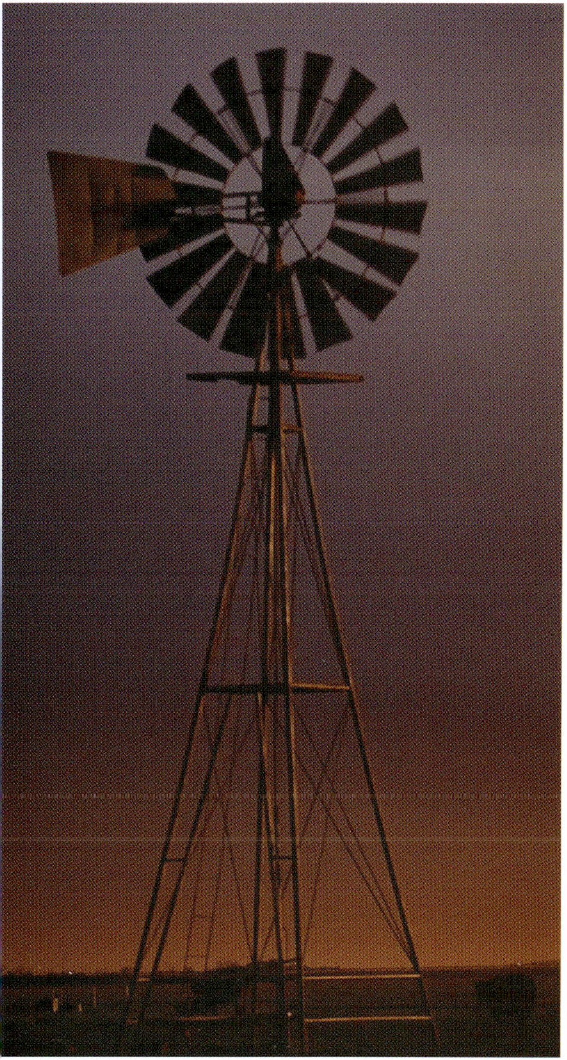

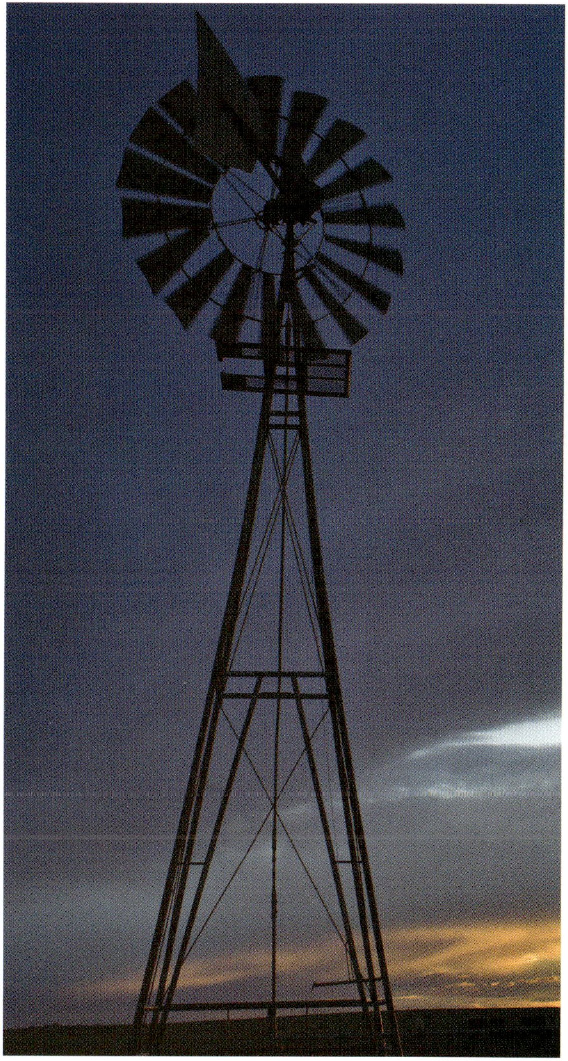

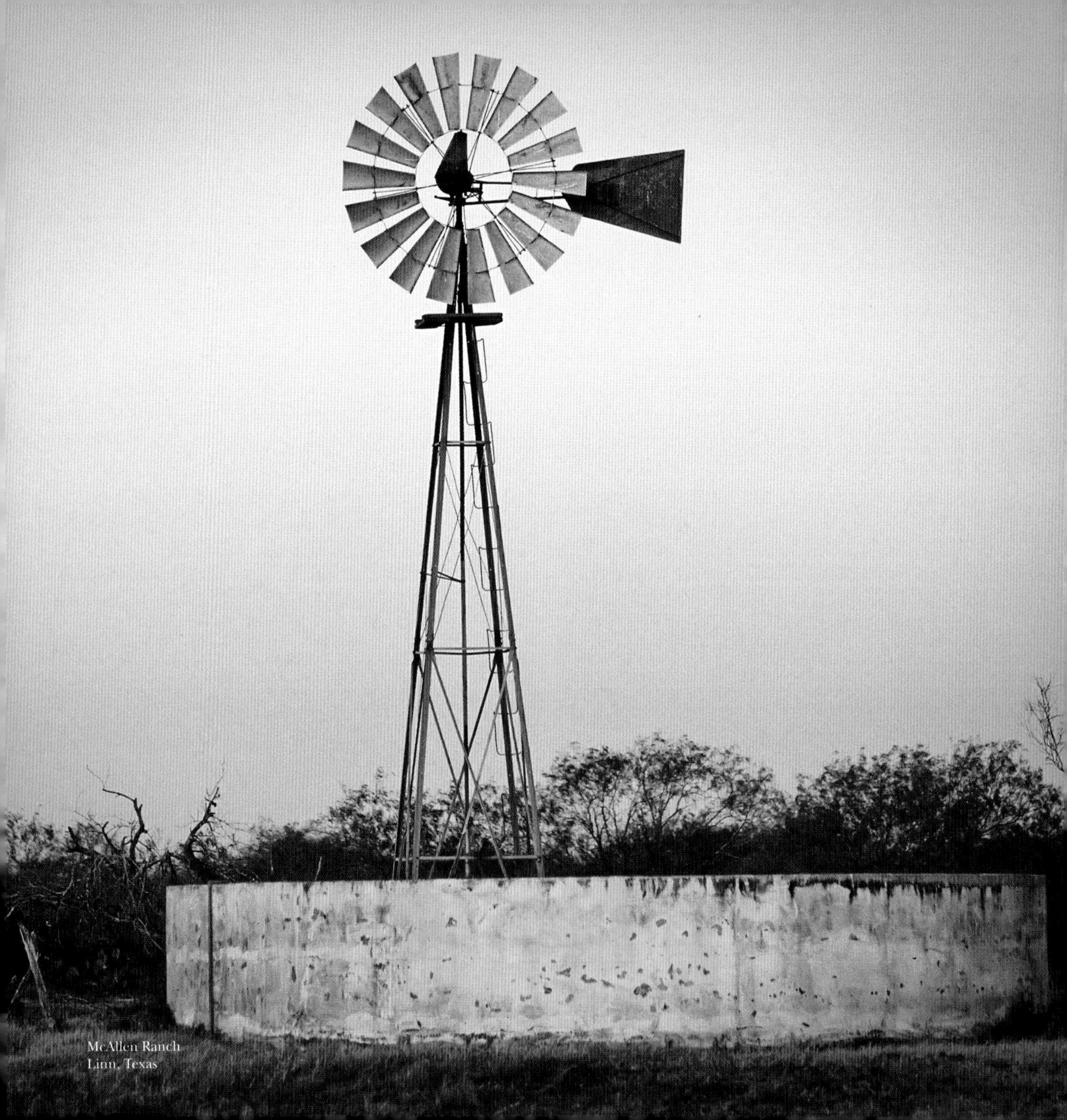

McAllen Ranch
Linn, Texas

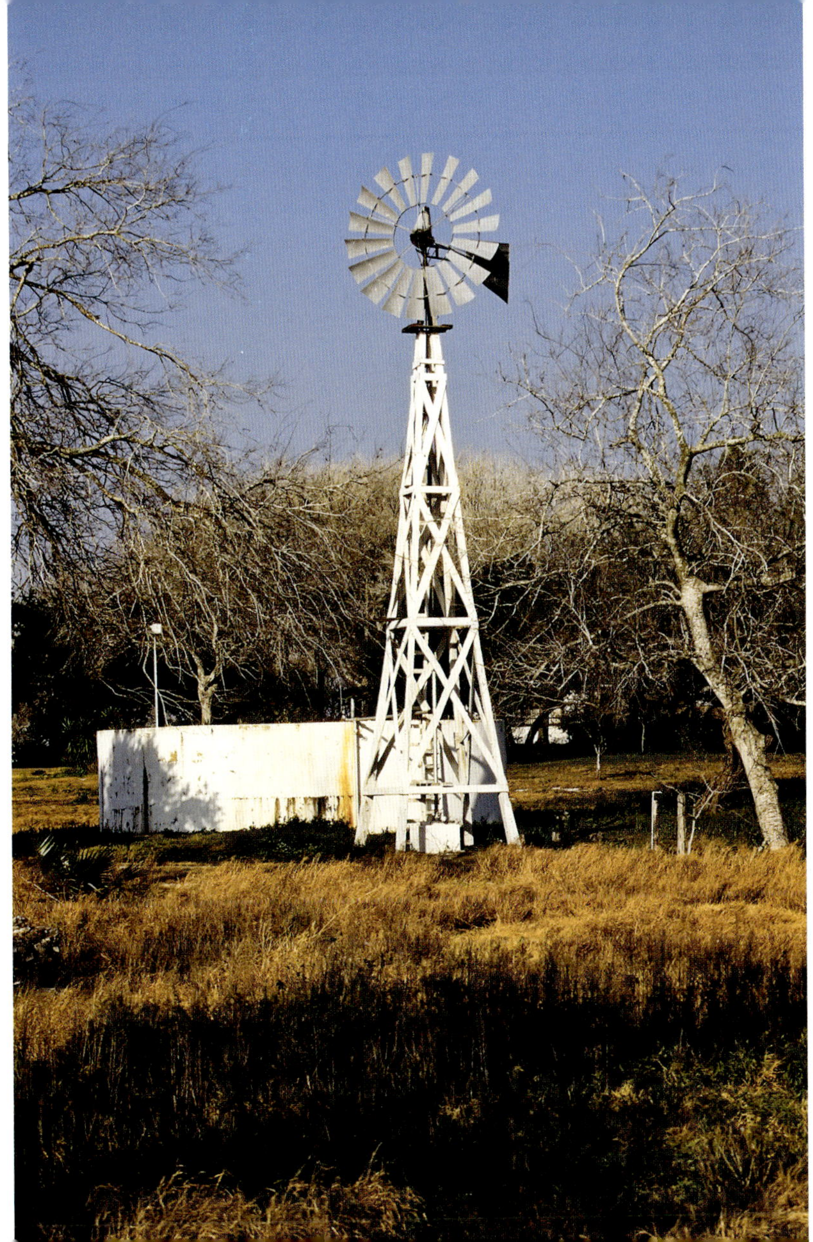

McAllen Ranch
Linn, Texas

*Windmills are often used in American folk art and as toys…
they are a symbol of the American spirit.*

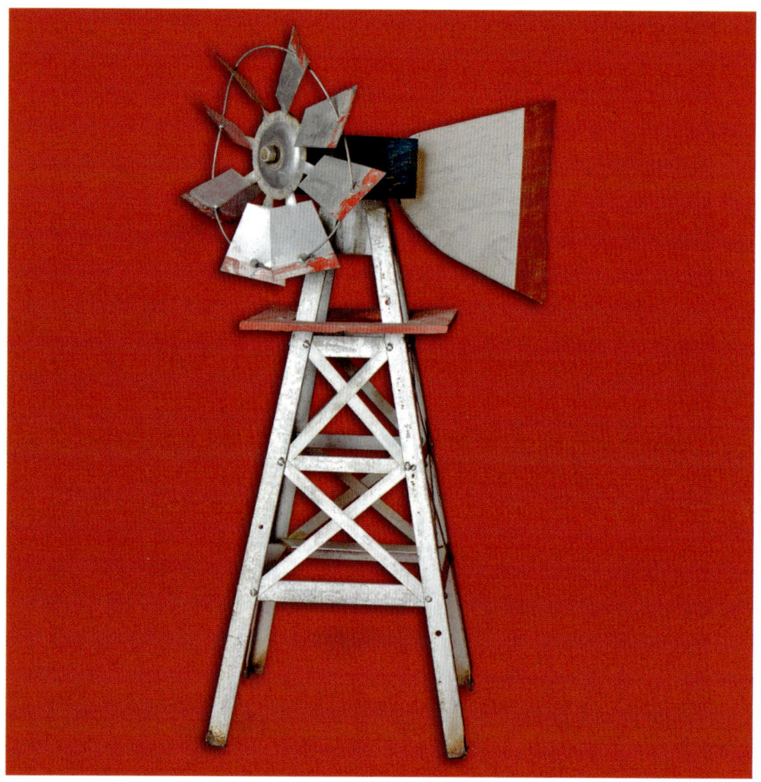

Homemade Folk Art Windmill

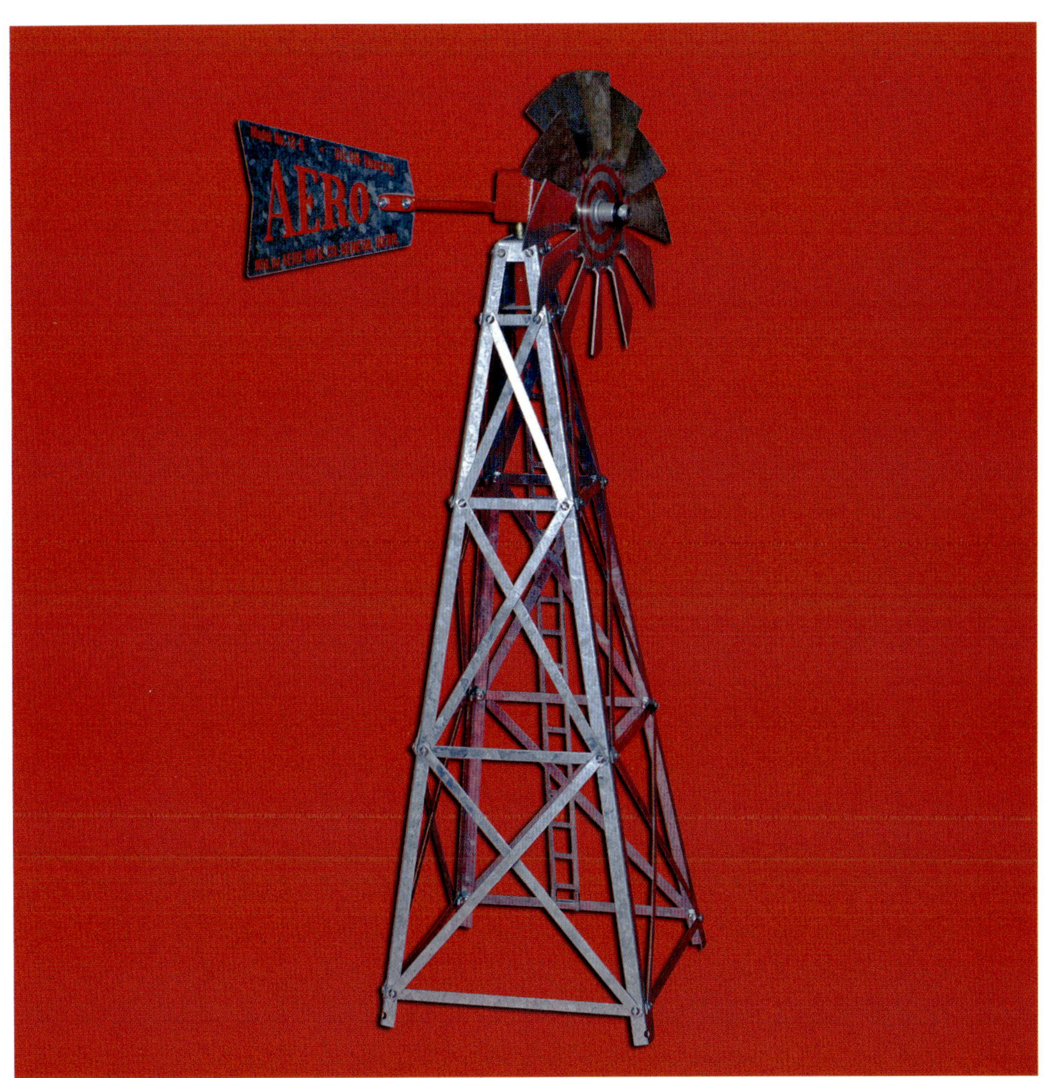

Windmill Toy Assembled from a Kit

May the Wind Always Blow...

Working on the Mill
Jim Detten
Harrell Cattle Company, Claude, Texas

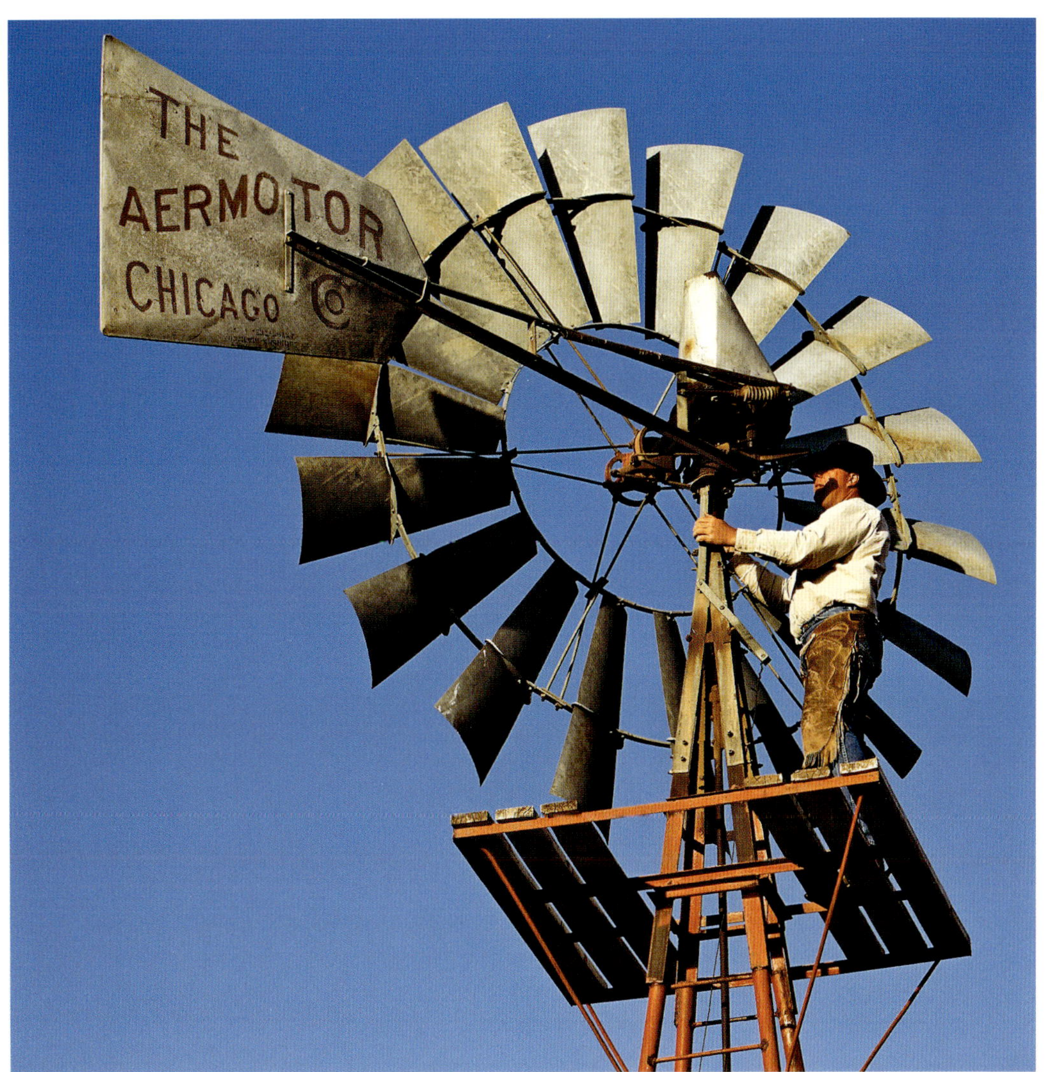
THE
AERMOTOR
CHICAGO
Co

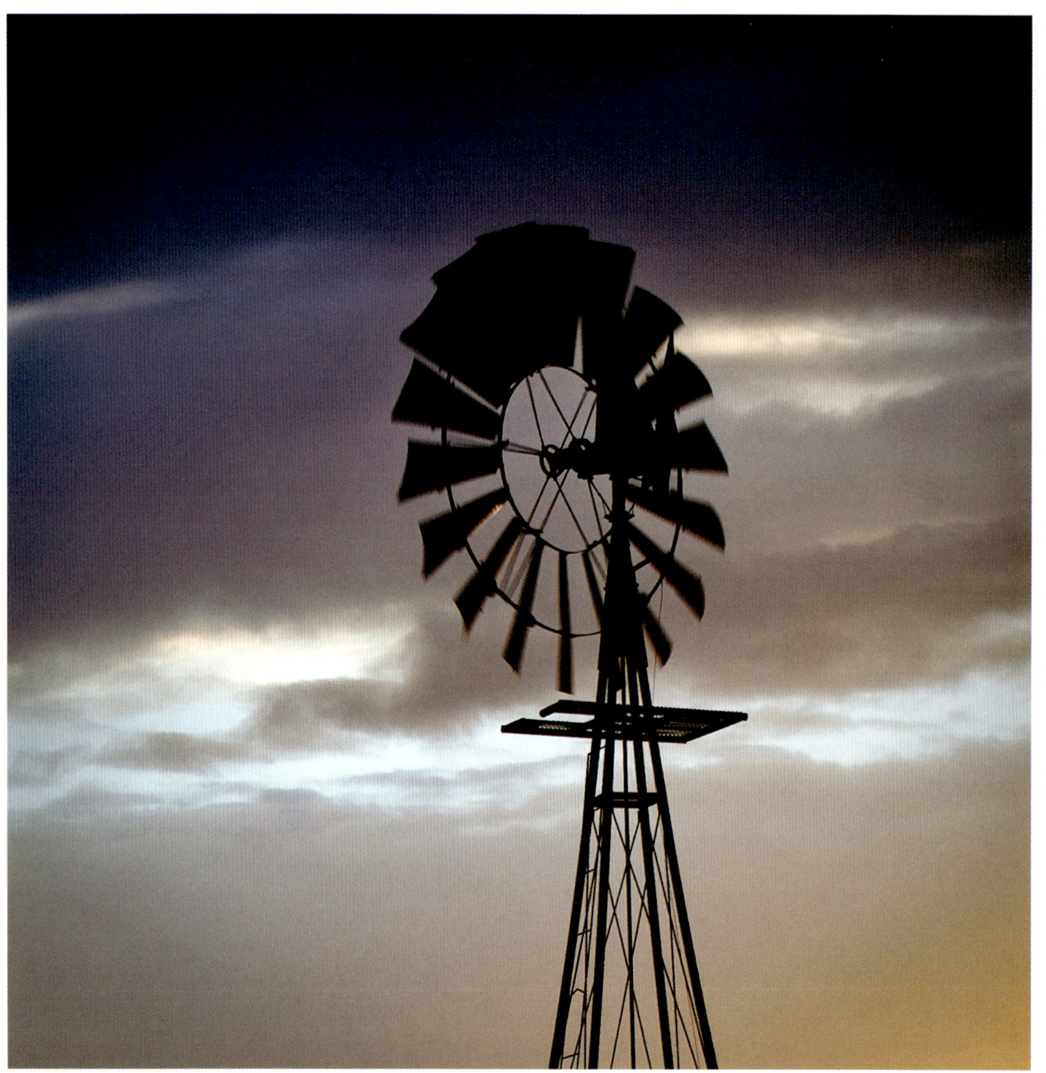

Technical Notes

David exclusively uses Canon cameras and lenses. He is one of the distinguished Canon "Explorers of Light" photographers and is extremely grateful to have all the great people at Canon USA as a support team while he travels around documenting the West.

David switched from film to the digital format about five years ago. He truly believes that digital photography has opened up a whole new world to him. "Since shooting digitally, I have taken some of the best photos of my career," he says.

David uses the Canon EOS 1D Mark III and Canon EOS 1Ds Mark III cameras and the following lenses: 70-200mm f/2.8L IS USM, 20mm f2.8L IS USM, 35mm f/2.8L IS USM, 400mm f/2.8L IS USM, 300mm f/2.8L IS USM, 200mm f/2.8L IS USM.

All photographs in the Stoecklein Collection are available as stock images and as fine art prints made with Canon paper and ink as well as printers.

Flying in the Wind
Cluck Ranches
Gruver, Texas

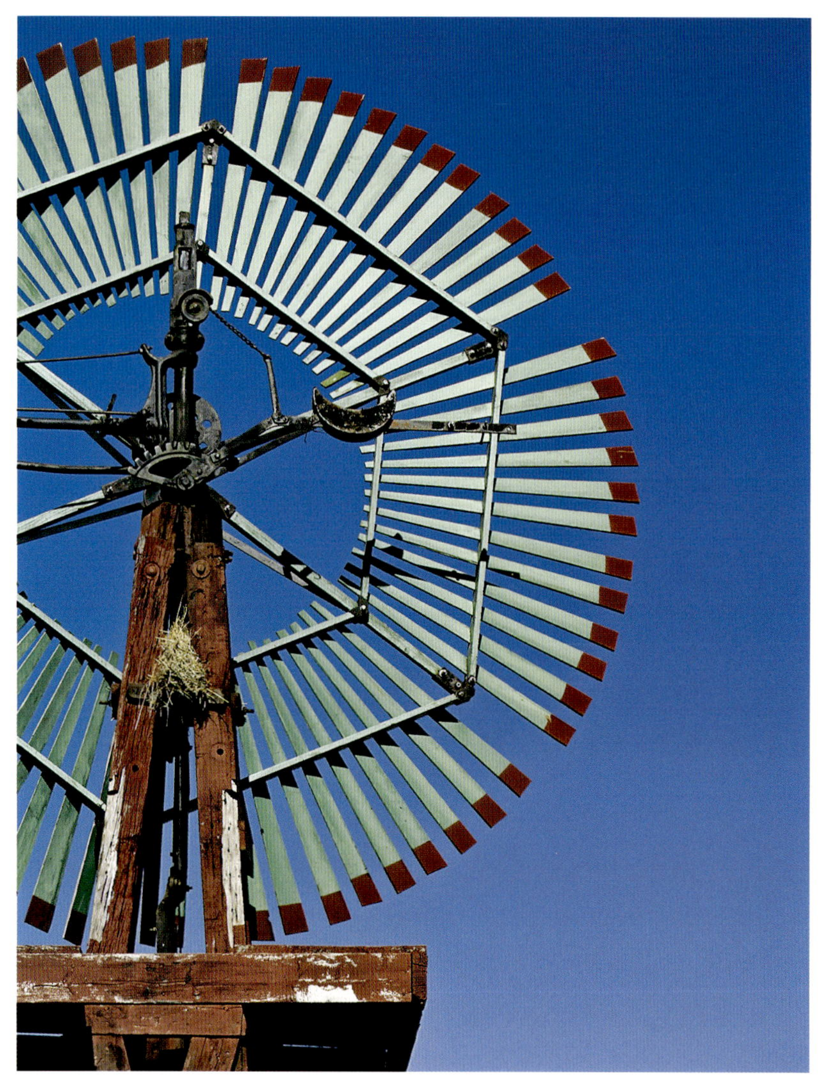

Antique Dempster Windmill
J.B. Buchanan Windmill Park
Spearman, Texas

Other Books by Stoecklein Publishing

The Western Buckle
The Cowboy Hat
The Cowboy Boot
Fly Fishing in Idaho
Ranch Style
Waiting for Daylight
Outhouses
Barns of the American West
Brands of the West
Cattle
Western Fences
Cowboy Ethics
Cowboy Wisdom
California Missions
Saddles of the West
The American Quarter Horse
The Horse Doctors

Cowgirls in Heaven
The Performance Horse
Lil' Buckaroos
Cow Dogs
Spirit of the West
The American Paint Horse
The California Cowboy
The Idaho Cowboy
Cowboy Gear
The Montana Cowboy
Don't Fence Me In
Cowgirls
The Texas Cowboys
The Western Horse
Sun Valley Images
Sun Valley Signatures I, II, III

www.thestoeckleincollection.com

Special Thanks From the Author

I would like to thank three very pretty ladies:

Rosemary Goddard, my wife, for keeping me honest and still loving me; Mary Stoecklein, for keeping David home long enough to put this book together; Carrie Lightner, for her astute editing of this cowboy's ramblings.

In addition:

Calvary Chapel pastors Dave Messenger and Gordon Boyle, for the music to the schoolyard rhyme.

Also, the following reference sources:

Power from Wind: A History of Windmill Technology by Richard L. Hills
Windmill Weights by Milt Simpson
American Windmills: An Album of Historic Photographs by T. Lindsay Baker
Wikipedia Online Encyclopedia

—Jack Goddard

"As long as there is wind, people will try to harness it."
—DRS

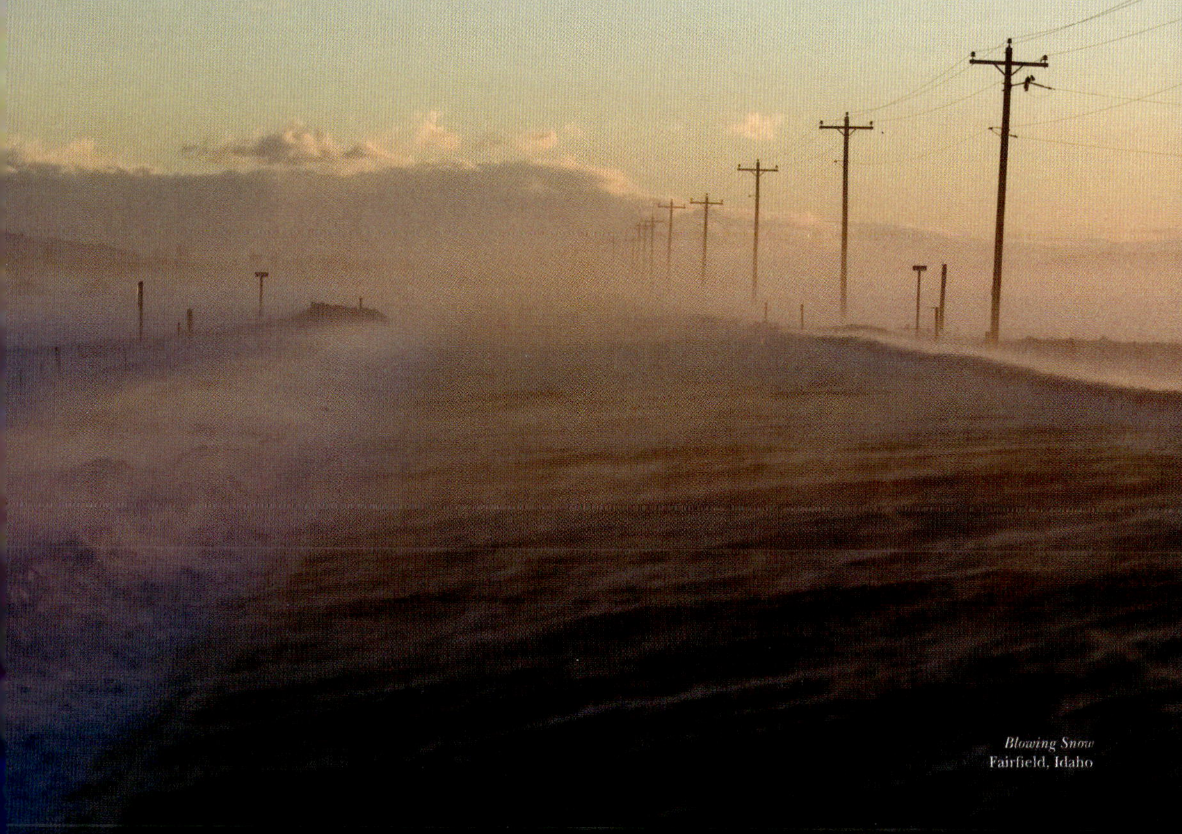

Blowing Snow
Fairfield, Idaho

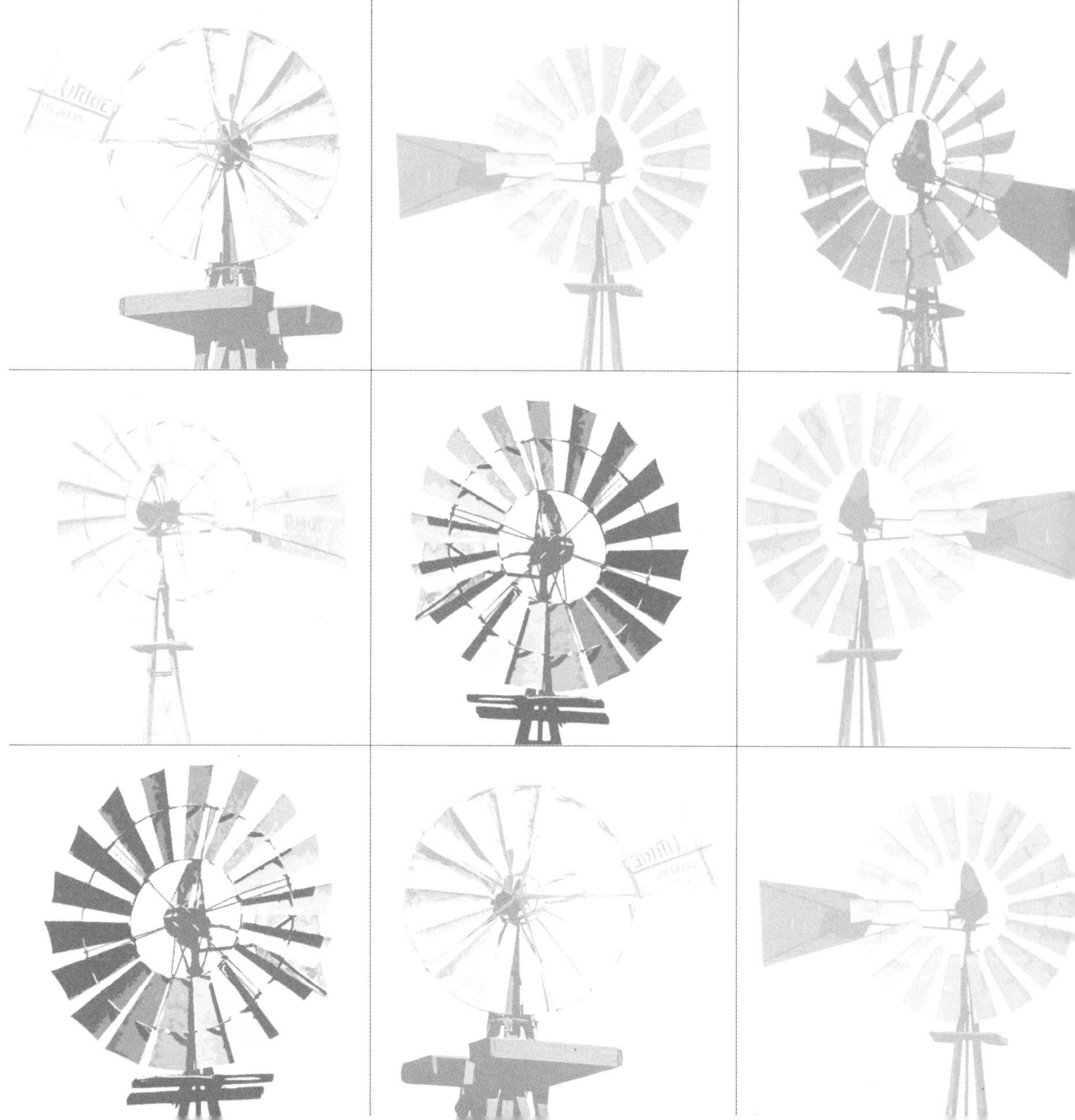